I0883511

Daily 6-Trait Writing

GRADE 6

Manufacturer	Evan-Moor Corporation 10 Harris Court, Suite C-3 Monterey, CA 93940, USA www.evan-moor.com
EU Rep.	Authorised Rep Compliance Ltd., Ground Floor, 71 Lower Baggot Street, Dublin, D02 P593, Ireland www.arccompliance.com

Editorial Development: Roseann Erwin
Gretchen McBride
Leslie Sorg
Andrea Weiss
Copy Editing: Cathy Harber
Art Direction: Cheryl Puckett
Cover Design: Liliana Potigian
Design/Production: Susan Bigger
Carolina Caird

EVAN-MOOR Educational Publishers

EMC 6026

Visit *teaching-standards.com* to view a correlation of this book.

Correlated to Current Standards

Congratulations on your purchase of some of the finest teaching materials in the world.

For information about other Evan-Moor products, call 1-800-777-4362, fax 1-800-777-4332, or visit our website, www.evan-moor.com.

10 Harris Court, Suite C-3, Monterey, CA 93940-5773. Printed in China.

007

CPSIA: Asia Pacific Offset Ltd, Kowloon, Hong Kong, China [6/2025]

Contents

How to Use This Book

Daily 6-Trait Writing contains 25 weeks of mini-lessons divided into five units. Each unit provides five weeks of scaffolded instruction focused on one of the following traits: **Ideas, Organization, Word Choice, Sentence Fluency,** and **Voice**. (See pages 6–9 for more information about each of these, as well as the sixth trait, **Conventions**.) You may wish to teach each entire unit in consecutive order, or pick and choose the lessons within the unit.

Each week of *Daily 6-Trait Writing* focuses on a specific skill within the primary trait, as well as one Convention skill. The weeks follow a consistent five-day format, making *Daily 6-Trait Writing* easy to use.

Teacher Overview Pages

Trait Skill

A specific writing skill for each trait is targeted.

Reduced Pages

Reduced student pages provide sample answers.

Convention Skill

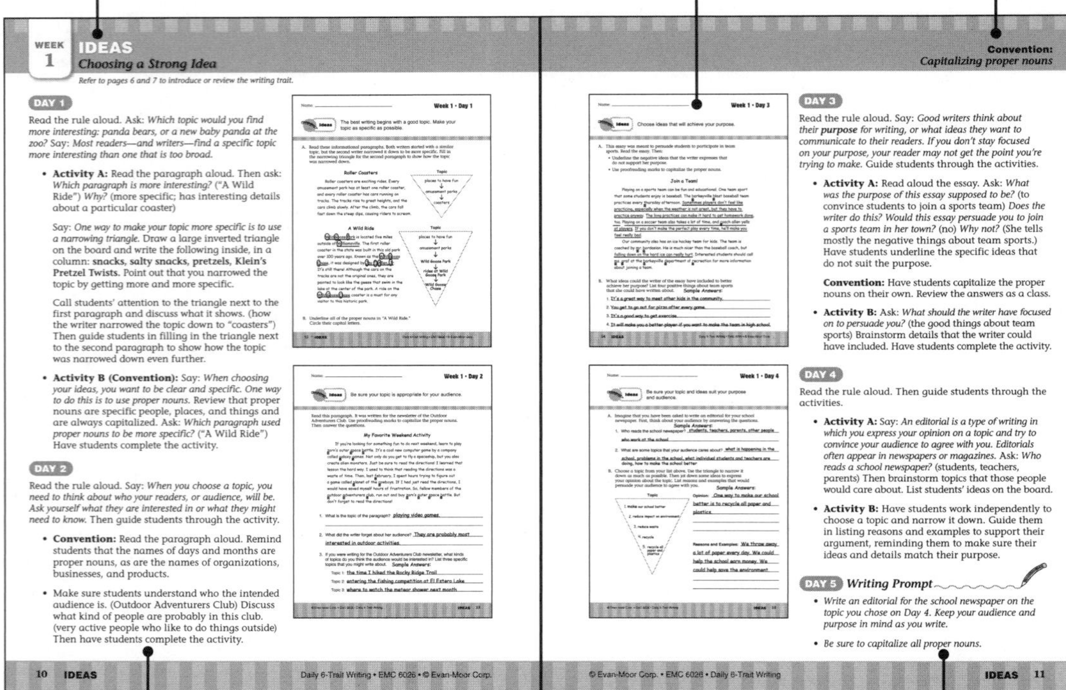

WEEK 1 IDEAS
Choosing a Strong Idea
Refer to pages 6 and 7 to introduce or review the writing trait.

Convention:
Capitalizing proper nouns

DAY 1
Read the rule aloud. Ask: *Which topic would you find more interesting: panda bears, or a new baby panda at the zoo?* Say: *Most readers—and writers—find a specific topic more interesting than one that is too broad.*

- **Activity A:** Read the paragraph aloud. Then ask: *Which paragraph is more interesting?* ("A Wild Ride") *Why?* (more specific; has interesting details about a particular coaster)

  Say: *One way to make your topic more specific is to use a narrowing triangle.* Draw a large inverted triangle on the board and write the following inside, in a column: **snacks, salty snacks, pretzels, Klein's Pretzel Twists.** Point out that you narrowed the topic by getting more and more specific.

  Call students' attention to the triangle next to the first paragraph and discuss what it shows. (how the writer narrowed the topic down to "coasters") Then guide students in filling in the triangle next to the second paragraph to show how the topic was narrowed down even further.

- **Activity B (Convention):** Say: *When choosing your ideas, you want to be clear and specific. One way to do this is to use proper nouns.* Review that proper nouns are specific people, places, and things and are always capitalized. Ask: *Which paragraph used proper nouns to be more specific?* ("A Wild Ride") Have students complete the activity.

DAY 2
Read the rule aloud. Say: *When you choose a topic, you need to think about who your readers, or audience, will be. Ask yourself what they are interested in or what they might need to know.* Then guide students through the activity.

- **Convention:** Read the paragraph aloud. Remind students that the names of days and months are proper nouns, as are the names of organizations, businesses, and products.
- Make sure students understand who the intended audience is. (Outdoor Adventurers Club) Discuss what kind of people are probably in this club. (very active people who like to do things outside) Then have students complete the activity.

DAY 3
Read the rule aloud. Say: *Good writers think about their* ***purpose*** *for writing, or what ideas they want to communicate to their readers. If you don't stay focused on your purpose, your reader may not get the point you're trying to make.* Guide students through the activities.

- **Activity A:** Read aloud the essay. Ask: *What was the purpose of this essay supposed to be?* (to convince students to join a sports team) *Does the writer do this? Would this essay persuade you to join a sports team in her town?* (no) *Why not?* (She tells mostly the negative things about team sports.) Have students underline the specific ideas that do not suit the purpose.

  Convention: Have students capitalize the proper nouns on their own. Review the answers as a class.

- **Activity B:** Ask: *What should the writer have focused on to persuade you?* (the good things about team sports) Brainstorm details that the writer could have included. Have students complete the activity.

DAY 4
Read the rule aloud. Then guide students through the activities.

- **Activity A:** Say: *An editorial is a type of writing in which you express your opinion on a topic and try to convince your audience to agree with you. Editorials often appear in newspapers or magazines.* Ask: *Who reads a school newspaper?* (students, teachers, parents) Then brainstorm topics that those people would care about. List students' ideas on the board.
- **Activity B:** Have students work independently to choose a topic and narrow it down. Guide them in listing reasons and examples to support their argument, reminding them to make sure their ideas and details match their purpose.

DAY 5 *Writing Prompt*

- *Write an editorial for the school newspaper on the topic you chose on Day 4. Keep your audience and purpose in mind as you write.*
- *Be sure to capitalize all proper nouns.*

10 IDEAS Daily 6-Trait Writing • EMC 6026 • © Evan-Moor Corp.

© Evan-Moor Corp. • EMC 6026 • Daily 6-Trait Writing IDEAS 11

Lesson Plans

Use the lesson plans to teach the trait and Convention skills and guide students through the activities on Days 1–4. The plans are structured to enable you to differentiate and tailor lessons for your own class, but still provide the explanation and support you need. You may choose to have students complete the activities as a class, in small groups, or independently.

Day 5 Writing Prompt

Give your students the writing prompt to apply the trait and Convention skills in their own writing. Provide students with paper, or use the page provided for Day 5 in the student practice book. You may also wish to expand the writing prompt into a more fully developed assignment that takes students through the writing process.

Student Activity Pages

Trait and Rule (Skill Summary)

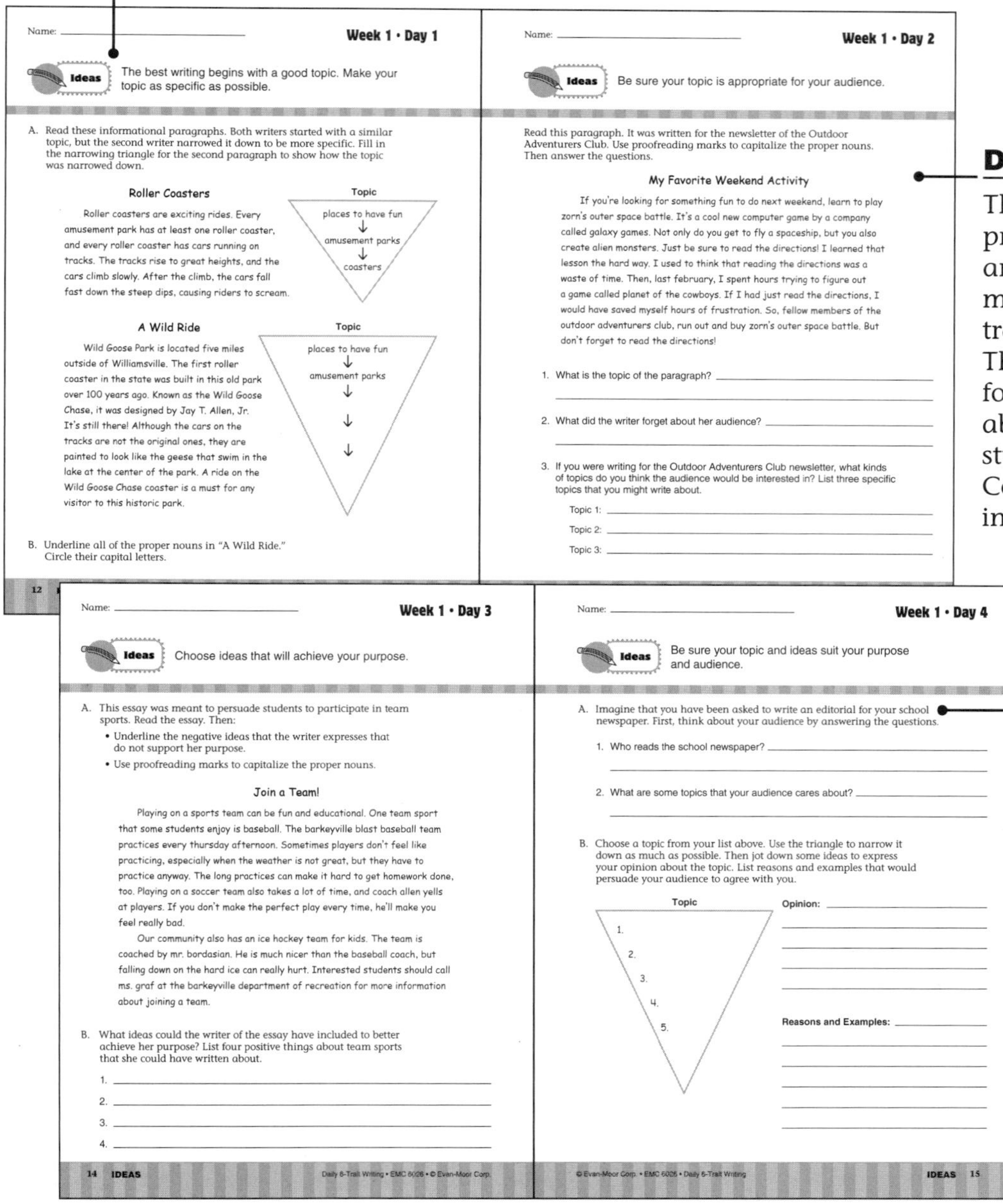

Name: ______ **Week 1 • Day 1**

Ideas — The best writing begins with a good topic. Make your topic as specific as possible.

A. Read these informational paragraphs. Both writers started with a similar topic, but the second writer narrowed it down to be more specific. Fill in the narrowing triangle for the second paragraph to show how the topic was narrowed down.

Roller Coasters

Roller coasters are exciting rides. Every amusement park has at least one roller coaster, and every roller coaster has cars running on tracks. The tracks rise to great heights, and the cars climb slowly. After the climb, the cars fall fast down the steep dips, causing riders to scream.

Topic: places to have fun → amusement parks → coasters

A Wild Ride

Wild Goose Park is located five miles outside of Williamsville. The first roller coaster in the state was built in this old park over 100 years ago. Known as the Wild Goose Chase, it was designed by Jay T. Allen, Jr. It's still there! Although the cars on the tracks are not the original ones, they are painted to look like the geese that swim in the lake at the center of the park. A ride on the Wild Goose Chase coaster is a must for any visitor to this historic park.

Topic: places to have fun → amusement parks → → →

B. Underline all of the proper nouns in "A Wild Ride." Circle their capital letters.

Name: ______ **Week 1 • Day 2**

Ideas — Be sure your topic is appropriate for your audience.

Read this paragraph. It was written for the newsletter of the Outdoor Adventurers Club. Use proofreading marks to capitalize the proper nouns. Then answer the questions.

My Favorite Weekend Activity

If you're looking for something fun to do next weekend, learn to play zorn's outer space battle. It's a cool new computer game by a company called galaxy games. Not only do you get to fly a spaceship, but you also create alien monsters. Just be sure to read the directions! I learned that lesson the hard way. I used to think that reading the directions was a waste of time. Then, last february, I spent hours trying to figure out a game called planet of the cowboys. If I had just read the directions, I would have saved myself hours of frustration. So, fellow members of the outdoor adventurers club, run out and buy zorn's outer space battle. But don't forget to read the directions!

1. What is the topic of the paragraph? ______
2. What did the writer forget about her audience? ______
3. If you were writing for the Outdoor Adventurers Club newsletter, what kinds of topics do you think the audience would be interested in? List three specific topics that you might write about.

Topic 1: ______
Topic 2: ______
Topic 3: ______

Name: ______ **Week 1 • Day 3**

Ideas — Choose ideas that will achieve your purpose.

A. This essay was meant to persuade students to participate in team sports. Read the essay. Then:
- Underline the negative ideas that the writer expresses that do not support her purpose.
- Use proofreading marks to capitalize the proper nouns.

Join a Team!

Playing on a sports team can be fun and educational. One team sport that some students enjoy is baseball. The barkeyville blast baseball team practices every thursday afternoon. Sometimes players don't feel like practicing, especially when the weather is not great, but they have to practice anyway. The long practices can make it hard to get homework done, too. Playing on a soccer team also takes a lot of time, and coach allen yells at players. If you don't make the perfect play every time, he'll make you feel really bad.

Our community also has an ice hockey team for kids. The team is coached by mr. bordasian. He is much nicer than the baseball coach, but falling down on the hard ice can really hurt. Interested students should call ms. graf at the barkeyville department of recreation for more information about joining a team.

B. What ideas could the writer of the essay have included to better achieve her purpose? List four positive things about team sports that she could have written about.

1. ______
2. ______
3. ______
4. ______

14 IDEAS Daily 6-Trait Writing • EMC 6026 • © Evan-Moor Corp.

Name: ______ **Week 1 • Day 4**

Ideas — Be sure your topic and ideas suit your purpose and audience.

A. Imagine that you have been asked to write an editorial for your school newspaper. First, think about your audience by answering the questions.

1. Who reads the school newspaper? ______
2. What are some topics that your audience cares about? ______

B. Choose a topic from your list above. Use the triangle to narrow it down as much as possible. Then jot down some ideas to express your opinion about the topic. List reasons and examples that would persuade your audience to agree with you.

Topic: 1. 2. 3. 4. 5.

Opinion: ______

Reasons and Examples: ______

© Evan-Moor Corp. • EMC 6026 • Daily 6-Trait Writing IDEAS 15

Days 1–3 Activities

The activities on Days 1–3 provide models for students to analyze, revise, or add to. These models expose students to the traits in many forms of writing. They also provide opportunities for students to think critically about writing, enhancing students' own proficiency. The Convention skill is integrated into the activities.

Day 4 Activity

The Day 4 activity provides a prewriting form for the Day 5 writing prompt.

Ways to Use

There are many ways to integrate *Daily 6-Trait Writing* into your classroom:

- Teach the lessons trait by trait.
- Target and practice specific skills students need help with.
- Use the lessons to enhance writing workshops.
- Incorporate the lessons into your other writing programs.

Introducing the Six Traits

Use these ideas to introduce or review the trait at the beginning of each unit.

Ideas

Explain to students that good writing starts with good ideas.

Say: *A good idea is clear, interesting, and original. It makes the reader say, "Wow!" or "I never would have thought of that!" Without good ideas, your writing would not have much of a point. Your reader would be bored!*

Organization

Explain to students that good writing is organized in a way that helps the reader understand the information and follow what the writer is saying.

Say: *The organization of your writing is what holds everything together. It puts your ideas in an order that makes sense, and it gives your writing a strong introduction, body, and conclusion. When your writing is not organized, your reader can grow confused and lose interest.*

Word Choice

Explain to students that good writers choose their words carefully in order to get their ideas across.

Say: *When you write, choose just the right words and use them correctly. Make them fun and interesting so they help your readers "see" what you are talking about. Try not to use the same words over and over again. If you don't choose your words carefully, your reader may not understand what you're trying to say.*

Sentence Fluency

Explain to students that good writers make their writing flow by using different kinds of sentences.

Say: *You want your writing to be easy to read and follow. It should flow so smoothly and sound so interesting that people want to read it aloud! When your sentences don't flow, your writing sounds choppy and flat. Your reader would not want to read it aloud.*

Voice

Explain to students that when they write, their personality, or who they are, should shine through.

Say: *You want your writing to sound like you, and no one else! When you write, you show who you are through words. No matter what type of writing you do, always make sure it sounds like you. Otherwise, your reader may not care about what you have to say. In fact, your reader may not even know who wrote it!*

Conventions

Explain to students that good writers follow all the rules, or conventions, of writing, so their readers can easily read and understand the writing.

Say: *Using correct grammar, spelling, and punctuation when you write is important. When you don't follow the rules, your reader can become lost or confused. He or she may not know where one idea starts and another begins.*

Using the Rubric

Use the rubric on pages 8 and 9 to evaluate and assess your students' skill acquisition.

- Each week, evaluate students' responses to the Day 5 writing prompt using the criteria that correspond to the skills taught that week.
- For Week 5, use all the trait criteria to assess students' understanding of that trait as a whole.
- Use the entire set of criteria to occasionally assess students' writing across the traits.
- In student- and parent-teacher conferences, use the rubric to accurately and clearly explain what a student does well in writing, as well as what he or she needs to improve.

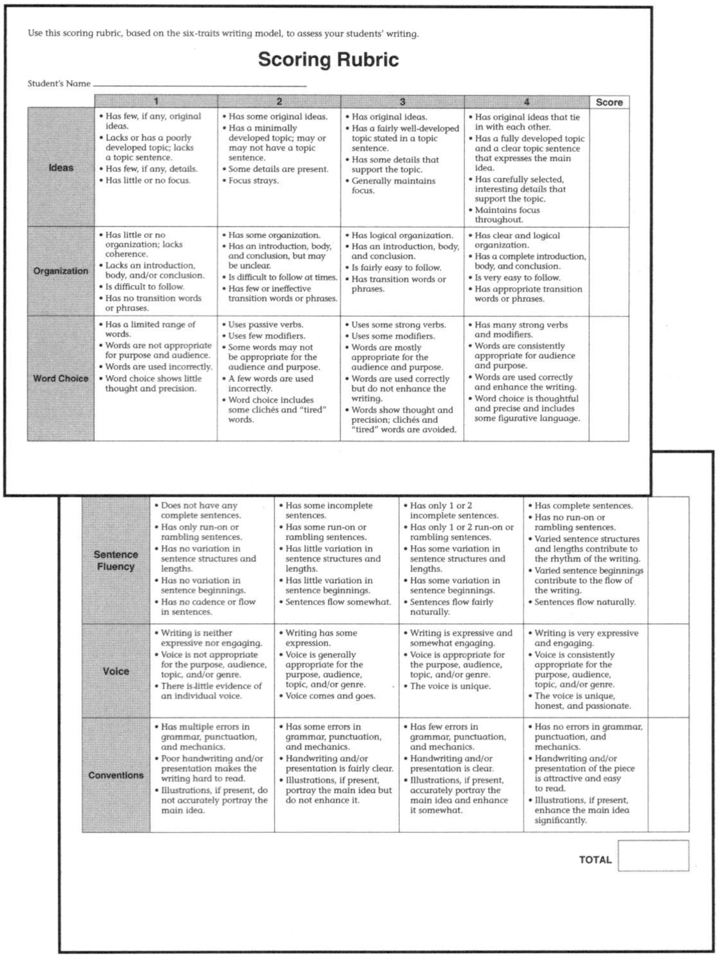

Use this scoring rubric, based on the six-traits writing model, to assess your students' writing.

Scoring Rubric

Student's Name ____________________

	1	2	3	4	Score
Ideas	• Has few, if any, original ideas. • Lacks or has a poorly developed topic; lacks a topic sentence. • Has few, if any, details. • Has little or no focus.	• Has some original ideas. • Has a minimally developed topic; may or may not have a topic sentence. • Some details are present. • Focus strays.	• Has original ideas. • Has a fairly well-developed topic stated in a topic sentence. • Has some details that support the topic. • Generally maintains focus.	• Has original ideas that tie in with each other. • Has a fully developed topic and a clear topic sentence that expresses the main idea. • Has carefully selected, interesting details that support the topic. • Maintains focus throughout.	
Organization	• Has little or no organization; lacks coherence. • Lacks an introduction, body, and/or conclusion. • Is difficult to follow. • Has no transition words or phrases.	• Has some organization. • Has an introduction, body, and conclusion, but may be unclear. • Is difficult to follow at times. • Has few or ineffective transition words or phrases.	• Has logical organization. • Has an introduction, body, and conclusion. • Is fairly easy to follow. • Has transition words or phrases.	• Has clear and logical organization. • Has a complete introduction, body, and conclusion. • Is very easy to follow. • Has appropriate transition words or phrases.	
Word Choice	• Has a limited range of words. • Words are not appropriate for purpose and audience. • Words are used incorrectly. • Word choice shows little thought and precision.	• Uses passive verbs. • Uses few modifiers. • Some words may not be appropriate for the audience and purpose. • A few words are used incorrectly. • Word choice includes some clichés and "tired" words.	• Uses some strong verbs. • Uses some modifiers. • Words are mostly appropriate for the audience and purpose. • Words are used correctly but do not enhance the writing. • Words show thought and precision; clichés and "tired" words are avoided.	• Has many strong verbs and modifiers. • Words are consistently appropriate for audience and purpose. • Words are used correctly and enhance the writing. • Word choice is thoughtful and precise and includes some figurative language.	
Sentence Fluency	• Does not have any complete sentences. • Has only run-on or rambling sentences. • Has no variation in sentence structures and lengths. • Has no variation in sentence beginnings. • Has no cadence or flow in sentences.	• Has some incomplete sentences. • Has some run-on or rambling sentences. • Has little variation in sentence structures and lengths. • Has little variation in sentence beginnings. • Sentences flow somewhat.	• Has only 1 or 2 incomplete sentences. • Has only 1 or 2 run-on or rambling sentences. • Has some variation in sentence structures and lengths. • Has some variation in sentence beginnings. • Sentences flow fairly naturally.	• Has complete sentences. • Has no run-on or rambling sentences. • Varied sentence structures and lengths contribute to the rhythm of the writing. • Varied sentence beginnings contribute to the flow of the writing. • Sentences flow naturally.	
Voice	• Writing is neither expressive nor engaging. • Voice is not appropriate for the purpose, audience, topic, and/or genre. • There is little evidence of an individual voice.	• Writing has some expression. • Voice is generally appropriate for the purpose, audience, topic, and/or genre. • Voice comes and goes.	• Writing is expressive and somewhat engaging. • Voice is appropriate for the purpose, audience, topic, and/or genre. • The voice is unique.	• Writing is very expressive and engaging. • Voice is consistently appropriate for the purpose, audience, topic, and/or genre. • The voice is unique, honest, and passionate.	
Conventions	• Has multiple errors in grammar, punctuation, and mechanics. • Poor handwriting and/or presentation makes the writing hard to read. • Illustrations, if present, do not accurately portray the main idea.	• Has some errors in grammar, punctuation, and mechanics. • Handwriting and/or presentation is fairly clear. • Illustrations, if present, portray the main idea but do not enhance it.	• Has few errors in grammar, punctuation, and mechanics. • Handwriting and/or presentation is clear. • Illustrations, if present, accurately portray the main idea and enhance it somewhat.	• Has no errors in grammar, punctuation, and mechanics. • Handwriting and/or presentation of the piece is attractive and easy to read. • Illustrations, if present, enhance the main idea significantly.	

TOTAL ______

Use this scoring rubric, based on the six-traits writing model, to assess your students' writing.

Scoring Rubric

Student's Name ______________________________

	1	2	3	4	Score
Ideas	• Has few, if any, original ideas. • Lacks or has a poorly developed topic; lacks a topic sentence. • Has few, if any, details. • Has little or no focus.	• Has some original ideas. • Has a minimally developed topic; may or may not have a topic sentence. • Some details are present. • Focus strays.	• Has original ideas. • Has a fairly well-developed topic stated in a topic sentence. • Has some details that support the topic. • Generally maintains focus.	• Has original ideas that tie in with each other. • Has a fully developed topic and a clear topic sentence that expresses the main idea. • Has carefully selected, interesting details that support the topic. • Maintains focus throughout.	
Organization	• Has little or no organization; lacks coherence. • Lacks an introduction, body, and/or conclusion. • Is difficult to follow. • Has no transition words or phrases.	• Has some organization. • Has an introduction, body, and conclusion, but may be unclear. • Is difficult to follow at times. • Has few or ineffective transition words or phrases.	• Has logical organization. • Has an introduction, body, and conclusion. • Is fairly easy to follow. • Has transition words or phrases.	• Has clear and logical organization. • Has a complete introduction, body, and conclusion. • Is very easy to follow. • Has appropriate transition words or phrases.	
Word Choice	• Has a limited range of words. • Words are not appropriate for purpose and audience. • Words are used incorrectly. • Word choice shows little thought and precision.	• Uses passive verbs. • Uses few modifiers. • Some words may not be appropriate for the audience and purpose. • A few words are used incorrectly. • Word choice includes some clichés and "tired" words.	• Uses some strong verbs. • Uses some modifiers. • Words are mostly appropriate for the audience and purpose. • Words are used correctly but do not enhance the writing. • Words show thought and precision; clichés and "tired" words are avoided.	• Has many strong verbs and modifiers. • Words are consistently appropriate for audience and purpose. • Words are used correctly and enhance the writing. • Word choice is thoughtful and precise and includes some figurative language.	

Sentence Fluency	• Does not have any complete sentences. • Has only run-on or rambling sentences. • Has no variation in sentence structures and lengths. • Has no variation in sentence beginnings. • Has no cadence or flow in sentences.	• Has some incomplete sentences. • Has some run-on or rambling sentences. • Has little variation in sentence structures and lengths. • Has little variation in sentence beginnings. • Sentences flow somewhat.	• Has only 1 or 2 incomplete sentences. • Has only 1 or 2 run-on or rambling sentences. • Has some variation in sentence structures and lengths. • Has some variation in sentence beginnings. • Sentences flow fairly naturally.	• Has complete sentences. • Has no run-on or rambling sentences. • Varied sentence structures and lengths contribute to the rhythm of the writing. • Varied sentence beginnings contribute to the flow of the writing. • Sentences flow naturally.	
Voice	• Writing is neither expressive nor engaging. • Voice is not appropriate for the purpose, audience, topic, and/or genre. • There is little evidence of an individual voice.	• Writing has some expression. • Voice is generally appropriate for the purpose, audience, topic, and/or genre. • Voice comes and goes.	• Writing is expressive and somewhat engaging. • Voice is appropriate for the purpose, audience, topic, and/or genre. • The voice is unique.	• Writing is very expressive and engaging. • Voice is consistently appropriate for the purpose, audience, topic, and/or genre. • The voice is unique, honest, and passionate.	
Conventions	• Has multiple errors in grammar, punctuation, and mechanics. • Poor handwriting and/or presentation makes the writing hard to read. • Illustrations, if present, do not accurately portray the main idea.	• Has some errors in grammar, punctuation, and mechanics. • Handwriting and/or presentation is fairly clear. • Illustrations, if present, portray the main idea but do not enhance it.	• Has few errors in grammar, punctuation, and mechanics. • Handwriting and/or presentation is clear. • Illustrations, if present, accurately portray the main idea and enhance it somewhat.	• Has no errors in grammar, punctuation, and mechanics. • Handwriting and/or presentation of the piece is attractive and easy to read. • Illustrations, if present, enhance the main idea significantly.	

TOTAL ____

IDEAS
Choosing a Strong Idea

Refer to pages 6 and 7 to introduce or review the writing trait.

DAY 1

Read the rule aloud. Ask: *Which topic would you find more interesting: panda bears, or a new baby panda at the zoo?* Say: *Most readers—and writers—find a specific topic more interesting than one that is too broad.*

- **Activity A:** Read the paragraph aloud. Then ask: *Which paragraph is more interesting?* ("A Wild Ride") *Why?* (more specific; has interesting details about a particular coaster)

  Say: *One way to make your topic more specific is to use a narrowing triangle.* Draw a large inverted triangle on the board and write the following inside, in a column: **snacks, salty snacks, pretzels, Klein's Pretzel Twists.** Point out that you narrowed the topic by getting more and more specific.

  Call students' attention to the triangle next to the first paragraph and discuss what it shows. (how the writer narrowed the topic down to "coasters") Then guide students in filling in the triangle next to the second paragraph to show how the topic was narrowed down even further.

- **Activity B (Convention):** Say: *When choosing your ideas, you want to be clear and specific. One way to do this is to use proper nouns.* Review that proper nouns are specific people, places, and things and are always capitalized. Ask: *Which paragraph used proper nouns to be more specific?* ("A Wild Ride") Have students complete the activity.

DAY 2

Read the rule aloud. Say: *When you choose a topic, you need to think about who your readers, or audience, will be. Ask yourself what they are interested in or what they might need to know.* Then guide students through the activity.

- **Convention:** Read the paragraph aloud. Remind students that the names of days and months are proper nouns, as are the names of organizations, businesses, and products.

- Make sure students understand who the intended audience is. (Outdoor Adventurers Club) Discuss what kind of people are probably in this club. (very active people who like to do things outside) Then have students complete the activity.

Name: ______________________ **Week 1 • Day 1**

Ideas The best writing begins with a good topic. Make your topic as specific as possible.

A. Read these informational paragraphs. Both writers started with a similar topic, but the second writer narrowed it down to be more specific. Fill in the narrowing triangle for the second paragraph to show how the topic was narrowed down.

Roller Coasters

Roller coasters are exciting rides. Every amusement park has at least one roller coaster, and every roller coaster has cars running on tracks. The tracks rise to great heights, and the cars climb slowly. After the climb, the cars speed down the steep dips, causing riders to scream.

Topic
places to have fun
↓
amusement parks
↓
coasters

A Wild Ride

Wild Goose Park is located five miles outside of Williamsville. The first roller coaster in the state was built in this old park over 100 years ago. Known as the Wild Goose Chase, it was designed by Toby T. Allen, Jr. It's still there! Although the cars on the tracks are not the original ones, they are painted to look like the geese that swim in the lake at the center of the park. A ride on the Wild Goose Chase coaster is a must for any visitor to this historic park.

Topic
places to have fun
↓
amusement parks
↓
Wild Goose Park
↓
rides at Wild Goose Park
↓
Wild Goose Chase

B. Underline all of the proper nouns in "A Wild Ride." Circle their capital letters.

12 IDEAS Daily 6-Trait Writing • EMC 6026 • © Evan-Moor Corp.

Name: ______________________ **Week 1 • Day 2**

Ideas Be sure your topic is appropriate for your audience.

Read this paragraph. It was written for the newsletter of the Outdoor Adventurers Club. Use proofreading marks to capitalize the proper nouns. Then answer the questions.

My Favorite Weekend Activity

If you're looking for something fun to do next weekend, learn to play zorn's outer space battle. It's a cool new computer game by a company called galaxy games. Not only do you get to fly a spaceship, but you also create alien monsters. Just be sure to read the directions! I learned that lesson the hard way. I used to think that reading the directions was a waste of time. Then, last february, I spent hours trying to figure out a game called planet of the cowboys. If I had just read the directions, I would have saved myself hours of frustration. So, fellow members of the outdoor adventurers club, run out and buy zorn's outer space battle. But don't forget to read the directions!

1. What is the topic of the paragraph? playing video games
2. What did the writer forget about her audience? They are probably most interested in outdoor activities.
3. If you were writing for the Outdoor Adventurers Club newsletter, what kinds of topics do you think the audience would be interested in? List three specific topics that you might write about. **Sample Answers:**
   Topic 1: the time I hiked the Rocky Ridge Trail
   Topic 2: entering the fishing competition at El Estero Lake
   Topic 3: where to watch the meteor shower next month

© Evan-Moor Corp. • EMC 6026 • Daily 6-Trait Writing IDEAS 13

Name: ____________________ **Week 1 • Day 3**

Ideas Choose ideas that will achieve your purpose.

A. This essay was meant to persuade students to participate in team sports. Read the essay. Then:

- Underline the negative ideas that the writer expresses that do not support her purpose.
- Use proofreading marks to capitalize the proper nouns.

Join a Team!

Playing on a sports team can be fun and educational. One team sport that some students enjoy is baseball. The barkeyville blast baseball team practices every thursday afternoon. Sometimes players don't feel like practicing, especially when the weather is not great, but they have to practice anyway. The long practices can make it hard to get homework done, too. Playing on a soccer team also takes a lot of time, and coach allen yells at players. If you don't make the perfect play every time, he'll make you feel really bad.

Our community also has an ice hockey team for kids. The team is coached by mr. bordasian. He is much nicer than the baseball coach, but falling down on the hard ice can really hurt. Interested students should call ms. graf at the barkeyville department of recreation for more information about joining a team.

B. What ideas could the writer of the essay have included to better achieve her purpose? List four positive things about team sports that she could have written about. Sample Answers:

1. It's a great way to meet other kids in the community.
2. You get to go out for pizza after every game.
3. It's a good way to get exercise.
4. It will make you a better player if you want to make the team in high school.

14 IDEAS Daily 6-Trait Writing • EMC 6026 • © Evan-Moor Corp.

DAY 3

Read the rule aloud. Say: *Good writers think about their* ***purpose*** *for writing, or what ideas they want to communicate to their readers. If you don't stay focused on your purpose, your reader may not get the point you're trying to make.* Guide students through the activities.

- **Activity A:** Read aloud the essay. Ask: *What was the purpose of this essay supposed to be?* (to convince students to join a sports team) *Does the writer do this? Would this essay persuade you to join a sports team in her town?* (no) *Why not?* (She tells mostly the negative things about team sports.) Have students underline the specific ideas that do not suit the purpose.

  Convention: Have students capitalize the proper nouns on their own. Review the answers as a class.

- **Activity B:** Ask: *What should the writer have focused on to persuade you?* (the good things about team sports) Brainstorm details that the writer could have included. Have students complete the activity.

Name: ____________________ **Week 1 • Day 4**

Ideas Be sure your topic and ideas suit your purpose and audience.

A. Imagine that you have been asked to write an editorial for your school newspaper. First, think about your audience by answering the questions.
Sample Answers:

1. Who reads the school newspaper? students, teachers, parents, other people who work at the school
2. What are some topics that your audience cares about? what is happening in the school, problems in the school, what individual students and teachers are doing, how to make the school better

B. Choose a topic from your list above. Use the triangle to narrow it down as much as possible. Then jot down some ideas to express your opinion about the topic. List reasons and examples that would persuade your audience to agree with you.
Sample Answers:

Topic

1. make our school better
2. reduce impact on environment
3. reduce waste
4. recycle
5. recycle all paper and plastics

Opinion: One way to make our school better is to recycle all paper and plastics.

Reasons and Examples: We throw away a lot of paper every day. We could help the school earn money. We could help save the environment.

© Evan-Moor Corp. • EMC 6026 • Daily 6-Trait Writing IDEAS 15

DAY 4

Read the rule aloud. Then guide students through the activities.

- **Activity A:** Say: *An editorial is a type of writing in which you express your opinion on a topic and try to convince your audience to agree with you. Editorials often appear in newspapers or magazines.* Ask: *Who reads a school newspaper?* (students, teachers, parents) Then brainstorm topics that those people would care about. List students' ideas on the board.

- **Activity B:** Have students work independently to choose a topic and narrow it down. Guide them in listing reasons and examples to support their argument, reminding them to make sure their ideas and details match their purpose.

DAY 5 *Writing Prompt*

- *Write an editorial for the school newspaper on the topic you chose on Day 4. Keep your audience and purpose in mind as you write.*
- *Be sure to capitalize all proper nouns.*

Name: ______________________________ **Week 1 • Day 1**

Ideas The best writing begins with a good topic. Make your topic as specific as possible.

A. Read these informational paragraphs. Both writers started with a similar topic, but the second writer narrowed it down to be more specific. Fill in the narrowing triangle for the second paragraph to show how the topic was narrowed down.

Roller Coasters

Roller coasters are exciting rides. Every amusement park has at least one roller coaster, and every roller coaster has cars running on tracks. The tracks rise to great heights, and the cars climb slowly. After the climb, the cars speed down the steep dips, causing riders to scream.

Topic

places to have fun
↓
amusement parks
↓
coasters

A Wild Ride

Wild Goose Park is located five miles outside of Williamsville. The first roller coaster in the state was built in this old park over 100 years ago. Known as the Wild Goose Chase, it was designed by Jay T. Allen, Jr. It's still there! Although the cars on the tracks are not the original ones, they are painted to look like the geese that swim in the lake at the center of the park. A ride on the Wild Goose Chase coaster is a must for any visitor to this historic park.

Topic

places to have fun
↓
amusement parks
↓

↓

↓

B. Underline all of the proper nouns in "A Wild Ride." Circle their capital letters.

Name: ________________________________

Week 1 • Day 2

Ideas Be sure your topic is appropriate for your audience.

Read this paragraph. It was written for the newsletter of the Outdoor Adventurers Club. Use proofreading marks to capitalize the proper nouns. Then answer the questions.

My Favorite Weekend Activity

If you're looking for something fun to do next weekend, learn to play zorn's outer space battle. It's a cool new computer game by a company called galaxy games. Not only do you get to fly a spaceship, but you also create alien monsters. Just be sure to read the directions! I learned that lesson the hard way. I used to think that reading the directions was a waste of time. Then, last february, I spent hours trying to figure out a game called planet of the cowboys. If I had just read the directions, I would have saved myself hours of frustration. So, fellow members of the outdoor adventurers club, run out and buy zorn's outer space battle. But don't forget to read the directions!

1. What is the topic of the paragraph? ________________________________

____

2. What did the writer forget about her audience? ________________________________

____

3. If you were writing for the Outdoor Adventurers Club newsletter, what kinds of topics do you think the audience would be interested in? List three specific topics that you might write about.

   Topic 1: ________________________________

   Topic 2: ________________________________

   Topic 3: ________________________________

Name: ___________________________

Ideas Choose ideas that will achieve your purpose.

A. This essay was meant to persuade students to participate in team sports. Read the essay. Then:

- Underline the negative ideas that the writer expresses that do not support her purpose.
- Use proofreading marks to capitalize the proper nouns.

Join a Team!

Playing on a sports team can be fun and educational. One team sport that some students enjoy is baseball. The barkeyville blast baseball team practices every thursday afternoon. Sometimes players don't feel like practicing, especially when the weather is not great, but they have to practice anyway. The long practices can make it hard to get homework done, too. Playing on a soccer team also takes a lot of time, and coach allen yells at players. If you don't make the perfect play every time, he'll make you feel really bad.

Our community also has an ice hockey team for kids. The team is coached by mr. bordasian. He is much nicer than the baseball coach, but falling down on the hard ice can really hurt. Interested students should call ms. graf at the barkeyville department of recreation for more information about joining a team.

B. What ideas could the writer of the essay have included to better achieve her purpose? List four positive things about team sports that she could have written about.

1. ___________________________
2. ___________________________
3. ___________________________
4. ___________________________

Ideas Be sure your topic and ideas suit your purpose and audience.

A. Imagine that you have been asked to write an editorial for your school newspaper. First, think about your audience by answering the questions.

1. Who reads the school newspaper? ______________________________

____

2. What are some topics that your audience cares about? ______________________________

____

B. Choose a topic from your list above. Use the triangle to narrow it down as much as possible. Then jot down some ideas to express your opinion about the topic. List reasons and examples that would persuade your audience to agree with you.

Topic

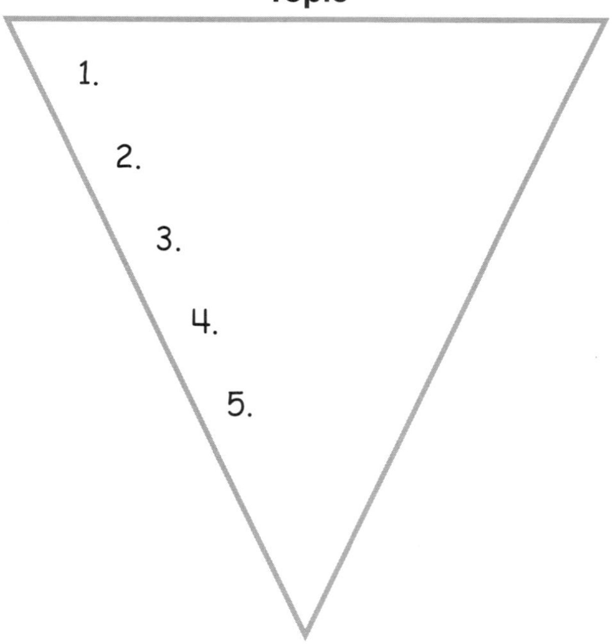

Opinion: ______________________________

____

____

____

____

Reasons and Examples: ______________________________

____

____

____

____

____

WEEK 2

IDEAS

Writing a Topic Sentence and Supporting Details

DAY 1

Read the rule aloud. Then guide students through the activities.

- **Activity A:** Have students read the paragraph. Then ask: *What is the topic of the paragraph?* (Dr. Ross) *What is the writer's main idea about the doctor?* (He was helpful.) *Which sentence is the topic sentence?* (the first) Say: *The other sentences provide details about the topic.* Have students complete the activity. Then review the details, discussing how each one supports the topic sentence.
- **Activity B:** Read the paragraph aloud. Ask: *What is the topic of this paragraph?* (Dr. Ross's patients) *What is the main idea?* (His patients helped him when he was sick.) Have students write and share their topic sentences.
- **Convention:** Write the words **girl's family** on the board. Say: *When we add an apostrophe and s to a word, it becomes a possessive noun. The word* ***girl's*** *shows that the family belongs to the girl.* Have students look for the other possessive nouns in Activity A. (**Dr. Ross's, daughter's, child's**)

DAY 2

Read the rule aloud. Then guide students through the activities.

- **Activity A:** Read the paragraph aloud. Then ask: *What is the topic of the report?* (The Secret of the Mansion) Then ask: *Which sentence is the topic sentence?* ("The Secret of the Mansion by Julie Campbell...") Say: *The topic sentence often comes at the beginning of a paragraph, but you should place it where it makes the most sense.* To determine where the topic sentence belongs (at the beginning, in this case), tell students to ask themselves what the reader needs to know first in order to understand the paragraph.

  Then point out the sentence beginning "I can't wait..." Ask: *Does this sentence support the topic?* (no) Say: *Details that don't support your topic will confuse your reader.* Have students cross out the irrelevant sentences.
- **Activity B (Convention):** Have students complete the activity. Review the answers.

Name: ______________________ **Week 2 • Day 1**

Ideas A good topic sentence clearly states the main idea of the paragraph and is supported by interesting details.

A. Read this paragraph from a biography. Circle the topic sentence and underline the details that support it.

John Ross: An Old-Fashioned Country Doctor

Dr. John Ross was well-known for going out of his way to help his patients. Many of his patients were poor farmers, and they could not always afford to pay Dr. Ross's small fee. The good doctor would accept vegetables, eggs, or even a simple "thank you" in payment. One winter afternoon, he made a house call to see a child with a fever. The girl's family had run out of the firewood they needed to keep their tiny house warm. Dr. Ross grabbed a spare blanket from his car and told the father to bathe his daughter's forehead with cool water. Then Dr. Ross left to take care of other patients. After setting a broken leg, delivering a baby, and cleaning an infected finger, he returned to the sick child's house with a load of firewood. He built a roaring fire for the little girl and her family.

B. The topic sentence is missing from this paragraph. Write a topic sentence that states the main idea of the paragraph.

One former patient, who had paid Dr. Ross many times in eggs, brought homemade chicken soup for the sick doctor. Another patient fixed a hole in his roof, and another drove to town to buy medicine for the doctor. The little girl who had suffered from the fever was all grown up, and she made sure that the doctor's faithful dog enjoyed a walk every day.

Sample Answer:

Topic Sentence: Many years later, when Dr. Ross became ill himself, his patients had a chance to repay his kindness.

18 IDEAS Daily 6-Trait Writing • EMC 6026 • © Evan-Moor Corp.

Name: ______________________ **Week 2 • Day 2**

Ideas Make sure all of your details support your main idea.

A. Read this book report. Use proofreading marks to:

- move the topic sentence to a better place.
- delete details that do not support the topic sentence.

A Good Mystery

Trixie Belden is a thirteen-year-old who solves mysteries with her friends. ~~I can't wait to be thirteen~~. In The Secret of the Mansion, Trixie meets Honey, a girl who becomes her best friend. ~~I have always wanted to live on a farm like Trixie's family does.~~ The Secret of the Mansion by Julie Campbell is the first in a series of mysteries featuring Trixie Belden. Trixie and Honey work together to find out what is going on in a spooky old mansion that is supposed to be empty—but it's not! Trixie and Honey find a boy named Jim in one of the rooms. ~~Old houses are scary and full of cobwebs~~. Jim has run away from his mean stepfather to live in the mansion, which used to be his great-uncle's home. Supposedly, his great-uncle hid thousands of dollars in the house, so the search is on for the missing treasure! I won't give away the book's ending, because not knowing is part of the fun. But if you want a great mystery, read The Secret of the Mansion. ~~My brother thought this book was boring~~.

B. Find the three possessive nouns in the book report. Use them to complete these sentences.

1. The __book's__ two main characters are Trixie and Honey.
2. Jim really wants to find his __great-uncle's__ treasure.
3. __Trixie's__ first name is actually Beatrix.

© Evan-Moor Corp. • EMC 6026 • Daily 6-Trait Writing IDEAS 19

Name: ____________________ **Week 2 • Day 3**

Ideas Include details that your reader would want to know and that support your main idea.

A. Read this beginning of a newspaper article. Fill in the blank with the name of your favorite author. Then provide supporting details by answering the questions.

Author Visits Local Library
Last Saturday, Colton Public Library delighted the community by hosting a party for the famous author Kate DiCamillo.

Sample Answers:

1. What books did the author talk about? What else did he or she do at the party? She read from Because of Winn-Dixie, signed her new book, and talked about writing.
2. How many people were there? There were over 50 people.
3. What did the people at the party think about the author? She was very nice and funny.
4. What was the best part of the party? She brought a dog who looked just like Winn-Dixie!

B. Use proofreading marks to correct the use of apostrophes in this paragraph.

Colton Public Library offers free tutoring to student's of all ages. The tutoring centers hours are from 3:00 to 6:00 p.m. on Tuesday's and Fridays. The center is located to the right of the librarys main door's.

20 IDEAS Daily 6-Trait Writing • EMC 6026 • © Evan-Moor Corp.

Name: ____________________ **Week 2 • Day 4**

Ideas State your main idea in a topic sentence. Then provide interesting details that support the main idea.

Plan a report about the funniest or scariest book you have read. In the center of the web, write a topic sentence for your report. In the outer circles, write details that support your main idea.

Sample Answers:

- The Queen tricks Edmund with promises of Turkish Delight and power.
- His actions put his family in danger.
- The Queen almost kills Edmund.

Topic Sentence: In The Lion, The Witch, and The Wardrobe by C.S. Lewis, Edmund learns that family and love is more important than wealth and power.

- Aslan rescues him and dies in his place.
- Edmund is very sorry.
- Aslan and his family forgive him.

© Evan-Moor Corp. • EMC 6026 • Daily 6-Trait Writing IDEAS 21

DAY 3

Read the rule aloud. Then guide students through the activities.

- **Activity A:** Have a volunteer read the beginning of the article. Point out that it is the topic sentence. Have students suggest authors they would like to meet to complete the sentence. Then ask: *What details would you expect to read about in this article?* (who was at the party, what they said and did, etc.)

  Say: *To think of details to write about, pretend you are the reader. Ask yourself what you would want to know about the topic.* Model this by using the sample answers on the reduced page to the left. Point out how each detail also relates to the main idea stated in the topic sentence.

- **Activity B (Convention):** Say: *Many people confuse possessive and plural nouns when they write.* Read the paragraph aloud. Point out the word **student's** and ask: *Should this word have an apostrophe?* (no) *Why not?* (It's a plural noun, not a possessive.) Have students complete the activity.

DAY 4

Read the rule aloud. Then guide students through the activity.

- Say: *You know that a web helps you plan your writing. But it also shows you if you have supporting details that relate to your topic.*
- Have students think of a funny or scary book they have read. Then have students craft a topic sentence for their book report. Ask prompting questions, such as: *What is the story mainly about?* Then have students fill in the circles with related details about the plot, characters, and setting. Have students exchange papers with a partner to make sure their details stick to the main idea.

DAY 5 *Writing Prompt*

- *Use your ideas from Day 4 to write a book report. Include a topic sentence and supporting details.*
- *Be sure to spell possessive nouns correctly.*

Name: ____________________

Ideas A good topic sentence clearly states the main idea of the paragraph and is supported by interesting details.

A. Read this paragraph from a biography. Circle the topic sentence and underline the details that support it.

John Ross: An Old-Fashioned Country Doctor

Dr. John Ross was well-known for going out of his way to help his patients. Many of his patients were poor farmers, and they could not always afford to pay Dr. Ross's small fee. The good doctor would accept vegetables, eggs, or even a simple "thank you" in payment. One winter afternoon, he made a house call to see a child with a fever. The girl's family had run out of the firewood they needed to keep their tiny house warm. Dr. Ross grabbed a spare blanket from his car and told the father to bathe his daughter's forehead with cool water. Then Dr. Ross left to take care of other patients. After setting a broken leg, delivering a baby, and cleaning an infected finger, he returned to the sick child's house with a load of firewood. He built a roaring fire for the little girl and her family.

B. The topic sentence is missing from this paragraph. Write a topic sentence that states the main idea of the paragraph.

One former patient, who had paid Dr. Ross many times in eggs, brought homemade chicken soup for the sick doctor. Another patient fixed a hole in his roof, and another drove to town to buy medicine for the doctor. The little girl who had suffered from the fever was all grown up, and she made sure that the doctor's faithful dog enjoyed a walk every day.

Topic Sentence: ____________________

____

Name: ______________________________

Ideas Make sure all of your details support your main idea.

A. Read this book report. Use proofreading marks to:

- move the topic sentence to a better place.
- delete details that do not support the topic sentence.

A Good Mystery

Trixie Belden is a thirteen-year-old who solves mysteries with her friends. I can't wait to be thirteen. In The Secret of the Mansion, Trixie meets Honey, a girl who becomes her best friend. I have always wanted to live on a farm like Trixie's family does. The Secret of the Mansion by Julie Campbell is the first in a series of mysteries featuring Trixie Belden. Trixie and Honey work together to find out what is going on in a spooky old mansion that is supposed to be empty—but it's not! Trixie and Honey find a boy named Jim in one of the rooms. Old houses are scary and full of cobwebs. Jim has run away from his mean stepfather to live in the mansion, which used to be his great-uncle's home. Supposedly, his great-uncle hid thousands of dollars in the house, so the search is on for the missing treasure! I won't give away the book's ending, because not knowing is part of the fun. But if you want a great mystery, read The Secret of the Mansion. My brother thought this book was boring.

B. Find the three possessive nouns in the book report. Use them to complete these sentences.

1. The ______________ two main characters are Trixie and Honey.
2. Jim really wants to find his ______________ treasure.
3. ______________ first name is actually Beatrix.

Ideas Include details that your reader would want to know and that support your main idea.

A. Read this beginning of a newspaper article. Fill in the blank with the name of your favorite author. Then provide supporting details by answering the questions.

Author Visits Local Library

Last Saturday, Colton Public Library delighted the community by hosting a party for the famous author ______________________.

1. What books did the author talk about? What else did he or she do at the party?

____

____

2. How many people were there? ______________________________

____

3. What did the people at the party think about the author? ______________

____

4. What was the best part of the party? ______________________________

____

B. Use proofreading marks to correct the use of apostrophes in this paragraph.

Colton Public Library offers free tutoring to student's of all ages. The tutoring centers hours are from 3:00 to 6:00 p.m. on Tuesday's and Fridays. The center is located to the right of the librarys' main door's.

Name: ______________________________

Ideas

State your main idea in a topic sentence. Then provide interesting details that support the main idea.

Plan a report about the funniest or scariest book you have read. In the center of the web, write a topic sentence for your report. In the outer circles, write details that support your main idea.

Topic Sentence:

WEEK 3

IDEAS

Developing Character, Setting, and Plot Ideas

DAY 1

Review the basic story elements. (character, setting, and plot) Then read the rule aloud. Explain that a well-developed setting can enhance a story. It enables readers to picture the story in their minds. Discuss the setting of a book that students have recently read. Then guide students through the activity.

- Tell students that they are going to change an ordinary setting into one that a reader could see, smell, hear, and feel. Say: *Including sensory details helps your reader picture the setting.* Read the paragraph and brainstorm possible details with students to guide them through the questions.
- **Convention:** Review: *When the characters in a story speak, it is called* ***dialogue****. When writing dialogue, always use quotation marks around the exact words spoken.* Point out the dialogue in the last line of the paragraph. Copy it onto the board, pointing out that the quotation marks go after the comma and the end punctuation.

Name: ____________ **Week 3 • Day 1**

Ideas Use vivid sensory details to develop your setting and to make your reader feel as if he or she is there.

Read the description of this setting for a story. Then use your imagination to answer the questions. Your answers should give details that develop the setting.

Felix spent hours in his new bedroom. The walls were a bright color, which he loved. Air came through the slightly open window. The sound of some music came from the room next door. Sounds came from the kitchen downstairs, too, and a smell filled the room. Some stuff was piled on the dresser, and more stuff was piled on the bed. Shelves on the wall held Felix's prized collection. Felix moved the stuff from the bed and sat down. He wrapped himself in his favorite blanket and called out to his brother in the next room, "Hey, Pete, turn that music down!"

Sample Answers:

1. In what time period and location could the story take place? present day, farmhouse in Nebraska
2. What color could the walls of Felix's room be? Why does Felix love that color? The room is painted orange. He loves that color because it's one of the colors of his favorite football team.
3. What kind of "stuff" is in the room? What kind of collection is on the shelves? Clothes and books are scattered about. A collection of tiny cars fills the shelves.
4. What might the air coming through the window feel like? A cool spring breeze comes through the open window.
5. What sounds can Felix hear? What kind of smells might be filling the room? He can hear loud rock music, a barking dog, and the banging of pots and pans. He can smell freshly cut grass.

24 IDEAS Daily 6-Trait Writing • EMC 6026 • © Evan-Moor Corp.

DAY 2

Review the definition of **dialogue.** Then read the rule aloud and guide students through the activities.

- **Activity A:** Read aloud Version 1. Ask: *What do we know about Veronica and Squeak?* (They're stepsiblings who don't get along.) Then read Version 2. Ask: *Which version makes the characters more interesting? How does dialogue help us know the characters better?* (It shows their emotions and personalities.) Discuss what students learned specifically about the characters from the dialogue.
- **Activity B (Convention):** Point out how each time a different character speaks, a new paragraph begins and the first line is indented. This convention makes it easier for the reader to follow who is speaking.

  Brainstorm with students what the characters could say to each other at the end. Then have students write their own lines of dialogue. Remind them to indent the first line and place quotation marks after the punctuation.

Name: ____________ **Week 3 • Day 2**

Ideas Use dialogue to develop your characters. Make them come alive through what they say and think.

A. Read these two versions of a scene from a story. Which version gives you a clearer picture of the characters? Check the box.

Version 1

☐ Veronica tugged at the hood of the little boy's sweatshirt. Veronica told him to slow down. She called him by his nickname, Squeak. The boy, who was her stepbrother, didn't like that.

Veronica sighed. She wondered if her stepbrother would ever accept her as his big sister. She called him by his real name, Gerald, but reminded him that his mom calls him Squeak. Her stepbrother told her that she wasn't his mother. Veronica could see the tears in the boy's eyes, yet she felt herself getting angry anyway.

Version 2

☒ Veronica tugged at the hood of the little boy's sweatshirt. "Please slow down, Squeak," she pleaded.

"My name is not Squeak, and you can't tell me what to do," the little boy muttered, "because you're not really my sister!" His voice rose to a shout.

Veronica sighed. She wondered if her stepbrother would ever accept her as his big sister. "OK, Gerald," she said. "Your name's not really Squeak, but that's what your mom calls you."

"Yeah, but you're not my mother, are you?"

Veronica could see the tears in Squeak's eyes, yet she felt herself getting angry anyway. "No," she sighed, "but I'm still a part of your family."

B. Write one more line of dialogue for each character to say to the other at the end of the story. Use quotation marks correctly.

Sample Answer:

"Well, I don't like it!" Squeak shouted at her.

"Oh, you're so annoying!" fumed Veronica.

© Evan-Moor Corp. • EMC 6026 • Daily 6-Trait Writing IDEAS 25

Name: ______________________ **Week 3 • Day 3**

Ideas Develop a strong plot by planning a sequence of events that is detailed and interesting.

A. Read the introduction for a story. Then answer the questions to develop each stage of the plot.

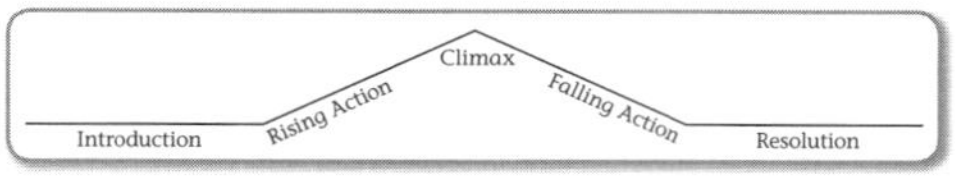

Introduction: *Martin is a 12-year-old boy living in a city apartment with his grandmother. For the first time, he is allowed to ride his bike to the store on his own. Then he realizes his bike is missing.*

Sample Answers:

Rising Action: What does Martin do when he realizes his bike is gone?

Martin runs around the building, searching for his bike.

Climax: What is the story's turning point? Does Martin find out where his bike is?

His grandmother needs butter to bake cookies, so he decides to walk to the store. When Martin arrives at the store, he sees his bike leaning against the wall!

Falling Action: What happens as a result of the climax? He grabs his bike and races home.

Resolution: How does the story end? He doesn't get cookies, but he buys a bike lock the next day.

B. What might Martin say to his grandma at the end? Write it in dialogue form.

Sample Answer: "I'd rather have my bike than your cookies," Martin admitted to his grandmother.

26 **IDEAS** Daily 6-Trait Writing • EMC 6026 • © Evan-Moor Corp.

Name: ______________________ **Week 3 • Day 4**

Ideas Develop your setting, characters, and plot to make your story interesting and detailed.

Read the story idea and the list of possible problems for the characters to face. Choose one idea to develop into a short story.

Story Idea: *A scientist and her assistant are on a mission in a submarine.*

Possible Problems:

- [x] *A mysterious monster arrives.*
- [ ] *Pirates are spotted.*
- [ ] *A spy is found on the submarine.*
- [ ] *A terrible hurricane hits.*

Introduction (Describe the main characters and setting.) Sample Answers:

She is a scientist who believes that a monster lives in the deepest waters of the ocean. She's determined and brave.

Rising Action (Describe the characters' main problem and how it gets worse.)

The submarine reaches deep water and the scientist spots the monster, but it grabs the submarine with its tentacles.

Climax (Describe what happens when the problem is at its worst.)

The submarine is losing power and the monster won't let go. The scientist tries flashing bright lights at the creature in the hope of scaring it away.

Falling Action (Describe what happens as a result of the climax.)

The scientist figures out that the creature hates bright light. The creature swims away. The sub has enough power to rise to the surface.

Resolution (Describe how the story ends.)

The scientist becomes famous, and the creature is named after her.

© Evan-Moor Corp. • EMC 6026 • Daily 6-Trait Writing **IDEAS** 27

DAY 3

Read the rule aloud. Then call students' attention to the plot diagram. Say: *A plot is a sequence of events. In the* ***introduction****, the reader learns about the characters and setting. The* ***rising action*** *is what happens that leads up to the* ***climax****, which is the turning point of the story. This is usually where the most important action happens, or where the characters face and solve a problem. The* ***falling action*** *is a result of the climax, and the* ***resolution*** *is how the story ends.* Then guide students through the activities.

- **Activity A:** Say: *Sometimes we start with a general idea, or even the introduction, for a story, but we don't know where to go next.* Read the introduction aloud. Then use the questions to help the class brainstorm each part of the plot. Encourage students to be creative, but remind them that each part of the story should make sense with the other parts. Prompt students to use specific details when answering the questions.

- **Activity B (Convention):** Remind students to indent and use proper punctuation. Invite students to read their lines of dialogue aloud.

DAY 4

Read the rule aloud. Then guide students through the activity.

- Say: *Every story includes a problem, or something that the main characters face and resolve.* Read the story idea and possible problems aloud. Brainstorm other problems the characters might have. Then have students choose one to develop into a story.

- Have students complete the activity to generate plot development and details. Circulate to assist as needed.

DAY 5 *Writing Prompt*

- *Use your plot outline from Day 4 to write a short story about scientists working on a submarine.*

- *Give each character at least one line of dialogue. Be sure to use correct punctuation.*

Ideas

Use vivid sensory details to develop your setting and to make your reader feel as if he or she is there.

Read the description of this setting for a story. Then use your imagination to answer the questions. Your answers should give details that develop the setting.

Felix spent hours in his new bedroom. The walls were a bright color, which he loved. Air came through the slightly open window. The sound of some music came from the room next door. Sounds came from the kitchen downstairs, too, and a smell filled the room. Some stuff was piled on the dresser, and more stuff was piled on the bed. Shelves on the wall held Felix's prized collection. Felix moved the stuff from the bed and sat down. He wrapped himself in his favorite blanket and called out to his brother in the next room, "Hey, Pete, turn that music down!"

1. In what time period and location could the story take place? ____________________

2. What color could the walls of Felix's room be? Why does Felix love that color?

3. What kind of "stuff" is in the room? What kind of collection is on the shelves?

4. What might the air coming through the window feel like? ____________________

5. What sounds can Felix hear? What kind of smells might be filling the room?

Name: ______________________________

Ideas

Use dialogue to develop your characters. Make them come alive through what they say and think.

A. Read these two versions of a scene from a story. Which version gives you a clearer picture of the characters? Check the box.

Version 1

☐ Veronica tugged at the hood of the little boy's sweatshirt. Veronica told him to slow down. She called him by his nickname, Squeak. The boy, who was her stepbrother, didn't like that.

Veronica sighed. She wondered if her stepbrother would ever accept her as his big sister. She called him by his real name, Gerald, but reminded him that his mom calls him Squeak. Her stepbrother told her that she wasn't his mother. Veronica could see the tears in the boy's eyes, yet she felt herself getting angry anyway.

Version 2

☐ Veronica tugged at the hood of the little boy's sweatshirt. "Please slow down, Squeak," she pleaded.

"My name is not Squeak, and you can't tell me what to do," the little boy muttered, "because you're not really my sister!" His voice rose to a shout.

Veronica sighed. She wondered if her stepbrother would ever accept her as his big sister. "OK, Gerald," she said. "Your name's not really Squeak, but that's what your mom calls you."

"Yeah, but you're not my mother, are you?"

Veronica could see the tears in Squeak's eyes, yet she felt herself getting angry anyway. "No," she sighed, "but I'm still a part of your family."

B. Write one more line of dialogue for each character to say to the other at the end of the story. Use quotation marks correctly.

____

____

____

____

Name: ____________________

Week 3 • Day 3

Ideas

Develop a strong plot by planning a sequence of events that is detailed and interesting.

A. Read the introduction for a story. Then answer the questions to develop each stage of the plot.

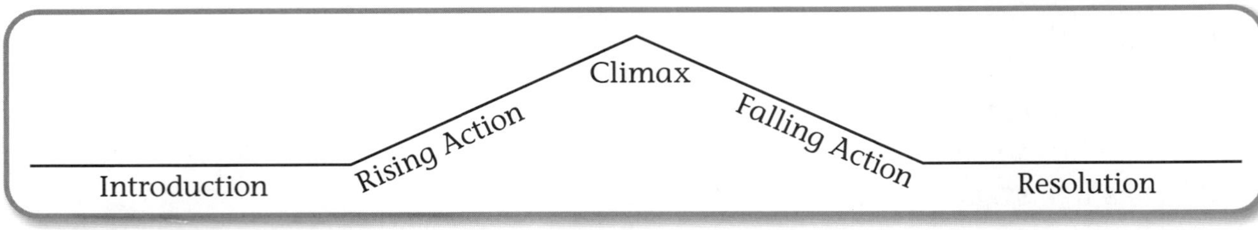

Introduction: *Martin is a 12-year-old boy living in a city apartment with his grandmother. For the first time, he is allowed to ride his bike to the store on his own. Then he realizes his bike is missing.*

Rising Action: What does Martin do when he realizes his bike is gone?

____

____

Climax: What is the story's turning point? Does Martin find out where his bike is?

____

____

Falling Action: What happens as a result of the climax? ____________________

____

Resolution: How does the story end? ____________________

____

B. What might Martin say to his grandma at the end? Write it in dialogue form.

____

____

Name: ________________________________

Ideas

Develop your setting, characters, and plot to make your story interesting and detailed.

Read the story idea and the list of possible problems for the characters to face. Choose one idea to develop into a short story.

Story Idea: *A scientist and her assistant are on a mission in a submarine.*

Possible Problems:

- ☐ *A mysterious monster arrives.*
- ☐ *A spy is found on the submarine.*
- ☐ *Pirates are spotted.*
- ☐ *A terrible hurricane hits.*

Introduction (Describe the main characters and setting.)

____

____

Rising Action (Describe the characters' main problem and how it gets worse.)

____

____

Climax (Describe what happens when the problem is at its worst.)

____

____

Falling Action (Describe what happens as a result of the climax.)

____

____

Resolution (Describe how the story ends.)

____

____

WEEK 4

IDEAS

Elaborating on Ideas and Details

DAY 1

Read the rule aloud. Say: *To **elaborate** means to develop further or tell more about something.* Then guide students through the activities.

- **Activity A:** Have students read both drafts of the narrative. Then compare the two to point out the elaboration. For example, say: *Look at the first sentence in both paragraphs. In the revision, we learn how much time (a week) was spent with which relatives (Uncle Richard and Aunt Joan).* Have students look for and underline additional examples of elaboration to complete the activity.
- **Activity B (Convention):** Say: *Using multiple adjectives to describe something can help you elaborate.* Point out **cozy** and **little** in the first sentence of the second narrative. Say: *Adding **cozy** to **little** gives the apartment a warm, snug feel.* Then point out the comma between the words. Say: *When you put two adjectives in front of a noun, you usually need a comma between the adjectives.* Have students circle the commas between adjectives in the revision. Then have them complete the activity.

DAY 2

Read the rule aloud. Say: *Trying to anticipate the questions your reader may have will help you know what details to include.* Guide students through the activities.

- **Activity A:** Read the letter aloud. Ask: *What questions do you think the recipient of this letter would have?* (e.g., What was Jamie busy with in school? What did she do after school?) Have students write their own questions to complete the activity.
- **Activity B:** Say: *Pretend that you're writing back to Jamie about yourself. What details might you share? What specific activities or people could you tell her about?* Use the sample answers on the reduced page to model writing the note. Then have students write their own notes and share them with the class.
- **Activity C (Convention):** Review the use of commas between adjectives. Then have students complete the activity.

Name: ____________________ **Week 4 • Day 1**

Ideas Good writers elaborate on ideas and details to make their writing clearer and more interesting.

A. Read the two versions of this personal narrative. Underline the details in the revision that show how the writer elaborated on his ideas.

First Draft

Last summer, I spent time with some relatives. They live in an apartment in the town where my uncle goes to college. Before he went to college, my uncle had a good job, but he decided that he wanted to do something else. He was nervous about going to college, but now he likes what he is learning. He told Aunt Joan and me a lot of stories. I learned interesting stuff from him last summer, and now I want to learn more.

Revision

Last summer, I spent a week with my Uncle Richard and Aunt Joan in their cozy, little apartment. They live just down the street from Hart College, where Uncle Richard goes to school. Until two years ago, my uncle was a construction worker. It was a good, steady job. But then he decided that he wanted to be a history teacher and inspire curious, young students. At first, he was nervous about going to college, but soon he was enjoying it too much to be nervous.

Uncle Richard told my aunt and me stories about what he was studying, such as ancient Greece, the Roman Empire, and the Egyptian pharaohs. Pretty soon, she and I both wanted to read more about these fascinating, fun topics. I learned a lot from Uncle Richard. What I really learned, though, was that the more you learn, the more you want to find out!

B. Circle the comma between the adjectives in each sentence.

1. I want to read more about the heroic, short-lived Alexander the Great.
2. Aunt Joan wants to learn about the wise, scholarly Greek philosophers.
3. My uncle's best stories were about the ruthless, powerful pharaohs.

30 IDEAS Daily 6-Trait Writing • EMC 6026 • © Evan-Moor Corp.

Name: ____________________ **Week 4 • Day 2**

Ideas As you write, think about the questions your reader might have, and how you can answer those questions by elaborating more.

A. Read Jamie's letter. Then write three questions you might ask Jamie to help her elaborate on her ideas so she gives more information.

Hi!

I have been busy since I last wrote to you. In school, I have been especially busy. After school, I like to do fun, different things. I love weekends. My friends are great. One of my friends is really fun. What have you been doing?

Your friend,
Jamie

Sample Answers:

Questions: Why have you been busy? What are you doing in school? What do you do after school? Why do you love weekends? Why are your friends great? Which friend is really fun?

B. Write back to Jamie, telling her what you've been doing lately. Think about your questions from above to help you elaborate on your own ideas.

Hi Jamie, Sample Answer:

I've been busy since I last wrote to you. I've had two volleyball tournaments, and I tried out for the school play. Also, I went camping last weekend with my Scout troop! One of my friends, Kasey, is also in Scouts. She showed us how to make homemade rope from plant stalks!

Your friend,

C. Write a comma between the adjectives in each sentence.

1. We're making realistic, life-sized models of skeletons in science.
2. The hard, round skull is the most difficult part to make!

© Evan-Moor Corp. • EMC 6026 • Daily 6-Trait Writing IDEAS 31

Name: ______________________ **Week 4 • Day 3**

Ideas Develop your writing by elaborating on ideas and details.

Look at the picture and read the description of the room. Then revise the description by adding details about the room and elaborating on what is happening in it. Be sure to use commas between adjectives.

A person is reading in her living room. She is sitting on a couch. The walls of the room have photographs on them. Against one wall is a fireplace with a cat lying in front of it. There are some prized possessions displayed on the mantelpiece. There is a rocking chair facing the couch, but it is empty.

Sample Answer: An elderly woman wearing glasses and fuzzy house slippers sits comfortably on her couch, reading a book. She is glad to be sitting down because it's hard for her to walk. She keeps her cane next to her in case she needs to get up. Behind the couch rises a steep, narrow staircase. Its walls are dotted with pictures of the woman's family. She misses them, but she has a telephone nearby if she wants to call them. Also, she has her cat to keep her company. He is lying happily on a woven, striped rug in front of a roaring fire. The warm, cozy room is filled with happy memories.

32 IDEAS Daily 6-Trait Writing • EMC 6026 • © Evan-Moor Corp.

DAY 3

Read the rule aloud. Then guide students through the activity.

- Have students read the description of the picture. Ask: *Does this description tell us much about what's going on in the picture?* (no) *What details could be elaborated on?* (e.g., who the person is and why she's there) Brainstorm other details that could be added to the description.
- Use the sample description on the reduced page to model writing about the scene. Point out that it is important not just to list what's in the room, but to elaborate on how the items are related or why they are there. Say: *As you write, use your imagination to elaborate on what is happening in the picture.*
- **Convention:** Encourage students to use two adjectives in a row to describe the items in the picture. Remind students to place commas between the adjectives.

Name: ______________________ **Week 4 • Day 4**

Ideas Make your writing richer by elaborating on ideas and details.

What is your favorite possession? Plan a paragraph to describe what makes it special. Answer the questions to help you elaborate and add details to your description. **Sample Answers:**

What is your favorite possession? my oldest stuffed animal, a dog with floppy ears

What size and shape is the object? It's about one foot high.

What is it made of? cloth covered with fake fur

What color is the object? used to be bright red, but now it's pink

Where do you keep it? on my bed

When or where did you get it? when I was four, for my birthday

Why do you like the object? Why is it important to you?
I've had it a long time. It's very cute and huggable. It reminds me of my grandma, who gave it to me.

© Evan-Moor Corp. • EMC 6026 • Daily 6-Trait Writing IDEAS 33

DAY 4

Read the rule aloud. Then guide students through the activity.

- Say: *Think of your most prized possession. Is it a game? An article of clothing? A present someone gave you? A trophy or photo? What is special about it? How would you describe it?*
- After students have chosen a possession to write about, have them answer the questions. Then have them exchange papers with a partner and ask each other questions to prompt further elaboration.

DAY 5 *Writing Prompt*

- *Using your answers to the questions from Day 4, write a description about your most prized possession. Be sure to elaborate on your ideas and details to make your writing interesting.*
- *If you use two adjectives in a row, remember to write a comma between them.*

Name: ______________________________

Week 4 • Day 1

Ideas Good writers elaborate on ideas and details to make their writing clearer and more interesting.

A. Read the two versions of this personal narrative. Underline the details in the revision that show how the writer elaborated on his ideas.

First Draft

Last summer, I spent time with some relatives. They live in an apartment in the town where my uncle goes to college. Before he went to college, my uncle had a good job, but he decided that he wanted to do something else. He was nervous about going to college, but now he likes what he is learning. He told Aunt Joan and me a lot of stories. I learned interesting stuff from him last summer, and now I want to learn more.

Revision

Last summer, I spent a week with my Uncle Richard and Aunt Joan in their cozy, little apartment. They live just down the street from Hart College, where Uncle Richard goes to school. Until two years ago, my uncle was a construction worker. It was a good, steady job. But then he decided that he wanted to be a history teacher and inspire curious, young students. At first, he was nervous about going to college, but soon he was enjoying it too much to be nervous.

Uncle Richard told my aunt and me stories about what he was studying, such as ancient Greece, the Roman Empire, and the Egyptian pharaohs. Pretty soon, she and I both wanted to read more about these fascinating, fun topics. I learned a lot from Uncle Richard. What I really learned, though, was that the more you learn, the more you want to find out!

B. Circle the comma between the adjectives in each sentence.

1. I want to read more about the heroic, short-lived Alexander the Great.
2. Aunt Joan wants to learn about the wise, scholarly Greek philosophers.
3. My uncle's best stories were about the ruthless, powerful pharaohs.

Name: ____________________

Week 4 • Day 2

Ideas

As you write, think about the questions your reader might have, and how you can answer those questions by elaborating more.

A. Read Jamie's letter. Then write three questions you might ask Jamie to help her elaborate on her ideas so she gives more information.

> Hi!
>
> I have been busy since I last wrote to you. In school, I have been especially busy. After school, I like to do fun, different things. I love weekends. My friends are great. One of my friends is really fun. What have you been doing?
>
> Your friend,
> Jamie

Questions: ____________________

____

____

B. Write back to Jamie, telling her what you've been doing lately. Think about your questions from above to help you elaborate on your own ideas.

> Hi Jamie,
>
> I've been busy since I last wrote to you. ____________________
>
> ____________________
>
> ____________________
>
> ____________________
>
> ____________________
>
> ____________________

C. Write a comma between the adjectives in each sentence.

1. We're making realistic life-sized models of skeletons in science.
2. The hard round skull is the most difficult part to make!

Ideas Develop your writing by elaborating on ideas and details.

Look at the picture and read the description of the room. Then revise the description by adding details about the room and elaborating on what is happening in it. Be sure to use commas between adjectives.

A person is reading in her living room. She is sitting on a couch. The walls of the room have photographs on them. Against one wall is a fireplace with a cat lying in front of it. There are some prized possessions displayed on the mantelpiece. There is a rocking chair facing the couch, but it is empty.

Name: ______________________________

Ideas

Make your writing richer by elaborating on ideas and details.

What is your favorite possession? Plan a paragraph to describe what makes it special. Answer the questions to help you elaborate and add details to your description.

What is your favorite possession? ______________________________

____

What size and shape is the object? ______________________________

____

What is it made of? ______________________________

____

What color is the object? ______________________________

Where do you keep it? ______________________________

____

When or where did you get it? ______________________________

____

____

Why do you like the object? Why is it important to you?

____

____

____

IDEAS
Maintaining Your Focus

DAY 1

Read the rule aloud. Explain that to stay focused on your topic, you only include details that support and directly relate to your main idea. Then guide students through the activities.

- **Activity A:** Remind students that the purpose of an autobiography is to tell about the events in your life. Read aloud "My Early Years." Ask: *Was this autobiography easy to follow and understand?* (yes) *This author stayed on topic. All of the details support the main idea.*

  Read aloud "My Childhood." Ask: *What is the main idea of this paragraph?* (hard to say, because the writer did not stay focused on one topic) Ask: *Which details are off topic? Which ones do not tell about the author's early childhood?* (the details about the hospitals, wanting to be a doctor, and taking a trip next year) Have students cross out the sentences.

- **Activity B (Convention):** Use the commas in the first two sentences of "My Early Years" to review where to place a comma in a date and in the name of a city and state. Then point out the date in the first sentence of "My Childhood." Say: *When the date falls in the middle of a sentence, it needs a comma before* <u>*and*</u> *after the year.* Repeat for the name of a city and state, using **Columbus, Ohio,** in the fifth sentence as an example.

DAY 2

Read the rule aloud. Then guide students through the activity.

- Say: *The writer, Dan, needs to persuade Mr. Diamond that he would make a good counselor-in-training. What should he include?* (details about his skills and experiences that relate to being a counselor)
- Have students read the letter. Then ask: *Does "but I did not have any time to write this letter because I was learning to ski" support Dan's purpose and main idea?* (no) Say: *That detail should be crossed out.*
- **Convention:** Point out that in an address, you place a comma between the city and state, but not between the state and the zip code. Have students complete the activity. Then review the answers.

Name: ______________________ **Week 5 • Day 1**

Ideas Stay focused on your topic so your reader doesn't get confused.

A. Read these two paragraphs from different autobiographies. Check the one that sticks to the topic. In the other one, cross out the details that do not belong in an autobiography.

☒ My Early Years

I was born on November 5, 1996. My mom and dad were living in a small apartment in Boston, Massachusetts. The apartment was so small that they had to move so there would be enough room for me. We moved to a bigger apartment in a different part of the city, and we still live there. Down the street from our apartment is a playground. I remember my dad taking me there to play with other little kids from the neighborhood. My dad said that it was at this playground that I said my first word, "doggy."

☐ My Childhood

I was born on October 4, 1996, in a hospital in Zoesville, West Virginia. ~~The hospital is a red building with a courtyard in the middle.~~ ~~It is not as big as the hospital where my dad works.~~ ~~He is a doctor.~~ We moved to Columbus, Ohio, last year. At first, I was nervous about leaving West Virginia, but now I like it here. ~~I hope to be a doctor someday.~~ ~~Also, we're taking a trip to New York City next year.~~

B. Write commas in the correct places.

1. March 16, 2006, was the first time I had ever been on an airplane.
2. My family flew to Little Rock, Arkansas, to visit my grandparents.
3. We celebrated my grandfather's birthday on March 18, 2006.
4. Then we flew home to Scranton, Pennsylvania, on March 23, 2006.

36 IDEAS Daily 6-Trait Writing • EMC 6026 • © Evan-Moor Corp.

Name: ______________________ **Week 5 • Day 2**

Ideas Eliminate details that do not support your purpose and main idea. Those details distract your reader.

Read this letter sent to the director of Camp Silver Hawk. Cross out the unnecessary details. Then use proofreading marks to insert commas in the date and addresses.

503 Putnam Avenue
Apollo, CT 05023

January 30, 2010

Mr. Spiro Diamond
14 Lake Road
Echo Valley, NH 02137

Dear Mr. Diamond:

I wish to apply for a place in Camp Silver Hawk's Junior Counselor-in-Training program. I first heard about the program last month, ~~but I did not have any time to write this letter because I was learning to ski~~. My cousin completed the Counselor-in-Training program last summer, and he told me all about it. ~~My cousin thought it was too cold in New Hampshire, so he will not be back.~~

There are several reasons why I would make a good junior counselor. First, I have been a member of the Outdoor Club for a year now. ~~I usually bring a snack with me when I hike.~~ During club hikes, I learned the names of many native plants, animals, and insects. Also, I help my soccer coach with the youngest kids in our soccer league. My coach says that I work well with small children. I enjoy teaching them to work together as a team. Finally, I am a good student, which shows that I am responsible. I hope that you will agree that I would be a great addition to Camp Silver Hawk. ~~If I don't go to Camp Silver Hawk, I will go to basketball camp.~~

Sincerely,
Dan Pinski

© Evan-Moor Corp. • EMC 6026 • Daily 6-Trait Writing IDEAS 37

Name: ______________________ **Week 5 • Day 3**

Ideas Eliminate details that do not support your purpose and main idea.

A. Read this newspaper advertisement for a summer camp. Cross out the details that do not support the purpose and main idea. Use proofreading marks to correct the use of commas in the date and address.

Give your children a summer to remember!

Send your kids to Camp Silver Hawk on the shores of beautiful Lake Echo!

At Silver Hawk, counselors lead campers in fun activities such as:

- hiking beautiful trails
- ~~washing dishes~~
- canoeing and kayaking
- ~~sweeping dead bugs out of cabins~~
- doing crafts such as pottery and woodcarving
- singing camp songs
- ~~picking up litter~~
- ~~repairing leaky boats~~

About Camp Silver Hawk:

- We're 80 years old this year, ~~and although our buildings are falling down~~, they're historical landmarks!
- ~~We're located right next to the freeway, across from the landfill.~~
- Kids from ages 6 to 16 are welcome.

To reserve a place at Camp Silver Hawk for your child, send a check for $50.00 to the following address. All checks must be received by May~~,~~ 15, 2010.

Camp Silver Hawk Office
14 Lake Road
Echo~~,~~ Valley, NH~~,~~ 42137

B. Replace three of the details you crossed out above with activities or other details that would make you want to go to Camp Silver Hawk.

Sample Answers:

1. roasting marshmallows over a campfire
2. sailing on the lake
3. swimming

38 IDEAS Daily 6-Trait Writing • EMC 6026 • © Evan-Moor Corp.

Name: ______________________ **Week 5 • Day 4**

Ideas When planning your writing, focus only on details that support your topic.

A. Pretend that you need a summer job. If you were old enough to work anywhere you wanted, where would it be? Use the questions below to plan a business letter in which you apply for a job. Sample Answers:

Where do you want to work? Moe's Guitar Store

What job do you want? to sell guitars

Why would you be good at this job? What previous experience do you have? have taken guitar lessons for 3 years, have taught some friends how to play, know about different kinds of guitars

What would you do in this job? help people pick the best guitar for their needs, show people different guitars, demonstrate how to play them

What are some other reasons you should be hired? friendly and outgoing, older brother is in a band and will bring in new customers, can work on the weekends when no one else wants to

B. Exchange papers with a classmate. Read each other's answers and discuss whether all of your details stick to your main idea. Cross out any details that don't belong.

© Evan-Moor Corp. • EMC 6026 • Daily 6-Trait Writing IDEAS 39

DAY 3

Read the rule aloud. Then guide students through the activities.

- **Activity A:** Ask: *What is the purpose of an ad?* (to sell something) Explain that people who write ads must stay focused on what the ad is selling. Otherwise, buyers may not want the product.

  Read the ad aloud. Ask: *Who is the audience of the ad?* (parents) *What is the purpose of the ad?* (to persuade parents to send their kids to Camp Silver Hawk) Ask: *Which details might persuade parents not to send their kids? Why?* (e.g., activities that don't sound fun, such as washing dishes; old buildings)

  Convention: If necessary, review the rules for comma placement in dates and addresses. Then have students complete the activity.

- **Activity B:** Have students work in pairs to brainstorm the kinds of activities or features that would make them want to go to a camp. (e.g., sailing, rock climbing, good food) Have students write their ideas and share them with the class.

DAY 4

Read the rule aloud. Then guide students through the activities.

- **Activity A:** Help students brainstorm places they would like to work or jobs they'd like to have. (e.g., cashier at a favorite store or restaurant, baby sitter, tutor, coach's assistant, library volunteer) Use one of the ideas or the sample answer on the reduced page to model answering the questions.
- **Activity B:** Have students exchange papers to make sure their details stick to their main idea.

DAY 5 *Writing Prompt*

- *Use your answers to the questions from Day 4 to write a business letter in which you apply for a job. Maintain your focus throughout the letter.*
- *Include the address of the person you are writing to, as well as the date. Be sure to place the commas correctly.*

Name: ______________________________

Ideas Stay focused on your topic so your reader doesn't get confused.

A. Read these two paragraphs from different autobiographies. Check the one that sticks to the topic. In the other one, cross out the details that do not belong in an autobiography.

☐ **My Early Years**

I was born on November 5, 1996. My mom and dad were living in a small apartment in Boston, Massachusetts. The apartment was so small that they had to move so there would be enough room for me. We moved to a bigger apartment in a different part of the city, and we still live there. Down the street from our apartment is a playground. I remember my dad taking me there to play with other little kids from the neighborhood. My dad said that it was at this playground that I said my first word, "doggy."

☐ **My Childhood**

I was born on October 4, 1996, in a hospital in Zoesville, West Virginia. The hospital is a red building with a courtyard in the middle. It is not as big as the hospital where my dad works. He is a doctor. We moved to Columbus, Ohio, last year. At first, I was nervous about leaving West Virginia, but now I like it here. I hope to be a doctor someday. Also, we're taking a trip to New York City next year.

B. Write commas in the correct places.

1. March 16 2006 was the first time I had ever been on an airplane.
2. My family flew to Little Rock Arkansas to visit my grandparents.
3. We celebrated my grandfather's birthday on March 18 2006.
4. Then we flew home to Scranton Pennsylvania on March 23 2006.

Name: ________________________________

Week 5 • Day 2

Ideas Eliminate details that do not support your purpose and main idea. Those details distract your reader.

Read this letter sent to the director of Camp Silver Hawk. Cross out the unnecessary details. Then use proofreading marks to insert commas in the date and addresses.

503 Putnam Avenue
Apollo CT 05023

January 30 2010

Mr. Spiro Diamond
14 Lake Road
Echo Valley NH 02137

Dear Mr. Diamond:

I wish to apply for a place in Camp Silver Hawk's Junior Counselor-in-Training program. I first heard about the program last month, but I did not have any time to write this letter because I was learning to ski. My cousin completed the Counselor-in-Training program last summer, and he told me all about it. My cousin thought it was too cold in New Hampshire, so he will not be back.

There are several reasons why I would make a good junior counselor. First, I have been a member of the Outdoor Club for a year now. I usually bring a snack with me when I hike. During club hikes, I learned the names of many native plants, animals, and insects. Also, I help my soccer coach with the youngest kids in our soccer league. My coach says that I work well with small children. I enjoy teaching them to work together as a team. Finally, I am a good student, which shows that I am responsible. I hope that you will agree that I would be a great addition to Camp Silver Hawk. If I don't go to Camp Silver Hawk, I will go to basketball camp.

Sincerely,
Dan Pinski

Ideas Eliminate details that do not support your purpose and main idea.

A. Read this newspaper advertisement for a summer camp. Cross out the details that do not support the purpose and main idea. Use proofreading marks to correct the use of commas in the date and address.

Give your children a summer to remember!

Send your kids to Camp Silver Hawk on the shores of beautiful Lake Echo!

At Silver Hawk, counselors lead campers in fun activities such as:

- hiking beautiful trails
- washing dishes
- canoeing and kayaking
- sweeping dead bugs out of cabins
- doing crafts such as pottery and woodcarving
- singing camp songs
- picking up litter
- repairing leaky boats

About Camp Silver Hawk:

- We're 80 years old this year, and although our buildings are falling down, they're historical landmarks!
- We're located right next to the freeway, across from the landfill.
- Kids from ages 6 to 16 are welcome.

To reserve a place at Camp Silver Hawk for your child, send a check for $50.00 to the following address. All checks must be received by May, 15 2010.

Camp Silver Hawk Office
14 Lake Road
Echo, Valley NH, 42137

B. Replace three of the details you crossed out above with activities or other details that would make you want to go to Camp Silver Hawk.

1. ____________________
2. ____________________
3. ____________________

Name: ____________________

Ideas When planning your writing, focus only on details that support your topic.

A. Pretend that you need a summer job. If you were old enough to work anywhere you wanted, where would it be? Use the questions below to plan a business letter in which you apply for a job.

Where do you want to work? ____________________

What job do you want? ____________________

____

Why would you be good at this job? What previous experience do you have?

____

____

____

What would you do in this job? ____________________

____

____

____

What are some other reasons you should be hired? ____________________

____

____

____

B. Exchange papers with a classmate. Read each other's answers and discuss whether all of your details stick to your main idea. Cross out any details that don't belong.

ORGANIZATION

Sequencing

Refer to pages 6 and 7 to introduce or review the writing trait.

DAY 1

Read the rule aloud. Say: *When you write, you have to organize your information. For example, if you're explaining how to do something or get somewhere, you have to describe the steps in the correct sequence, or your reader will get the wrong result!* Then guide students through the activities.

- **Activity A (Convention):** Read the paragraph aloud. Say: *These directions tell the reader exactly where to go, in sequential order.* Point out that the verbs are all in the present tense. Say: *When you give directions, you use* ***imperative verbs****, or verbs that give a command. These are always in the present tense.*

  Review the definition of **prepositional phrase.** (a phrase containing a preposition, its object, and any words in between) Say: *Prepositional phrases help you describe the position or direction of the object. So do direction words such as* ***right*** *and* ***left****.* Have students complete the activity.

- **Activity B:** Brainstorm with students different places in the school that they can give directions to. Then have them write the steps independently. When they are finished, ask volunteers to read aloud their steps and have classmates confirm that the steps are in the right order.

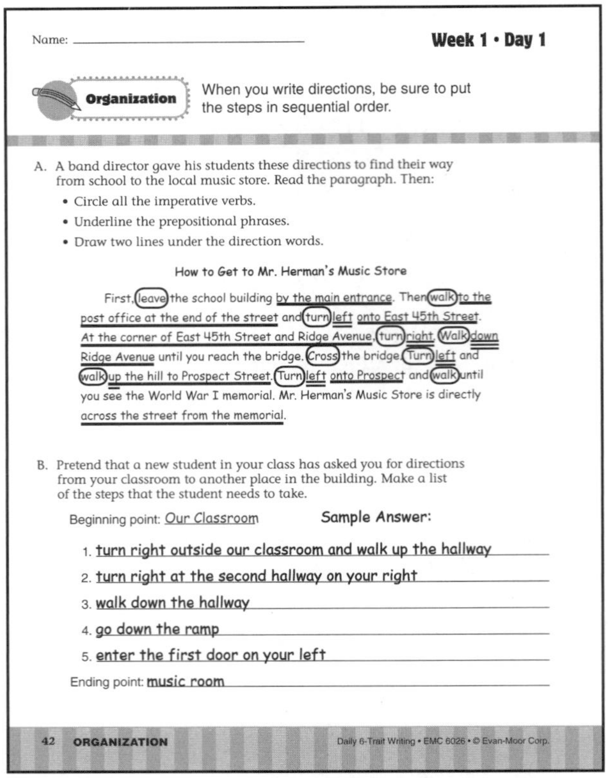

Name: ____________ **Week 1 • Day 1**

Organization When you write directions, be sure to put the steps in sequential order.

A. A band director gave his students these directions to find their way from school to the local music store. Read the paragraph. Then:
- Circle all the imperative verbs.
- Underline the prepositional phrases.
- Draw two lines under the direction words.

How to Get to Mr. Herman's Music Store

First, leave the school building by the main entrance. Then walk to the post office at the end of the street and turn left onto East 45th Street. At the corner of East 45th Street and Ridge Avenue, turn right. Walk down Ridge Avenue until you reach the bridge. Cross the bridge. Turn left and walk up the hill to Prospect Street. Turn left onto Prospect and walk until you see the World War I memorial. Mr. Herman's Music Store is directly across the street from the memorial.

B. Pretend that a new student in your class has asked you for directions from your classroom to another place in the building. Make a list of the steps that the student needs to take.

Beginning point: Our Classroom   Sample Answer:

1. turn right outside our classroom and walk up the hallway
2. turn right at the second hallway on your right
3. walk down the hallway
4. go down the ramp
5. enter the first door on your left

Ending point: music room

42 ORGANIZATION   Daily 6-Trait Writing • EMC 6026 • © Evan-Moor Corp.

DAY 2

Read the rule aloud. Review: ***Chronological order*** *means the order in which things happen in time.* Then guide students through the activities.

- **Activity A:** Read the description aloud. Ask: *Is this paragraph in chronological order?* (no) Say: *The writer wrote his thoughts as they came to him, instead of thinking of the order in which the events happened.*

  Convention: Ask: *The events in this description have already happened, so in what tense should they all be?* (past) Have students correct the verbs.

- **Activity B:** Point out the first box in the sequence map and ask: *What happened after the writer and his dad entered the theater?* (usher took their tickets) Have students write that in the second box. Then have them complete the activity on their own. Point out transition words and phrases such as "after" and "at the beginning" to use as clues to the order of events.

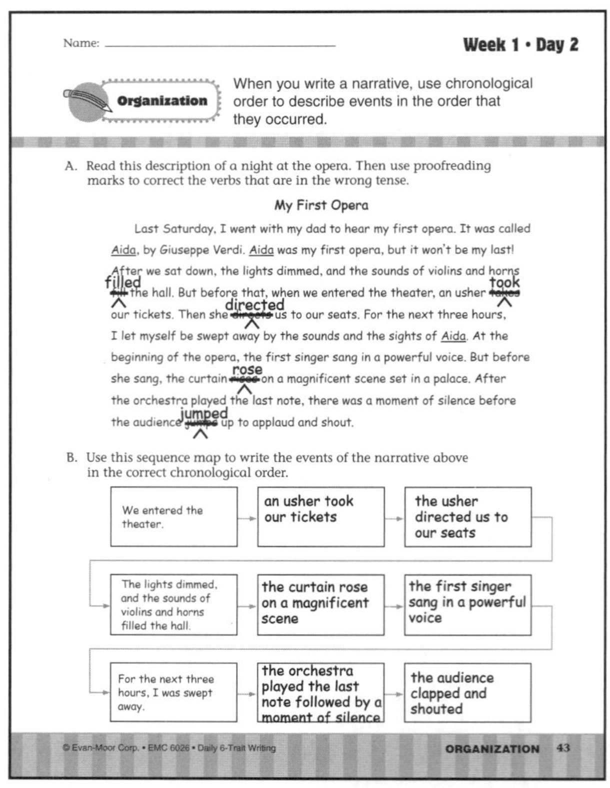

Name: ____________ **Week 1 • Day 2**

Organization When you write a narrative, use chronological order to describe events in the order that they occurred.

A. Read this description of a night at the opera. Then use proofreading marks to correct the verbs that are in the wrong tense.

My First Opera

Last Saturday, I went with my dad to hear my first opera. It was called Aida, by Giuseppe Verdi. Aida was my first opera, but it won't be my last! After we sat down, the lights dimmed, and the sounds of violins and horns ~~fill~~ filled the hall. But before that, when we entered the theater, an usher ~~takes~~ took our tickets. Then she ~~directs~~ directed us to our seats. For the next three hours, I let myself be swept away by the sounds and the sights of Aida. At the beginning of the opera, the first singer sang in a powerful voice. But before she sang, the curtain ~~rises~~ rose on a magnificent scene set in a palace. After the orchestra played the last note, there was a moment of silence before the audience ~~jumps~~ jumped up to applaud and shout.

B. Use this sequence map to write the events of the narrative above in the correct chronological order.

We entered the theater.	an usher took our tickets	the usher directed us to our seats
The lights dimmed, and the sounds of violins and horns filled the hall.	the curtain rose on a magnificent scene	the first singer sang in a powerful voice
For the next three hours, I was swept away.	the orchestra played the last note followed by a moment of silence	the audience clapped and shouted

© Evan-Moor Corp. • EMC 6026 • Daily 6-Trait Writing   ORGANIZATION 43

Name: ____________________ **Week 1 • Day 3**

Organization Use transition words and phrases to help your reader follow the sequence of events in your narrative.

Read this personal narrative. Then fill in the blanks with transition words and phrases that give clues to the order of events.

Transition Words and Phrases					
suddenly	then	at first	next	before long	finally
eventually	after	at last	soon	the next time	before

Answers may vary. Suggested answers:

My First Performance

The first time I played my guitar and sang in the school talent show, I was very nervous. Before I went on, I stood backstage shaking. It was my turn to perform next. While the audience was clapping, I slowly walked to the center of the empty stage. After everyone stopped, I lifted my guitar and started strumming. Soon, I began to sing. At first, my voice came out as a little squeak, but I decided to pretend that I was just standing in my bedroom playing for my biggest fan—my cat! Eventually, my voice grew stronger. I decided to concentrate on what the words of the song meant. "This land is your land," I sang with courage. Then, I noticed that the audience was swaying to the tune and singing along. So I led them in another round of the chorus. Before long, the song was over. I took a bow as the audience cheered.

Being on stage turned out to be a lot of fun. The next time, I wouldn't be as nervous!

44 ORGANIZATION Daily 6-Trait Writing • EMC 6026 • © Evan-Moor Corp.

Name: ____________________ **Week 1 • Day 4**

Organization Use chronological order to help your reader follow the sequence of events in your narrative.

Think about a time when you accomplished something special. Plan a narrative about it by using the sequence map to write the events in chronological order. Be sure to use only past tense verbs. Sample Answers:

received audition music from band director

↓

practiced for hours

↓

played the music for my director, who recorded it

↓

waited for two weeks

↓

Final accomplishment or result:
found out that I made the all-district middle school band

© Evan-Moor Corp. • EMC 6026 • Daily 6-Trait Writing ORGANIZATION 45

DAY 3

Read the rule aloud. Say: *Transition words and phrases help our readers understand the order of our ideas and of the events that happened.* Guide students through the activity.

- Read the transition words and phrases in the box. Say: *Often—but not always—these words and phrases come at the beginning of a sentence.* Then have students fill in the blanks. Point out that there may be more than one way to do so correctly, and that some words or phrases may not be used.
- Have volunteers read aloud their completed paragraphs. Discuss the different choices students may have made in filling in the blanks. For example, students may have written **Then**, **Finally**, or **At last** in front of "I began to sing."
- **Convention:** Ask: *What verb tense does the writer stick to throughout the narrative?* (past)

DAY 4

Read the rule aloud. Then guide students through the activity.

- Brainstorm with students what accomplishments they could write about. (e.g., mastering a new sport, passing a difficult test, giving a special performance) Then ask: *What led up to your accomplishment? What did you have to do?* (e.g., practice, rehearse, study) *Describe the events leading up to the final accomplishment or result.*
- **Convention:** Have students use the sequence map to list events in the order they happened. Remind students to keep their verbs in the past tense.

DAY 5 *Writing Prompt*

- *Use your sequence map from Day 4 to write a personal narrative about a special accomplishment. Use transition words and phrases to connect your ideas and to show the order of events.*
- *Be sure to use the same verb tense throughout your narrative.*

Name: ______________________________

Week 1 • Day 1

Organization

When you write directions, be sure to put the steps in sequential order.

A. A band director gave his students these directions to find their way from school to the local music store. Read the paragraph. Then:

- Circle all the imperative verbs.
- Underline the prepositional phrases.
- Draw two lines under the direction words.

How to Get to Mr. Herman's Music Store

First, leave the school building by the main entrance. Then walk to the post office at the end of the street and turn left onto East 45th Street. At the corner of East 45th Street and Ridge Avenue, turn right. Walk down Ridge Avenue until you reach the bridge. Cross the bridge. Turn left and walk up the hill to Prospect Street. Turn left onto Prospect and walk until you see the World War I memorial. Mr. Herman's Music Store is directly across the street from the memorial.

B. Pretend that a new student in your class has asked you for directions from your classroom to another place in the building. Make a list of the steps that the student needs to take.

Beginning point: Our Classroom

1. ______________________________
2. ______________________________
3. ______________________________
4. ______________________________
5. ______________________________

Ending point: ______________________________

Name: ____________________________________

Organization

When you write a narrative, use chronological order to describe events in the order that they occurred.

A. Read this description of a night at the opera. Then use proofreading marks to correct the verbs that are in the wrong tense.

My First Opera

Last Saturday, I went with my dad to hear my first opera. It was called Aida, by Giuseppe Verdi. Aida was my first opera, but it won't be my last! After we sat down, the lights dimmed, and the sounds of violins and horns fill the hall. But before that, when we entered the theater, an usher takes our tickets. Then she directs us to our seats. For the next three hours, I let myself be swept away by the sounds and the sights of Aida. At the beginning of the opera, the first singer sang in a powerful voice. But before she sang, the curtain rises on a magnificent scene set in a palace. After the orchestra played the last note, there was a moment of silence before the audience jumps up to applaud and shout.

B. Use this sequence map to write the events of the narrative above in the correct chronological order.

We entered the theater. →	→	
The lights dimmed, and the sounds of violins and horns filled the hall. →	→	
For the next three hours, I was swept away. →	→	

Name: ______________________________

Organization

Use transition words and phrases to help your reader follow the sequence of events in your narrative.

Read this personal narrative. Then fill in the blanks with transition words and phrases that give clues to the order of events.

Transition Words and Phrases					
suddenly	then	at first	next	before long	finally
eventually	after	at last	soon	the next time	before

My First Performance

The first time I played my guitar and sang in the school talent show, I was very nervous. ____________________ I went on, I stood backstage shaking. It was my turn to perform ____________________. While the audience was clapping, I slowly walked to the center of the empty stage. ____________________ everyone stopped, I lifted my guitar and started strumming. ____________________, I began to sing.

____________________, my voice came out as a little squeak, but I decided to pretend that I was just standing in my bedroom playing for my biggest fan—my cat! ____________________, my voice grew stronger. I decided to concentrate on what the words of the song meant. "This land is your land," I sang with courage. ____________________, I noticed that the audience was swaying to the tune and singing along. So I led them in another round of the chorus. ____________________, the song was over. I took a bow as the audience cheered.

Being on stage turned out to be a lot of fun. ____________________, I wouldn't be as nervous!

Name: ______________________

Organization

Use chronological order to help your reader follow the sequence of events in your narrative.

Think about a time when you accomplished something special. Plan a narrative about it by using the sequence map to write the events in chronological order. Be sure to use only past tense verbs.

↓

↓

↓

↓

Final accomplishment or result:

WEEK 2 ORGANIZATION
Organizing Information Logically

DAY 1

Read the rule aloud. Say: *By grouping similar ideas and details together, you'll make your writing easier to follow.* Guide students through the activities.

- **Activity A:** If necessary, review the definition of **main idea.** Then have students read the paragraphs and underline the main ideas. Then ask: *Does this essay have good organization?* (yes) *All of the details about a disorganized locker are in one paragraph, and all of the details about an organized locker are in the other.*

  Convention: Review: ***Homophones*** *are words that sound alike but have different spellings and meanings.* Write the homophones **its/it's** and **your/you're** on the board and discuss their meanings. Then say: *People often confuse these and other homophones when they write.* Have students find and correct the misspelled homophones.

- **Activity B:** Say: *Writing an outline can help you make sure your details are organized properly.* Review how outlines are formed. (e.g., Roman numerals for main ideas; capital letters for details) Use the answers on the reduced page to model filling in part of the outline. Then have students complete the activity.

DAY 2

Read the rule aloud. Review the definitions of **cause** (something that makes something else happen) and **effect** (the result of what happens). Then guide students through the activity.

- **Convention:** You may want to list the misspelled homophones on the board ahead of time to help students recognize and correct them.
- Read the report aloud. Then say: *The details in this report are organized around cause-and-effect relationships. That is, the writer identifies each cause and then describes its effect(s). The writer also uses transition words and phrases such as* ***so, therefore, as a result,*** *and* ***consequently*** *to guide the reader and make connections between the causes and effects.*
- Have students work in pairs to complete the chart. Review the answers as a class.

Name: ______________________ **Week 2 • Day 1**

Organization Use logical organization so your writing makes sense. Group similar ideas and details together.

A. Underline the main idea of this essay. Draw two lines under the main idea of each paragraph. Finally, cross out and correct the four misspelled homophones.

What's That Smell?

Keeping your locker clean and organized will make you a better and happier student. If your locker is disorganized, you will have a mess. You will lose important books and papers that you need for class. On a rainy day, your coat will never dry because ~~its~~ it's jammed in next to your dirty gym clothes. Your science project will be crushed when your library books fall on it. You'll never have sharp pencils because every ~~led~~ lead tip will be broken off. Someday, someone will ask, "What's that smell?" and you'll realize that the smell is coming from a forgotten sandwich at the bottom of your locker!

On the other hand, if you keep ~~you're~~ your locker clean and organized, your life will be much happier. Your books and papers will be easy to find. Your wet coat will be dry before lunchtime. You'll get a good grade on that science project and never ruin another pencil. Best of all, the next time someone asks, "What's that smell?" they won't be pointing at your locker. So don't ~~waist~~ waste another minute. Start cleaning!

B. Fill in the outline below with details from each paragraph.

I. Disorganized locker
- A. lose things
- B. coat stays wet
- C. project ruined
- D. no sharp pencils
- E. lost and smelly lunch

II. Organized locker
- A. things easy to find
- B. coat gets dry
- C. good grade on project
- D. never ruin another pencil
- E. no smell from lost lunch

48 ORGANIZATION Daily 6-Trait Writing • EMC 6026 • © Evan-Moor Corp.

Name: ______________________ **Week 2 • Day 2**

Organization You can organize your details by cause and effect to show how events are connected.

Read this report about the *Titanic*. Then:
- Cross out and correct the eight misspelled homophones.
- Complete the chart to help you see how the report is organized.

On April 14, 1912, the famous ship called the Titanic struck an iceberg, causing over 1,500 people to die. People have long wondered how this well-built ship, ~~witch~~ which had been called "practically unsinkable," could have sunk.

One cause was natural. There was no moon visible the night of the disaster, so the crew on watch did not ~~sea~~ see the iceberg until it was too late. Other causes were human error. The ship was moving ~~to~~ too fast in dangerous waters. Therefore, important parts of the ship were damaged when it struck the iceberg. Also, ~~their~~ there were not enough lifeboats for everyone on ~~bored~~ board, and many more people died than would have otherwise.

As a result of the Titanic disaster, safety improvements were ~~maid~~ made to ships, and new laws were ~~past~~ passed to protect passengers. The International Ice Patrol was formed to look out for icebergs in the northwest Atlantic Ocean. Consequently, there has never ~~bin~~ been another disaster as bad as the Titanic.

Cause	Effect
The Titanic struck an iceberg. →	Over 1,500 people died.
There was no moon visible. →	The crew couldn't see the iceberg until it was too late.
The ship was moving too fast in dangerous waters. →	Important parts of the ship were damaged.
There weren't enough lifeboats. →	Many more people died than would have otherwise.
No one wanted another Titanic disaster. →	Safety improvements were made, new laws were passed, and the International Ice Patrol was formed.

© Evan-Moor Corp. • EMC 6026 • Daily 6-Trait Writing ORGANIZATION 49

Name: ____________________ **Week 2 • Day 3**

Organization When you write a description of how something looks, you can use spatial order to organize your details.

A. Read Josefina's description of her grandmother's home. Then:
- Underline the prepositional phrases that show position or direction.
- Cross out and correct the four misspelled homophones.

Come with me to visit my grandmother. She is an artist who works with clay. We'll travel the dusty ~~rode~~ road that leads to her house. First, we must take a ~~plain~~ plane ride to Mexico and drive to the town where she lives. As we walk into her front yard, dozens of colorful clay figures greet us from both sides. My grandfather sits at a long table, painting faces on the dried figures with a tiny brush. A bright ~~blew~~ blue door leads from the yard into the patio. Just inside the door is a stool ~~wear~~ where my grandmother sits, shaping the clay. Across from her is my grandfather. A mound of wet clay is piled on a large cloth behind my grandmother, ready to be transformed.

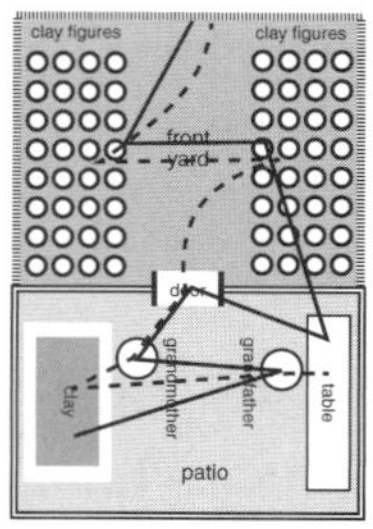

B. Some of the sentences in Josefina's description are not in spatial order. Rewrite the description in a more logical order, using the diagram for help.

Sample Answer:

Come with me to visit my grandmother. She is an artist who works with clay. First, we must take a plane ride to Mexico and drive to the town where she lives. Then, we'll travel the dusty road that leads to her house. As we walk into her front yard, dozens of colorful clay figures greet us from both sides. A bright blue door leads from the yard into the patio. Just inside the door is a stool where my grandmother sits, shaping the clay. A mound of wet clay is piled on a large cloth behind her, ready to be transformed. Across from her is my grandfather. He sits at a long table, painting faces on the dried figures with a tiny brush.

50 ORGANIZATION Daily 6-Trait Writing • EMC 6026 • © Evan-Moor Corp.

DAY 3

Read the rule aloud. Explain: ***Spatial order*** *means organizing details by where things are located in relation to each other. For example, details can be described from left to right, or top to bottom.* Then say: *Prepositions such as* ***across from, behind,*** *and* ***into*** *can help the reader picture what you are describing.* Guide students through the activities.

- **Activity A:** Have students read the description and underline the prepositional phrases. Review the answers as a class.

  Convention: You may want to list the misspelled homophones on the board before students look for them in the description.

- **Activity B:** Read the paragraph aloud, having students draw a line on their diagrams to show the order in which the details are described (solid line). Then have students draw another line to show a more logical order that the writer could have followed (dotted line). Have students rewrite the description, using that order.

Name: ____________________ **Week 2 • Day 4**

Organization Use spatial order to plan and organize your description of a place.

Draw a diagram of your bedroom. Then draw and label details in your bedroom that you want to write about. Plan the way you will organize your description by tracing a path through the room.

Drawings will vary.

© Evan-Moor Corp. • EMC 6026 • Daily 6-Trait Writing ORGANIZATION 51

DAY 4

Review the rule. Guide students through the activity.

- Explain that making a drawing of a room can serve as a visual organizer for a description. If necessary, model drawing a diagram of your classroom on the board. Then circulate to assist students in drawing their own diagrams.
- To help students plan their paths through the room, point out that they should first choose the place they wish to start their descriptions. Then say: *Make sure your path makes sense, and that it would guide someone through your room even if they couldn't see it. Don't jump from one side of the room to another.*

DAY 5 *Writing Prompt*

- *Use your diagram from Day 4 to write a description of your bedroom. Use spatial order and prepositional phrases.*
- *Exchange papers with a partner to check that you have not misspelled any homophones.*

Name: ______________________________

Week 2 • Day 1

Organization

Use logical organization so your writing makes sense. Group similar ideas and details together.

A. Underline the main idea of this essay. Draw two lines under the main idea of each paragraph. Finally, cross out and correct the four misspelled homophones.

What's That Smell?

Keeping your locker clean and organized will make you a better and happier student. If your locker is disorganized, you will have a mess. You will lose important books and papers that you need for class. On a rainy day, your coat will never dry because its jammed in next to your dirty gym clothes. Your science project will be crushed when your library books fall on it. You'll never have sharp pencils because every led tip will be broken off. Someday, someone will ask, "What's that smell?" and you'll realize that the smell is coming from a forgotten sandwich at the bottom of your locker!

On the other hand, if you keep you're locker clean and organized, your life will be much happier. Your books and papers will be easy to find. Your wet coat will be dry before lunchtime. You'll get a good grade on that science project and never ruin another pencil. Best of all, the next time someone asks, "What's that smell?" they won't be pointing at your locker. So don't waist another minute. Start cleaning!

B. Fill in the outline below with details from each paragraph.

I. Disorganized locker

A. ______________________

B. ______________________

C. ______________________

D. ______________________

E. ______________________

II. Organized locker

A. ______________________

B. ______________________

C. ______________________

D. ______________________

E. ______________________

Name: ____________________

Week 2 • Day 2

Organization

You can organize your details by cause and effect to show how events are connected.

Read this report about the *Titanic*. Then:

- Cross out and correct the eight misspelled homophones.
- Complete the chart to help you see how the report is organized.

On April 14, 1912, the famous ship called the Titanic struck an iceberg, causing over 1,500 people to die. People have long wondered how this well-built ship, witch had been called "practically unsinkable," could have sunk.

One cause was natural. There was no moon visible the night of the disaster, so the crew on watch did not sea the iceberg until it was too late. Other causes were human error. The ship was moving to fast in dangerous waters. Therefore, important parts of the ship were damaged when it struck the iceberg. Also, their were not enough lifeboats for everyone on bored, and many more people died than would have otherwise.

As a result of the Titanic disaster, safety improvements were maid to ships, and new laws were past to protect passengers. The International Ice Patrol was formed to look out for icebergs in the northwest Atlantic Ocean. Consequently, there has never bin another disaster as bad as the Titanic.

Cause	Effect
→	Over 1,500 people died.
There was no moon visible. →	
→	Important parts of the ship were damaged.
There weren't enough lifeboats. →	
No one wanted another Titanic disaster. →	

Name: ______________________

Organization

When you write a description of how something looks, you can use spatial order to organize your details.

A. Read Josefina's description of her grandmother's home. Then:

- Underline the prepositional phrases that show position or direction.
- Cross out and correct the four misspelled homophones.

Come with me to visit my grandmother. She is an artist who works with clay. We'll travel the dusty rode that leads to her house. First, we must take a plain ride to Mexico and drive to the town where she lives. As we walk into her front yard, dozens of colorful clay figures greet us from both sides. My grandfather sits at a long table, painting faces on the dried figures with a tiny brush. A bright blew door leads from the yard into the patio. Just inside the door is a stool wear my grandmother sits, shaping the clay. Across from her is my grandfather. A mound of wet clay is piled on a large cloth behind my grandmother, ready to be transformed.

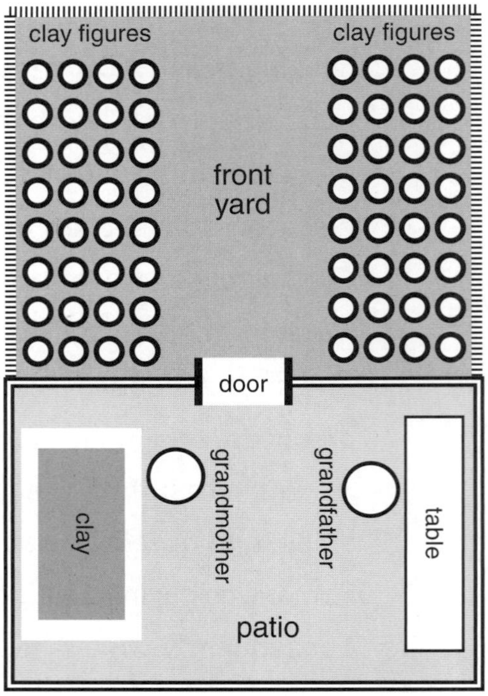

B. Some of the sentences in Josefina's description are not in spatial order. Rewrite the description in a more logical order, using the diagram for help.

____

____

____

____

____

____

____

Name: ____________________

Organization

Use spatial order to plan and organize your description of a place.

Draw a diagram of your bedroom. Then draw and label details in your bedroom that you want to write about. Plan the way you will organize your description by tracing a path through the room.

WEEK 3

ORGANIZATION

Organizing Information to Compare and Contrast

DAY 1

Read the rule aloud. Say: *There are three ways to organize your writing when you compare and contrast. You can tell all about one thing and then the other; you can describe all of the similarities between both things and then all of the differences; or, you can compare the two things point by point, giving one similarity and difference at a time.* Then guide students through the activities.

- **Activity A:** Have students read both reviews. Then explain: *In the first review, the writer discusses all the points about the first film and then all the points about the second film. In the second review, the writer compares the films point by point.* Have students complete the activity.

  Afterward, ask: *Which organization do you like better? Why?* Explain that there is no right answer. Depending on the topic, sometimes one way works better than the other, and writers have a choice of how they organize their writing.

- **Activity B (Convention):** Say: *Pronouns must always agree in number and gender with the nouns they replace.* Complete Sentence 1 together. Point out that **her** takes the place of **Ms. Smith's** because they are both singular, female, and possessive. Then have students complete the second sentence independently.

DAY 2

Read the rule aloud. Then guide students through the activity.

- **Convention:** Have students read the letter. To check the pronouns, have students find the **antecedents**, or nouns they replace. Point out the word **them** in the second sentence. Ask: *What is the antecedent of* **them**? (**liquid**) *Is* **liquid** *a plural noun?* (no) Have students complete the activity.

- Say: *The writer organized her letter by writing about each bubble liquid one at a time. However, she could have written about the liquid point by point.* Help students identify the four points of comparison. (wand, bubble size, bubble color, and how long the bubbles last) Then have students complete the outline.

Name: ______________________ **Week 3 • Day 1**

Organization When you compare and contrast, you can write all about one subject first and then all about the other. Or, you can alternate between subjects.

A. These reviews compare and contrast the same two movies, but they are organized differently. In each review, underline the details about the first movie. Draw a wavy line under the details about the sequel.

Review 1

Last year, the Future Moviemakers Club made its first film, The Great Chase. Mr. Piccarini's class wrote the script for the movie. It was a funny story about a crime-solving skateboarder named Scoop. However, the camera was not always in focus. Also, some actors spoke too quickly and were hard to understand. But in spite of the movie's problems, the audience loved it and hoped the club would make a sequel. Well, now they have!

In Rescued Again, Scoop is back on his skateboard, saving the day. Ms. Smith's class wrote the new script, and this time the camera stayed focused on the action. Also, most of the actors spoke clearly. The Great Chase was good, but Rescued Again is a masterpiece!

Review 2

Last year, the Future Moviemakers Club made its first film, The Great Chase. This year, the club is back with a sequel, Rescued Again. In the first one, which was written by Mr. Piccarini's class, a crime-solving skateboarder named Scoop finds a stolen treasure. In the sequel, which was written by Ms. Smith's class, Scoop is back on his skateboard, searching for a kidnapped millionaire.

This movie is much easier to follow than the first one. In The Great Chase, the camera was not always in focus, and not all the actors spoke clearly. But in Rescued Again, the camera stayed focused on the action and the actors were easier to understand. I really enjoyed The Great Chase, but Rescued Again is a masterpiece!

B. Read each sentence. Write the pronoun that would replace the underlined words.

1. Ms. Smith was proud of Ms. Smith's students. ___her___
2. Mr. Piccarini's students worked hard on the students' movie. ___their___

54 ORGANIZATION Daily 6-Trait Writing • EMC 6026 • © Evan-Moor Corp.

Name: ______________________ **Week 3 • Day 2**

Organization When you write to compare and contrast two or more things, use a clear organization to describe the similarities and differences.

Read this letter of complaint. Then:

- Use proofreading marks to fix the incorrect pronouns.
- Fill in the outline to show how the details in the letter could have been organized to compare the products point by point.

Dear Backyard Bubble Company:

I am writing to express my disappointment in your Super Backyard Bubble Liquid. You advertise ~~them~~ it as "new and improved." However, the original Backyard Bubble Liquid was much better. Last summer, my sister and I enjoyed making bubbles with the original Backyard Bubble. The sturdy bubble wand was easy to hold, and the bubbles came out huge and rainbow-colored. ~~It~~ They floated on the breeze for a long time. We had fun making bubbles all summer long.

In contrast, the bubbles we have made this summer with the new Super Backyard Bubble Liquid ~~is~~ are not very colorful. In addition, the new bubble wand is flimsy, and we could make only very small bubbles that pop immediately. If you want people to keep buying your Super Backyard Bubble Liquid, I urge you to return to the original formula and wand design.

Sincerely,
Kenzie Lawson

I. The wand
   A. Original: sturdy, easy to hold
   B. New: flimsy

II. Bubble size
   A. Original: huge
   B. New: very small

III. Bubble color
   A. Original: rainbow-colored
   B. New: not very colorful

IV. How long the bubbles last
   A. Original: a long time
   B. New: pop immediately

© Evan-Moor Corp. • EMC 6026 • Daily 6-Trait Writing ORGANIZATION 55

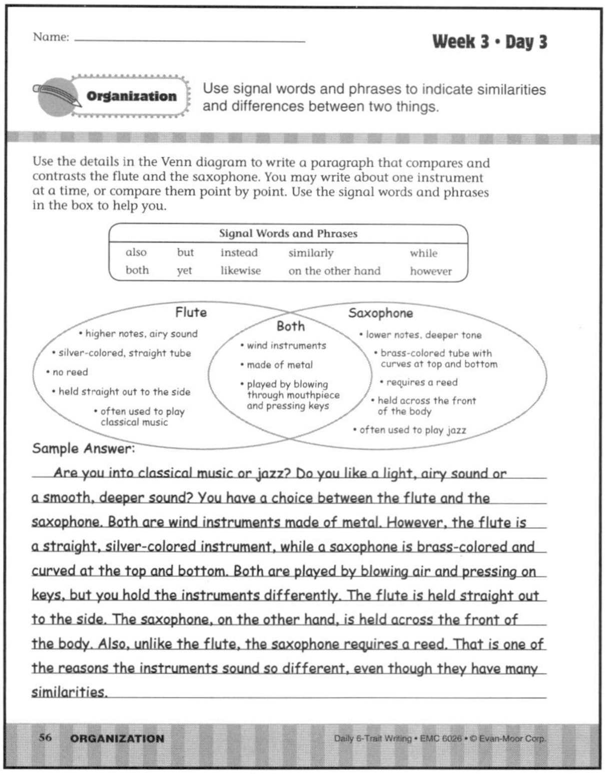

Name: ______________________ **Week 3 • Day 3**

Organization Use signal words and phrases to indicate similarities and differences between two things.

Use the details in the Venn diagram to write a paragraph that compares and contrasts the flute and the saxophone. You may write about one instrument at a time, or compare them point by point. Use the signal words and phrases in the box to help you.

Signal Words and Phrases				
also	but	instead	similarly	while
both	yet	likewise	on the other hand	however

Sample Answer:

Are you into classical music or jazz? Do you like a light, airy sound or a smooth, deeper sound? You have a choice between the flute and the saxophone. Both are wind instruments made of metal. However, the flute is a straight, silver-colored instrument, while a saxophone is brass-colored and curved at the top and bottom. Both are played by blowing air and pressing on keys, but you hold the instruments differently. The flute is held straight out to the side. The saxophone, on the other hand, is held across the front of the body. Also, unlike the flute, the saxophone requires a reed. That is one of the reasons the instruments sound so different, even though they have many similarities.

56 ORGANIZATION Daily 6-Trait Writing • EMC 6026 • © Evan-Moor Corp.

DAY 3

Read the rule aloud. Then guide students through the activity.

- Remind students that a Venn diagram shows the similarities and differences between two things. Read the details in the diagram and make sure students understand them. (e.g., reeds are thin strips of wood connected to the mouthpiece; keys are what you push to play different notes)
- Read aloud the signal words and phrases. Say: *These words guide your reader through your writing and make your ideas clearer.* Discuss which words or phrases indicate a similarity and which ones indicate a difference.
- Have students write their paragraphs. Then have volunteers share what they wrote and explain how they organized their writing.
- **Convention:** Have students exchange papers to check for noun-pronoun agreement.

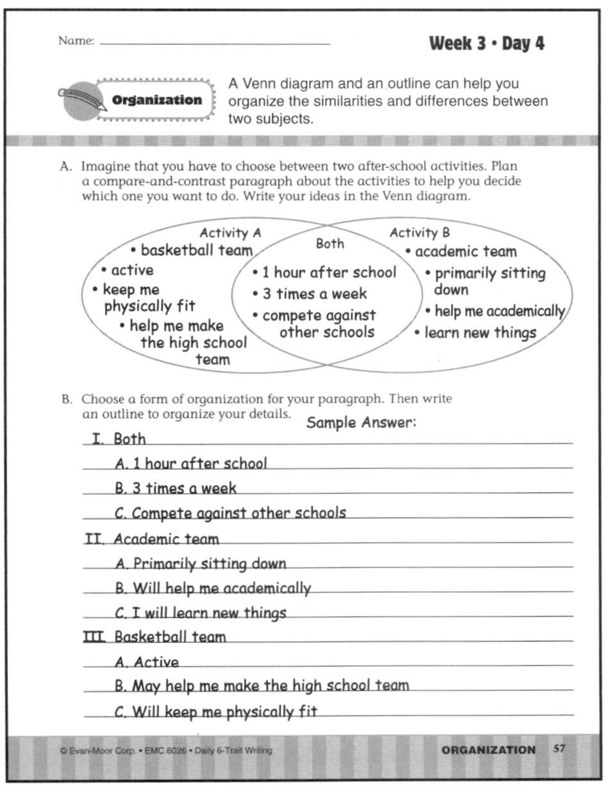

Name: ______________________ **Week 3 • Day 4**

Organization A Venn diagram and an outline can help you organize the similarities and differences between two subjects.

A. Imagine that you have to choose between two after-school activities. Plan a compare-and-contrast paragraph about the activities to help you decide which one you want to do. Write your ideas in the Venn diagram.

B. Choose a form of organization for your paragraph. Then write an outline to organize your details.

Sample Answer:

I. Both
A. 1 hour after school
B. 3 times a week
C. Compete against other schools
II. Academic team
A. Primarily sitting down
B. Will help me academically
C. I will learn new things
III. Basketball team
A. Active
B. May help me make the high school team
C. Will keep me physically fit

© Evan-Moor Corp. • EMC 6026 • Daily 6-Trait Writing ORGANIZATION 57

DAY 4

Review the rule. Guide students through the activities.

- **Activity A:** Say: *Imagine that you are trying to decide between two after-school activities. How are they alike? How are they different? What are the pros and cons of each? Use the Venn diagram to compare and contrast them.* Help students brainstorm different activities that they might write about. (e.g., Scouts, dance class, team sports, academic clubs)
- **Activity B:** Use the outline on Day 2 to review how to use Roman numerals and letters in outlines. Then say: *Remember to choose the form of organization that's best for your subject—will it be subject by subject or point by point?* Assist students as needed to create their outlines.

DAY 5 *Writing Prompt*

- *Compare and contrast two after-school activities. Use your Venn diagram and outline from Day 4.*
- *Be sure that your pronouns agree with your nouns.*

Name: ______________________________

Week 3 • Day 1

Organization

When you compare and contrast, you can write all about one subject first and then all about the other. Or, you can alternate between subjects.

A. These reviews compare and contrast the same two movies, but they are organized differently. In each review, underline the details about the first movie. Draw a wavy line under the details about the sequel.

Review 1

Last year, the Future Moviemakers Club made its first film, The Great Chase. Mr. Piccarini's class wrote the script for the movie. It was a funny story about a crime-solving skateboarder named Scoop. However, the camera was not always in focus. Also, some actors spoke too quickly and were hard to understand. But in spite of the movie's problems, the audience loved it and hoped the club would make a sequel. Well, now they have!

In Rescued Again, Scoop is back on his skateboard, saving the day. Ms. Smith's class wrote the new script, and this time the camera stayed focused on the action. Also, most of the actors spoke clearly. The Great Chase was good, but Rescued Again is a masterpiece!

Review 2

Last year, the Future Moviemakers Club made its first film, The Great Chase. This year, the club is back with a sequel, Rescued Again. In the first one, which was written by Mr. Piccarini's class, a crime-solving skateboarder named Scoop finds a stolen treasure. In the sequel, which was written by Ms. Smith's class, Scoop is back on his skateboard, searching for a kidnapped millionaire.

This movie is much easier to follow than the first one. In The Great Chase, the camera was not always in focus, and not all the actors spoke clearly. But in Rescued Again, the camera stayed focused on the action and the actors were easier to understand. I really enjoyed The Great Chase, but Rescued Again is a masterpiece!

B. Read each sentence. Write the pronoun that would replace the underlined words.

1. Ms. Smith was proud of Ms. Smith's students. ______________

2. Mr. Piccarini's students worked hard on the students' movie. ______________

Name: ____________________

Organization

When you write to compare and contrast two or more things, use a clear organization to describe the similarities and differences.

Read this letter of complaint. Then:

- Use proofreading marks to fix the incorrect pronouns.
- Fill in the outline to show how the details in the letter could have been organized to compare the products point by point.

Dear Backyard Bubble Company:

I am writing to express my disappointment in your Super Backyard Bubble Liquid. You advertise them as "new and improved." However, the original Backyard Bubble Liquid was much better. Last summer, my sister and I enjoyed making bubbles with the original Backyard Bubble. The sturdy bubble wand was easy to hold, and the bubbles came out huge and rainbow-colored. It floated on the breeze for a long time. We had fun making bubbles all summer long.

In contrast, the bubbles we have made this summer with the new Super Backyard Bubble Liquid is not very colorful. In addition, the new bubble wand is flimsy, and we could make only very small bubbles that pop immediately. If you want people to keep buying your Super Backyard Bubble Liquid, I urge you to return to the original formula and wand design.

Sincerely,
Kenzie Lawson

I. The wand

A. Original: ____________________

B. New: flimsy

II. ____________________

A. Original: huge

B. New: very small

III. ____________________

A. Original: rainbow-colored

B. New: ____________________

IV. How long the bubbles last

A. Original: ____________________

B. New: ____________________

Name: ____________________

Organization

Use signal words and phrases to indicate similarities and differences between two things.

Use the details in the Venn diagram to write a paragraph that compares and contrasts the flute and the saxophone. You may write about one instrument at a time, or compare them point by point. Use the signal words and phrases in the box to help you.

Signal Words and Phrases				
also	but	instead	similarly	while
both	yet	likewise	on the other hand	however

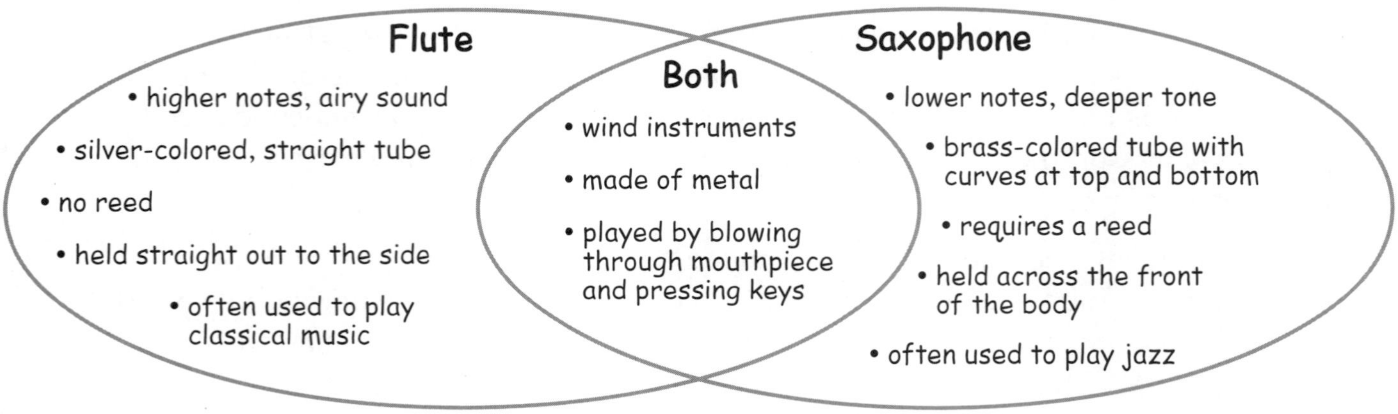

Name: ______________________________

Organization

A Venn diagram and an outline can help you organize the similarities and differences between two subjects.

A. Imagine that you have to choose between two after-school activities. Plan a compare-and-contrast paragraph about the activities to help you decide which one you want to do. Write your ideas in the Venn diagram.

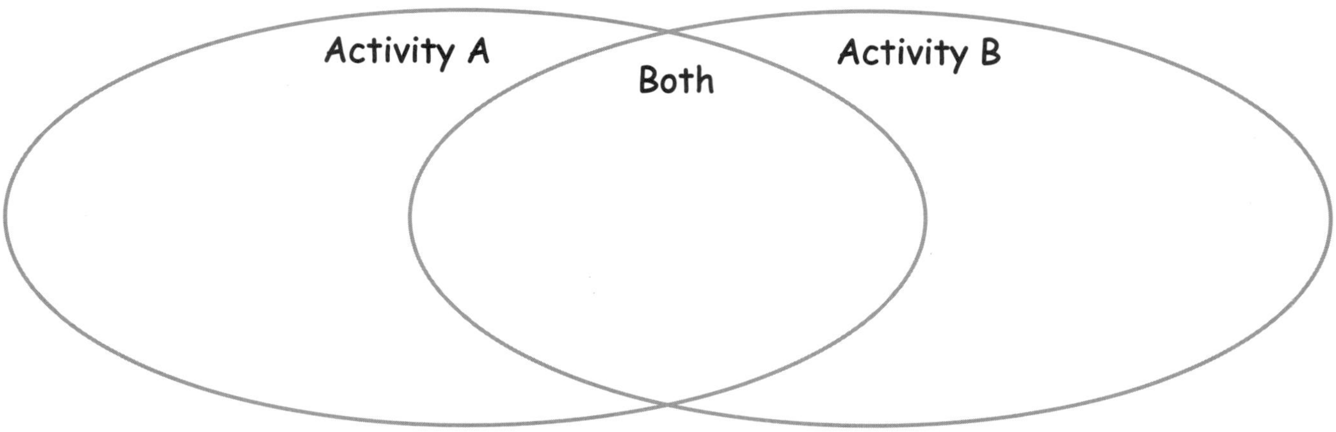

B. Choose a form of organization for your paragraph. Then write an outline to organize your details.

____

____

____

____

____

____

____

____

____

____

____

____

ORGANIZATION

Organizing to Persuade

DAY 1

Say: *The organization of your writing can affect how persuasive it is.* Then read the rule aloud and guide students through the activity.

- **Convention:** Have students read the paragraph. Then say: *People often confuse the words* ***good*** *and* ***well. Good*** *is an adjective that describes a noun or pronoun.* ***Well*** *is an adverb that describes a verb.* Have students find and correct the errors in the paragraph.
- Use the diagram to explain the parts of a persuasive argument. Say: *The* ***opinion statement*** *is like a topic sentence in which you clearly state your position or take a stand. You should then give* ***reasons*** *that support your opinion, including* ***supporting evidence*** *that backs up your reasons. A good argument also includes any* ***objections****, or reasons your reader may disagree with you, and then gives a* ***response*** *to those objections. Finally, give a* ***closing statement*** *that sums up your opinion.* Have students fill in the diagram.

Name: ______________________ **Week 4 • Day 1**

Organization When you want to be persuasive, organize your ideas to build your argument. State your opinion, and then give reasons with supporting evidence.

Read this persuasive paragraph. Then:

- Use proofreading marks to fix the incorrect uses of *good* and *well.*
- Fill in the opinion diagram to show how the writer organized her argument.

Our Most Important Meal

For students who want to do ~~good~~ well in school, breakfast is the most important meal of the day. When you skip breakfast, you are like a car trying to run without fuel. Experts say that a nutritious breakfast is the brain's fuel. A brain that is fully fueled concentrates better and solves problems faster. Some students say that getting an extra few minutes of sleep is more important than eating a bowl of oatmeal, but they're wrong. Of course, sleeping is important, but going to bed a half-hour earlier would be better than sleeping late and skipping breakfast. Give your brain the fuel it needs to run ~~good~~ well. To think clearer and faster, eat a ~~well~~ good breakfast.

Opinion Statement: For students who want to do well in school, breakfast is the most important meal of the day.

Reason: Not eating breakfast is like a car without fuel.

Supporting Evidence: Experts say that a nutritious breakfast is the brain's fuel. A brain with fuel concentrates better and solves problems faster.

Possible Objection: Some students think getting more sleep is more important.

Response to Objection: You can go to bed earlier to get the same amount of sleep.

Closing Statement: To think clearer and faster, eat a good breakfast.

60 ORGANIZATION Daily 6-Trait Writing • EMC 6026 • © Evan-Moor Corp.

DAY 2

Read the rule aloud. Say: *Your reasons and evidence make up the body of your argument. If they aren't well organized, they may not be effective.* Then guide students through the activity.

- **Convention:** Have students read the letter. Point out the phrases **feeling well** and **feel good** in the last two sentences. Explain: *Both are correct. Use* ***well*** *when you mean the opposite of* ***sick.*** *Use* ***good*** *when you mean* ***happy.*** Have students find the other uses of **good** and **well** and correct them.
- Say: *You can organize your reasons in two different ways—from most to least important, or least to most important. Starting with your most important reason is a good way to "hook" your reader. Building up to your most important reason is a good way to make it "stick" with your reader.* Have students fill in the diagram. Then ask: *Which order did David use in his letter?* (least to most important) *Why?* (He wanted to build up to Jessica's love of dogs, which he thought might be the most important thing to a dog owner.)

Name: ______________________ **Week 4 • Day 2**

Organization To persuade your reader, be sure to organize your reasons and evidence so that they clearly support your opinion.

Read the following letter of recommendation. Then:

- Use proofreading marks to fix the incorrect uses of *good* and *well.*
- Fill in the diagram to show how David organized his reasons and supporting evidence.

Dear Mr. and Ms. Trevino,

I know that you are looking for a dog walker for your poodle. You should hire my cousin, Jessica. She has the qualities that a ~~well~~ good dog walker needs. First of all, Jessica is very responsible. When she takes care of our dog, Bruno, she always feeds him on time and never forgets to walk him. Jessica also has experience as a dog trainer. In fact, Jessica trained Bruno very ~~good~~ well. He now knows how to sit, stay, and play ~~good~~ well with other dogs. Most importantly, Jessica loves dogs. She brings them treats, and she even visits them when they aren't feeling well. I promise you will feel good about hiring Jessica to walk your dog.

Your neighbor,
David Orloff

Reason 1: She is responsible.

Supporting Evidence: She feeds Bruno on time and remembers to walk him.

Reason 2: She has experience as a dog trainer.

Supporting Evidence: She trained Bruno to sit, stay, and play nicely.

Reason 3: She loves dogs.

Supporting Evidence: She brings them treats and visits them when they're sick.

© Evan-Moor Corp. • EMC 6026 • Daily 6-Trait Writing ORGANIZATION 61

Name: ______________________ **Week 4 • Day 3**

Organization To persuade your reader, be sure to organize your details carefully.

Read the details in this opinion diagram and notice how they're organized. Use the diagram to write an editorial about school cafeteria food.

Opinion Statement: It's time to stop making fun of the food our cafeteria serves.

- **Reason 1:** The food is a lot better than it used to be.
  - **Supporting Evidence:** Now serving healthier dishes, such as grilled chicken, whole wheat pasta, salads, and fresh fruit.
- **Reason 2:** The cafeteria staff works really hard.
  - **Supporting Evidence:** Must make lunch (and clean up!) for 400 students each day.
- **Possible Objection:** The food isn't always piping hot, and doesn't always look good.
  - **Response to Objection:** The food is a lot worse at many other schools.

Closing Statement: Students should stop making jokes about the food and start showing a little appreciation instead!

Sample Answer: It's time to stop making fun of the food our cafeteria serves. The food is so much better than it used to be. The cafeteria now serves healthier dishes, such as grilled chicken, whole wheat pasta, salads, and fresh fruit. Yum! In addition, our cafeteria staff works really hard. They have to prepare lunch (and clean up!) for more than 400 students each day. Can you imagine doing that? Now, I know that the food isn't always piping hot and doesn't always look perfect. But let me tell you, the food is a lot worse at many other schools. So stop making jokes about our cafeteria food and start showing a little appreciation instead!

62 **ORGANIZATION** Daily 6-Trait Writing • EMC 6026 • © Evan-Moor Corp.

Name: ______________________ **Week 4 • Day 4**

Organization To persuade your reader, be sure to organize your details carefully.

Plan an editorial to be published in your school or local newspaper. Choose one of the following topics, or think of your own.

- ☐ Students should join a new club that you started.
- ☐ Professional athletes should be paid less money.
- ☒ Restaurants should donate leftover food to homeless shelters.
- ☐ Your school should extend the school day by one hour so students can get help with homework.

Sample Answers:

Opinion Statement: Restaurants in Omaha should donate their leftover food to homeless shelters.

- **Reason:** There are many hungry, homeless people in our city who need the food.
  - **Supporting Evidence:** Homeless shelters never have enough food to feed everyone.
- **Reason:** This program could provide jobs for the homeless.
  - **Supporting Evidence:** Workers would be needed to collect and serve the donated food.
- **Reason:** reduce trash
  - **Supporting Evidence:** Restaurants throw out tons of good food each week. It takes up space in landfills.
- **Possible Objection:** The donated food might be old or spoiled.
  - **Response to Objection:** could set up strict rules for donations

Closing Statement: Quit wasting food and encourage your favorite restaurant to donate its leftover food.

© Evan-Moor Corp. • EMC 6026 • Daily 6-Trait Writing **ORGANIZATION** 63

DAY 3

Read the rule aloud. Then guide students through the activity.

- Remind students that an **editorial** expresses an opinion and tries to persuade readers to agree with that opinion. Then use the diagram to review the parts of a persuasive argument. (opinion statement, reasons, evidence, etc.)
- Remind students that it's important to anticipate your reader's objections. Say: *By acknowledging the objection, you can respond to it in a way that convinces the reader that it is not important.* Ask: *What objection does this writer address?* (sometimes food is cold, doesn't look good) *How does she answer, or contradict, that objection?* (it's a lot worse at other schools)
- Have students write the editorial. Then ask volunteers to read theirs aloud.

DAY 4

Review the rule. Then guide students through the activity.

- Have each student choose a topic and write an opinion statement. Remind students that they must take a strong, clear stand on the topic in their opinion statement. For example, write these two statements on the board and ask which one is better: *1) I think that it might be good if students wore uniforms to school. 2) Elementary school students should wear uniforms to school.* (the second—it takes a clearer stand on the topic)
- Circulate as students complete their diagrams, assisting as necessary. You may want students to work in pairs, having partners help each other brainstorm the parts of their arguments.

DAY 5 *Writing Prompt*

- *Use your diagram from Day 4 to write an editorial for your school or local newspaper.*
- *Be sure to use the words **good** and **well** correctly.*

Organization

When you want to be persuasive, organize your ideas to build your argument. State your opinion, and then give reasons with supporting evidence.

Read this persuasive paragraph. Then:

- Use proofreading marks to fix the incorrect uses of *good* and *well*.
- Fill in the opinion diagram to show how the writer organized her argument.

Our Most Important Meal

For students who want to do good in school, breakfast is the most important meal of the day. When you skip breakfast, you are like a car trying to run without fuel. Experts say that a nutritious breakfast is the brain's fuel. A brain that is fully fueled concentrates better and solves problems faster. Some students say that getting an extra few minutes of sleep is more important than eating a bowl of oatmeal, but they're wrong. Of course, sleeping is important, but going to bed a half-hour earlier would be better than sleeping late and skipping breakfast. Give your brain the fuel it needs to run good. To think clearer and faster, eat a well breakfast.

Opinion Statement:

Reason:

Supporting Evidence:

Possible Objection:

Response to Objection:

Closing Statement:

Name: ____________________

Organization

To persuade your reader, be sure to organize your reasons and evidence so that they clearly support your opinion.

Read the following letter of recommendation. Then:

- Use proofreading marks to fix the incorrect uses of *good* and *well*.
- Fill in the diagram to show how David organized his reasons and supporting evidence.

Dear Mr. and Ms. Trevino,

I know that you are looking for a dog walker for your poodle. You should hire my cousin, Jessica. She has the qualities that a well dog walker needs. First of all, Jessica is very responsible. When she takes care of our dog, Bruno, she always feeds him on time and never forgets to walk him. Jessica also has experience as a dog trainer. In fact, Jessica trained Bruno very good. He now knows how to sit, stay, and play good with other dogs. Most importantly, Jessica loves dogs. She brings them treats, and she even visits them when they aren't feeling well. I promise you will feel good about hiring Jessica to walk your dog.

Your neighbor,
David Orloff

Reason 1:

Supporting Evidence:

Reason 2:

Supporting Evidence:

Reason 3:

Supporting Evidence:

Name: ______________________________

Organization

To persuade your reader, be sure to organize your details carefully.

Read the details in this opinion diagram and notice how they're organized. Use the diagram to write an editorial about school cafeteria food.

Opinion Statement: It's time to stop making fun of the food our cafeteria serves.

- **Reason 1:** The food is a lot better than it used to be.
  - **Supporting Evidence:** Now serving healthier dishes, such as grilled chicken, whole wheat pasta, salads, and fresh fruit.
- **Reason 2:** The cafeteria staff works really hard.
  - **Supporting Evidence:** Must make lunch (and clean up!) for 400 students each day.
- **Possible Objection:** The food isn't always piping hot, and doesn't always look good.
  - **Response to Objection:** The food is a lot worse at many other schools.

Closing Statement: Students should stop making jokes about the food and start showing a little appreciation instead!

____

____

____

____

____

____

____

____

____

Name: ____________________

Organization

To persuade your reader, be sure to organize your details carefully.

Plan an editorial to be published in your school or local newspaper. Choose one of the following topics, or think of your own.

- ☐ Students should join a new club that you started.
- ☐ Professional athletes should be paid less money.
- ☐ Restaurants should donate leftover food to homeless shelters.
- ☐ Your school should extend the school day by one hour so students can get help with homework.

Opinion Statement:

Reason:

Supporting Evidence:

Reason:

Supporting Evidence:

Reason:

Supporting Evidence:

Possible Objection:

Response to Objection:

Closing Statement:

ORGANIZATION

Choosing Which Way to Organize Your Writing

DAY 1

Read the rule aloud. Say: *We've discussed many ways to organize your writing. Now, we'll talk about how to decide which type of organization to use.* Then guide students through the activity.

- Read aloud Paragraph 1. Then review each type of organization shown on the page. Ask: *Which type of organization did the writer of this paragraph use?* (persuasive) *How do you know?* (e.g., It gives an opinion, reasons, and examples.) Ask: *Which organizer would we use to plan a persuasive paragraph?* (the opinion diagram)
- Point out that the opinion diagram is incomplete. For example, it is missing the opinion statement. Ask: *What is the opinion statement in Paragraph 1?* ("Our school should have...") Have students write it in the diagram.
- Repeat the process for each paragraph, or have students complete the activity independently.
- **Convention:** Remind students that a series is a list of three or more items. Have students find the series in Paragraph 1 ("strength, balance, and coordination") and circle the commas. Say: *Commas help us separate the items in a series.*

DAY 2

Read the rule aloud. Then guide students through the activities.

- **Activity A:** Review the types of organization. Then read aloud Assignment 1. Say: *The words* ***compares, similar,*** *and* ***different*** *tell me that I would be writing about how daily life in the early Mesopotamian and Egyptian civilizations were similar and different. Which type of organization should I use?* (compare and contrast) Have students complete the activity independently.
- **Activity B (Convention):** Say: *A series isn't always just a list of three or more one-word items in a sentence.* Have students identify the series in Sentence 1. ("to encourage school spirit, to promote responsibility, and to prevent cheating") Ask: *Do the commas correctly separate the three things listed?* (no) Have students make the corrections and complete the activity.

Name: ____________________ **Week 5 • Day 1**

Organization The best way to organize your writing depends on your topic and purpose.

Decide which type of organization each paragraph uses. Write the correct letter on the line. Then fill in the missing parts of the organizers.

Paragraph

1. __c__ Our school should have a jump rope team. Jumping rope is an excellent form of exercise. It improves your strength, balance, and coordination. It also teaches teamwork because you have to time the jumping and rope turning with your teammates. Some people think that it isn't a real sport, but those people should try it sometime to see how challenging it is!
2. __a__ Many bones make up the human leg. It starts with the femur, or thighbone. Below the femur is the patella, or kneecap. Below that are the tibia and fibula. The tibia is in front of the fibula. Both connect to the talus, or anklebone, which is attached to the metatarsals. Protruding from the metatarsals are the phalanges.
3. __b__ Skateboards and surfboards have a lot in common. In addition to their similar shapes, both can carry you when you stand on them. However, a skateboard has wheels, while a surfboard has a fin. You can ride a skateboard on any hard surface, but you need ocean waves to ride a surfboard!

Organization

a.

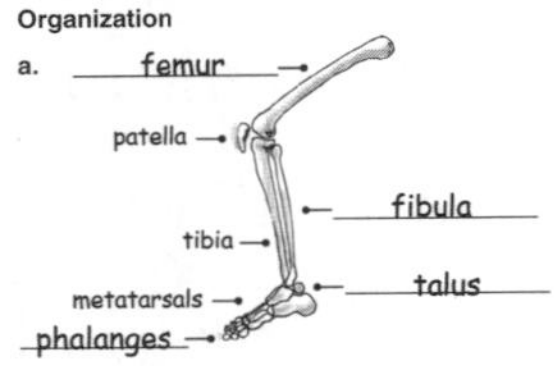

b.

Skateboard	Both	Surfboard
• ride on any hard surface • wheels	• board shape • stand on to ride	• fin • ride on water

c.

Opinion Statement: Our school should have a jump rope team.

Reason 1: excellent form of exercise
Example: improves strength, balance, coordination

Reason 2: teaches teamwork
Example: have to work with teammates to time jumping and rope turning

Possible Objection: not a real sport
Answer: People should try it themselves.

66 ORGANIZATION Daily 6-Trait Writing • EMC 6026 • © Evan-Moor Corp.

Name: ____________________ **Week 5 • Day 2**

Organization When you are given a writing assignment, decide which type of organization best fits the assignment.

A. Read each writing assignment. Which type of organization would you use to write the paragraph? Write it on the line. Circle the words that provide clues to the organization.

Types of Organization		
Spatial	Chronological	Compare-Contrast
Persuasive	Cause-Effect	

Assignment 1: *Write a paragraph that compares daily life in the early civilizations of Mesopotamia and Egypt. Describe the ways in which they were similar and different.*

Compare-Contrast

Assignment 2: *Write a paragraph that explains the reasons you believe your school should have an honor code.*

Persuasive

Assignment 3: *Write a paragraph that describes how earthquakes are caused by the movement of large plates beneath the Earth's surface.*

Cause-Effect

Assignment 4: *Write a paragraph describing the life of a famous historical figure you admire. Explain the events that led to his or her success.*

Chronological

B. Underline the series in each sentence. Use proofreading marks to correct the use of commas.

1. Rowland Middle School should have an honor code to, encourage school spirit, to promote, responsibility and, to, prevent cheating.
2. I will write about Cesar Chavez Susan B. Anthony, or, Sojourner Truth.

© Evan-Moor Corp. • EMC 6026 • Daily 6-Trait Writing ORGANIZATION 67

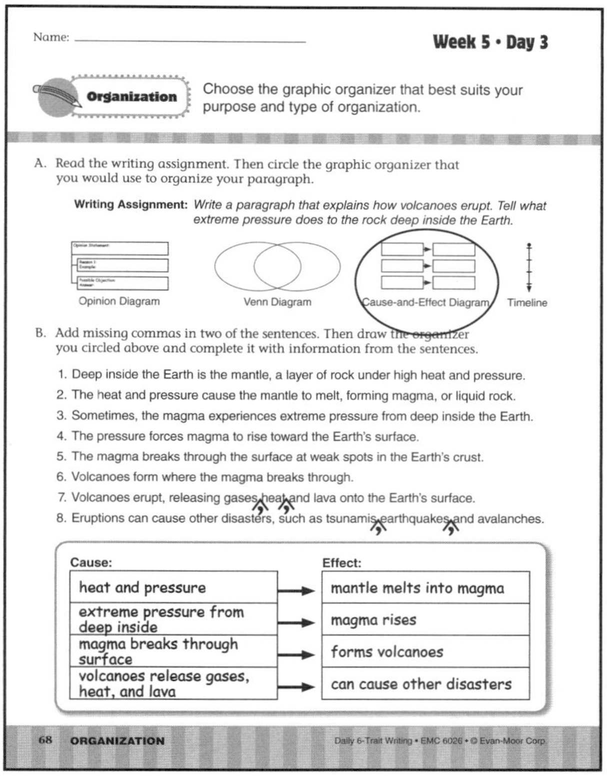
Name: ______________ **Week 5 • Day 3**

Organization Choose the graphic organizer that best suits your purpose and type of organization.

A. Read the writing assignment. Then circle the graphic organizer that you would use to organize your paragraph.

Writing Assignment: *Write a paragraph that explains how volcanoes erupt. Tell what extreme pressure does to the rock deep inside the Earth.*

B. Add missing commas in two of the sentences. Then draw the organizer you circled above and complete it with information from the sentences.

1. Deep inside the Earth is the mantle, a layer of rock under high heat and pressure.
2. The heat and pressure cause the mantle to melt, forming magma, or liquid rock.
3. Sometimes, the magma experiences extreme pressure from deep inside the Earth.
4. The pressure forces magma to rise toward the Earth's surface.
5. The magma breaks through the surface at weak spots in the Earth's crust.
6. Volcanoes form where the magma breaks through.
7. Volcanoes erupt, releasing gases, heat, and lava onto the Earth's surface.
8. Eruptions can cause other disasters, such as tsunamis, earthquakes, and avalanches.

Cause:	Effect:
heat and pressure	mantle melts into magma
extreme pressure from deep inside	magma rises
magma breaks through surface	forms volcanoes
volcanoes release gases, heat, and lava	can cause other disasters

68 ORGANIZATION Daily 6-Trait Writing • EMC 6026 • © Evan-Moor Corp.

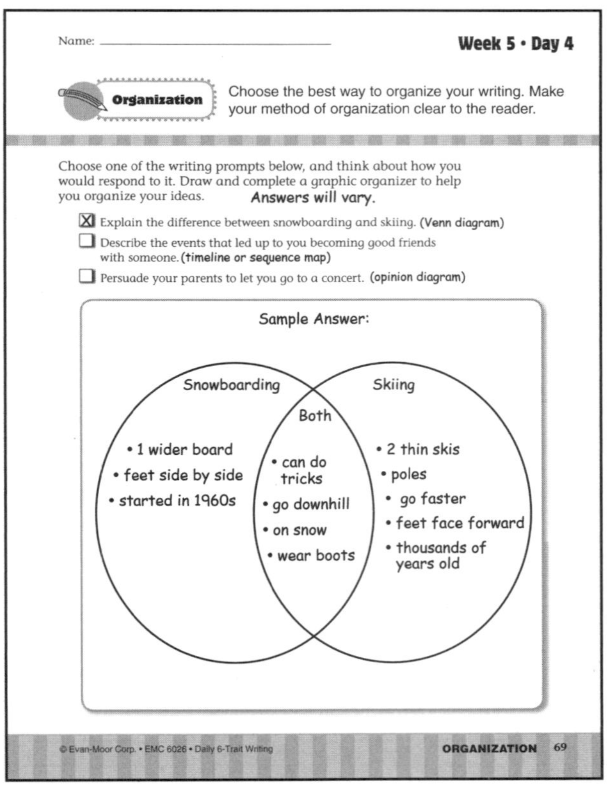
Name: ______________ **Week 5 • Day 4**

Organization Choose the best way to organize your writing. Make your method of organization clear to the reader.

Choose one of the writing prompts below, and think about how you would respond to it. Draw and complete a graphic organizer to help you organize your ideas. **Answers will vary.**

- [x] Explain the difference between snowboarding and skiing. **(Venn diagram)**
- [ ] Describe the events that led up to you becoming good friends with someone. **(timeline or sequence map)**
- [ ] Persuade your parents to let you go to a concert. **(opinion diagram)**

© Evan-Moor Corp. • EMC 6026 • Daily 6-Trait Writing ORGANIZATION 69

DAY 3

Read the rule aloud. Then guide students through the activities.

- **Activity A:** Read the assignment aloud. If necessary, review each organizer and its purpose. Then ask: *Which organizer would help you write the paragraph?* (cause-and-effect diagram) Ask: *Why?* (the assignment is to write about what causes volcanoes to erupt)

- **Activity B (Convention):** Read aloud the sentences. Ask: *Which ones include a series?* (sentences 7 and 8) Have students insert the commas and share their answers.

  Copy the circled diagram in Activity A onto the board and have students do the same on their papers. Say: *Sentence 1 tells what is under heat and pressure. That is a cause, so I'll write "heat and pressure" in the first box of the "Cause" column. What is the effect?* (magma is formed) *I'll write "mantle melts into magma" in the "Effect" column.* Have students complete the remainder of the activity independently.

DAY 4

Read the rule aloud. Then guide students through the activity.

- Have students read the writing prompts and discuss which graphic organizers might be used to plan each one. (Venn diagram; timeline or sequence map; opinion diagram)

- Have students choose a prompt, or think of their own idea, and complete an appropriate graphic organizer for it. Circulate to provide assistance as needed.

DAY 5 *Writing Prompt*

- *Write a paragraph based on the prompt you chose on Day 4. Use the diagram you completed to organize your paragraph.*

- *Be sure to write commas in a series correctly.*

Organization

The best way to organize your writing depends on your topic and purpose.

Decide which type of organization each paragraph uses. Write the correct letter on the line. Then fill in the missing parts of the organizers.

Paragraph

1. _____ Our school should have a jump rope team. Jumping rope is an excellent form of exercise. It improves your strength, balance, and coordination. It also teaches teamwork because you have to time the jumping and rope turning with your teammates. Some people think that it isn't a real sport, but those people should try it sometime to see how challenging it is!

2. _____ Many bones make up the human leg. It starts with the femur, or thighbone. Below the femur is the patella, or kneecap. Below that are the tibia and fibula. The tibia is in front of the fibula. Both connect to the talus, or anklebone, which is attached to the metatarsals. Protruding from the metatarsals are the phalanges.

3. _____ Skateboards and surfboards have a lot in common. In addition to their similar shapes, both can carry you when you stand on them. However, a skateboard has wheels, while a surfboard has a fin. You can ride a skateboard on any hard surface, but you need ocean waves to ride a surfboard!

Organization

a.

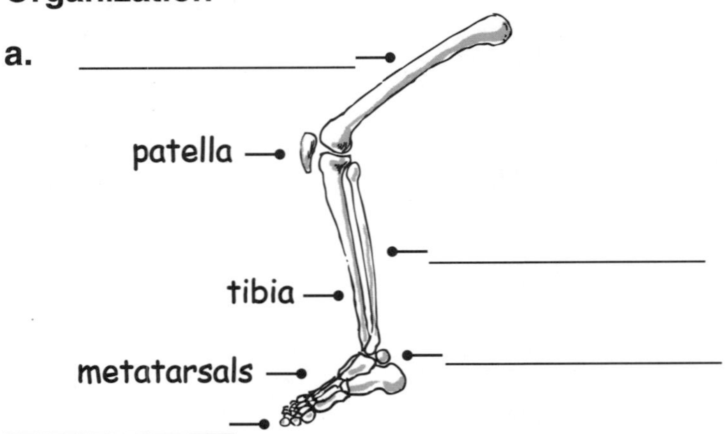

b.

Skateboard
- ride on any hard surface
-

Both
- board shape
-

Surfboard
- fin
-

c.

Opinion Statement:

Reason 1: excellent form of exercise
Example:

Reason 2:
Example: have to work with teammates to time jumping and rope turning

Possible Objection:
Answer: People should try it themselves.

Name: ______________________________

Organization

When you are given a writing assignment, decide which type of organization best fits the assignment.

A. Read each writing assignment. Which type of organization would you use to write the paragraph? Write it on the line. Circle the words that provide clues to the organization.

Types of Organization		
Spatial	Chronological	Compare-Contrast
Persuasive	Cause-Effect	

Assignment 1: *Write a paragraph that compares daily life in the early civilizations of Mesopotamia and Egypt. Describe the ways in which they were similar and different.*

____

Assignment 2: *Write a paragraph that explains the reasons you believe your school should have an honor code.*

____

Assignment 3: *Write a paragraph that describes how earthquakes are caused by the movement of large plates beneath the Earth's surface.*

____

Assignment 4: *Write a paragraph describing the life of a famous historical figure you admire. Explain the events that led to his or her success.*

____

B. Underline the series in each sentence. Use proofreading marks to correct the use of commas.

1. Rowland Middle School should have an honor code to, encourage school spirit, to promote, responsibility and, to, prevent cheating.
2. I will write about Cesar Chavez Susan B. Anthony, or, Sojourner Truth.

Name: ______________________________ **Week 5 • Day 3**

Organization

Choose the graphic organizer that best suits your purpose and type of organization.

A. Read the writing assignment. Then circle the graphic organizer that you would use to organize your paragraph.

Writing Assignment: *Write a paragraph that explains how volcanoes erupt. Tell what extreme pressure does to the rock deep inside the Earth.*

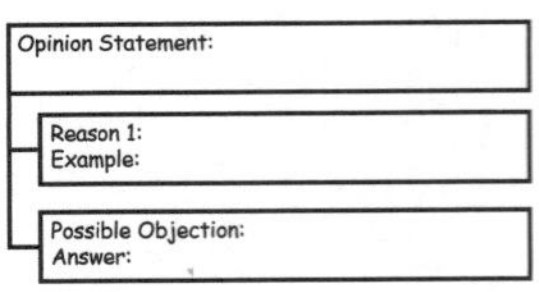

Opinion Diagram

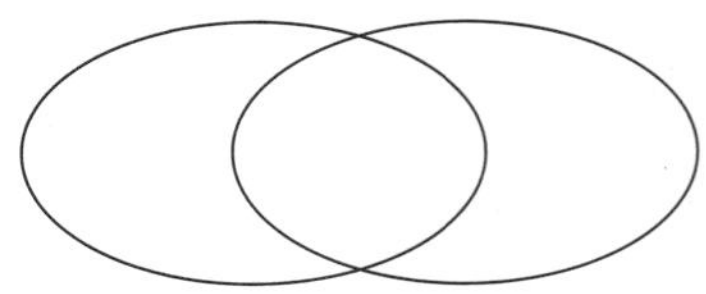

Venn Diagram

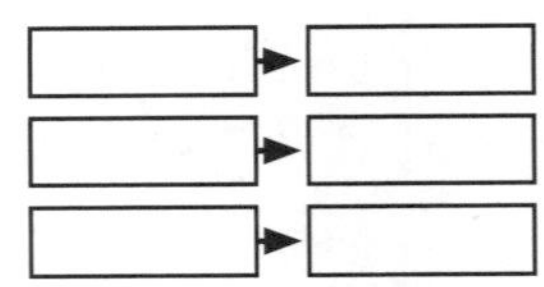

Cause-and-Effect Diagram

Timeline

B. Add missing commas in two of the sentences. Then draw the organizer you circled above and complete it with information from the sentences.

1. Deep inside the Earth is the mantle, a layer of rock under high heat and pressure.
2. The heat and pressure cause the mantle to melt, forming magma, or liquid rock.
3. Sometimes, the magma experiences extreme pressure from deep inside the Earth.
4. The pressure forces magma to rise toward the Earth's surface.
5. The magma breaks through the surface at weak spots in the Earth's crust.
6. Volcanoes form where the magma breaks through.
7. Volcanoes erupt, releasing gases heat and lava onto the Earth's surface.
8. Eruptions can cause other disasters, such as tsunamis earthquakes and avalanches.

Name: ______________________________

Organization

Choose the best way to organize your writing. Make your method of organization clear to the reader.

Choose one of the writing prompts below, and think about how you would respond to it. Draw and complete a graphic organizer to help you organize your ideas.

- ☐ Explain the difference between snowboarding and skiing.
- ☐ Describe the events that led up to you becoming good friends with someone.
- ☐ Persuade your parents to let you go to a concert.

WEEK 1

WORD CHOICE

Writing Precise Descriptions

Refer to pages 6 and 7 to introduce or review the writing trait.

DAY 1

Read the rule aloud. Then guide students through the activity.

- Have students read the draft. Ask: *Do the words in this article give precise, specific details?* If students think so, ask: *What kind of emergency vehicles went to the fire? How many?* (not specified)
- Have students read the revision. Call attention to the first sentence and have students underline the phrase that tells how many and what kind of emergency vehicles there were. Then have students work independently to underline the other specific words and phrases that were added to the article. Afterward, go over the answers, having students identify the words in the draft that were replaced in the revision.
- **Convention:** Point out the comma after "Late last night" at the beginning of the article. Explain: *The comma separates this phrase from the rest of the sentence.* Help students find the commas after the other introductory words or phrases in the article. (**Within minutes, However**) You may also want to point out the commas after the dependent clauses. ("Because the temperature..." and "When it was finally over...")

DAY 2

Read the rule aloud. Say: *Vague words, such as* ***nice*** *or* ***bad****, don't give your reader enough information.* Then guide students through the activities.

- **Activity A:** After students read the entry, say: *The events are easy to follow, but a lot of the details aren't very clear. For example, the writer describes the raincoat as old, but does that give you enough to picture it?* Have students underline other adjectives that they think could be more specific.

  Convention: Say: *A comma after an introductory word or phrase is not always necessary, but sometimes it helps the reader.* Have students circle the commas.
- **Activity B:** Use the first word to model completing the activity. Ask: *What better, more specific words could we use to describe a raincoat? How old is it? What makes it look old?* After students complete the activity, ask volunteers to share their answers. Make sure students haven't replaced vague words with other vague words. (e.g., **cool, interesting**)

Name: ______________________ **Week 1 • Day 1**

Word Choice A description should include carefully chosen, precise words to help your readers picture the topic.

Read this news article about a fire. Then read the revision. Underline the words in the revision that give a more accurate description of the event.

Draft

Fire at Factory

Late last night, some emergency vehicles went to a fire at the Sweets Candy Factory on Main Street. A call came into the fire station late. The caller smelled something and thought that there might be something wrong at the factory. Within minutes, people arrived at the factory. Flames were coming from windows as smoke rose from the roof. People went into the building. Other people aimed hoses at the roof of the big building. Because the night was cold, ice began to cover the sidewalk. People fell as they tried to put out the fire. When it was finally over, there wasn't much left. However, the owners of the factory plan to begin rebuilding in a few months.

Revision

Candy Factory Consumed by Blaze

Late last night, five fire trucks and one ambulance sped to a raging fire at the Sweets Candy Factory on Main Street. A call came into the fire station just after midnight. The worried caller smelled burning chocolate and thought there might be a fire at the factory. Within minutes, firefighters and other emergency workers arrived at the factory. Huge yellow flames were shooting from windows as thick black smoke curled from the roof. Firefighters rushed into the brick building. More firefighters aimed enormous hoses at the roof of the five-story building. Because the temperature was below zero, ice began to cover the sidewalk. Firefighters slipped and fell as they scrambled to put out the inferno. When it was finally over, nothing remained but charred, crumbling ruins. However, the owners of the factory plan to begin rebuilding in June.

72 WORD CHOICE Daily 6-Trait Writing • EMC 6026 • © Evan-Moor Corp.

Name: ______________________ **Week 1 • Day 2**

Word Choice Make your descriptions precise by using specific adjectives instead of vague ones.

A. Read this journal entry. Then:
- Circle the commas after introductory words and phrases.
- Underline any adjectives that seem vague or boring to you.

Thursday, March 4 — This morning, the weather was cold and rainy. I wore an old raincoat but carried a nice umbrella as I walked to the bus stop. Under a big tree, a group of unhappy kids stood waiting for the bus. I joined them under the tree.

Eventually, the bus arrived. I climbed the steps and sat down on a bad seat next to a nice girl from my street. She was wearing a raincoat, too, but she had still gotten soaking wet. Her nice hair was dripping all over her books. Suddenly, I realized how wet I was, too! Water had dripped down my back, and my good sneakers squished when I stood up to get off the bus. Of course, the rain stopped as soon as we were inside the school building. I had to spend the rest of the day in cold, wet shoes!

B. List some descriptive adjectives or phrases that the writer could have used to better describe the following objects or people in the journal entry.

Sample Answers:

1. raincoat yellow, dirty, ragged
2. umbrella flowered, rainbow-colored, bright orange
3. tree giant maple
4. kids cold, tired, grumpy
5. bus seat lumpy, ripped, full of holes
6. girl friendly, in eighth grade
7. hair long, curly, black
8. sneakers brand new, white

© Evan-Moor Corp. • EMC 6026 • Daily 6-Trait Writing WORD CHOICE 73

DAY 3

Read the rule aloud. Say: *When we talk to our friends, we often use general nouns such as **things** and **stuff**, but precise nouns are better to use in writing because they are more interesting and they tell the reader more.* Then guide students through the activity.

- Have students read the description. To model the activity, say: *Look at the word **bright** in the second sentence. What does that mean? How was the jacket bright? Was it sparkly? A bright color? What color?*
- **Convention:** Remind students that we often use a comma after an introductory word or phrase because it makes our sentences easier to read. Have students complete the activity.
- Have volunteers read aloud their revised descriptions. Discuss how each student's choice of words made the revision tell more about Aunt Nora. Check to be sure that students inserted commas in the correct places.

Name: ______________________ **Week 1 • Day 3**

Word Choice Choose specific nouns and adjectives to make your descriptions more precise.

Read this description of a person. Then:

- Replace the vague adjectives and general nouns with better words that could provide a more accurate description.
- Add commas after introductory words or phrases.

Sample Answers: My Aunt Nora

Last week, Aunt Nora arrived at our house for a family dinner. She was wearing a hot pink ~~bright~~ jacket and skirt. Everyone who meets Aunt Nora notices her clothes and her jewelry. For example, she always wears necklaces and big sparkly rings ~~stuff~~. She also wears pointy pink pumps ~~crazy shoes~~, and her long silver ~~pretty~~ hair is usually hidden under a hat decorated with cherries and plastic flowers ~~different things~~. My mom says that Aunt Nora likes to make a "fashion statement" wherever she goes.

At the dinner table, Aunt Nora passed around one of her famous casseroles. It smelled spicy ~~good~~, but I couldn't tell exactly what was in it. I was afraid it might be curried snails ~~something gross~~! Unfortunately, Aunt Nora always brings a "casserole surprise" to family dinners.

Aunt Nora chatted all through dinner, just like she does at every meal. She talked about politics and art ~~things~~ in her high-pitched ~~unusual~~ voice and waved her hands to show off her fluorescent orange ~~colored~~ fingernails. One thing is for sure — Aunt Nora is never boring. In fact, she is my favorite aunt!

74 WORD CHOICE Daily 6-Trait Writing • EMC 6026 • © Evan-Moor Corp.

DAY 4

Review the rule. Then guide students through the activities.

- **Activity A:** To help students choose a subject, ask: *Who are some of your favorite people? What makes them special? Who would be fun to write about?* Have students answer the questions. Circulate to assist as necessary, reminding students to be precise and descriptive.
- **Activity B:** Have students exchange papers. Say: *Read your partner's answers to the questions. Do you see any vague adjectives or general nouns? Do you have any more questions about the person being described?* Have students' partners discuss the vague adjectives and general nouns and offer suggestions about how to make them specific.

Name: ______________________ **Week 1 • Day 4**

Word Choice Choose specific nouns and adjectives to make your descriptions more precise.

A. Use these questions to help you plan a descriptive paragraph about one of your favorite people. Be sure to use vivid adjectives and precise nouns in your answers. **Sample Answers:**

Who is this person? my big sister

How would you describe his or her personality? outgoing, daring, fun to be with

What is the first thing that someone would notice about this person? her long, straight blond hair

How would you describe this person's appearance? short, athletic

What kind of clothes does this person wear? jeans, flip flops, T-shirts

What is the most important thing you want your reader to know about this person? She's always ready to try something new and crazy.

Why is this person one of your favorite people? She's a lot of fun, and we have many adventures together.

B. Trade papers with a partner. Have your partner circle any vague adjectives or general nouns you may have used. Then replace them with more precise words.

© Evan-Moor Corp. • EMC 6026 • Daily 6-Trait Writing WORD CHOICE 75

DAY 5 *Writing Prompt*

- *Write a description of one of your favorite people. Use precise nouns and vivid adjectives.*
- *Be sure to use a comma after introductory words and phrases.*

Word Choice A description should include carefully chosen, precise words to help your readers picture the topic.

Read this news article about a fire. Then read the revision. Underline the words in the revision that give a more accurate description of the event.

Draft

Fire at Factory

Late last night, some emergency vehicles went to a fire at the Sweets Candy Factory on Main Street. A call came into the fire station late. The caller smelled something and thought that there might be something wrong at the factory. Within minutes, people arrived at the factory. Flames were coming from windows as smoke rose from the roof. People went into the building. Other people aimed hoses at the roof of the big building. Because the night was cold, ice began to cover the sidewalk. People fell as they tried to put out the fire. When it was finally over, there wasn't much left. However, the owners of the factory plan to begin rebuilding in a few months.

Revision

Candy Factory Consumed by Blaze

Late last night, five fire trucks and one ambulance sped to a raging fire at the Sweets Candy Factory on Main Street. A call came into the fire station just after midnight. The worried caller smelled burning chocolate and thought there might be a fire at the factory. Within minutes, firefighters and other emergency workers arrived at the factory. Huge yellow flames were shooting from windows as thick black smoke curled from the roof. Firefighters rushed into the brick building. More firefighters aimed enormous hoses at the roof of the five-story building. Because the temperature was below zero, ice began to cover the sidewalk. Firefighters slipped and fell as they scrambled to put out the inferno. When it was finally over, nothing remained but charred, crumbling ruins. However, the owners of the factory plan to begin rebuilding in June.

Name: ________________________

Word Choice Make your descriptions precise by using specific adjectives instead of vague ones.

A. Read this journal entry. Then:

- Circle the commas after introductory words and phrases.
- Underline any adjectives that seem vague or boring to you.

Thursday, March 4 — This morning, the weather was cold and rainy. I wore an old raincoat but carried a nice umbrella as I walked to the bus stop. Under a big tree, a group of unhappy kids stood waiting for the bus. I joined them under the tree.

Eventually, the bus arrived. I climbed the steps and sat down on a bad seat next to a nice girl from my street. She was wearing a raincoat, too, but she had still gotten soaking wet. Her nice hair was dripping all over her books. Suddenly, I realized how wet I was, too! Water had dripped down my back, and my good sneakers squished when I stood up to get off the bus. Of course, the rain stopped as soon as we were inside the school building. I had to spend the rest of the day in cold, wet shoes!

B. List some descriptive adjectives or phrases that the writer could have used to better describe the following objects or people in the journal entry.

1. raincoat ________________________
2. umbrella ________________________
3. tree ________________________
4. kids ________________________
5. bus seat ________________________
6. girl ________________________
7. hair ________________________
8. sneakers ________________________

Word Choice Choose specific nouns and adjectives to make your descriptions more precise.

Read this description of a person. Then:

- Replace the vague adjectives and general nouns with better words that could provide a more accurate description.
- Add commas after introductory words or phrases.

My Aunt Nora

Last week Aunt Nora arrived at our house for a family dinner. She was wearing a bright jacket and skirt. Everyone who meets Aunt Nora notices her clothes and her jewelry. For example she always wears necklaces and stuff. She also wears crazy shoes, and her pretty hair is usually hidden under a hat decorated with different things. My mom says that Aunt Nora likes to make a "fashion statement" wherever she goes.

At the dinner table Aunt Nora passed around one of her famous casseroles. It smelled good, but I couldn't tell exactly what was in it. I was afraid it might be something gross! Unfortunately Aunt Nora always brings a "casserole surprise" to family dinners.

Aunt Nora chatted all through dinner, just like she does at every meal. She talked about things in her unusual voice and waved her hands to show off her colored fingernails. One thing is for sure — Aunt Nora is never boring. In fact she is my favorite aunt!

Name: ____________________

Word Choice Choose specific nouns and adjectives to make your descriptions more precise.

A. Use these questions to help you plan a descriptive paragraph about one of your favorite people. Be sure to use vivid adjectives and precise nouns in your answers.

Who is this person? ____________________

How would you describe his or her personality? ____________________

____

What is the first thing that someone would notice about this person? ____________________

____

How would you describe this person's appearance? ____________________

____

What kind of clothes does this person wear? ____________________

____

What is the most important thing you want your reader to know about this person?

____

____

Why is this person one of your favorite people? ____________________

____

B. Trade papers with a partner. Have your partner circle any vague adjectives or general nouns you may have used. Then replace them with more precise words.

WORD CHOICE
Writing About Action

DAY 1

Read the rule aloud. Then guide students through the activities.

- **Activity A:** Have students read the narrative and complete the activity on their own. Then go through the paragraph together, noting how many times the writer used forms of **walk.** (7)

  Convention: Have students find the sentence in the paragraph that contains two homophones. ("**There** were..., **their** leaves...") Review the meanings (**there**: where something is; **their**: belonging to them). Then ask: *What is another homophone for **there** and **their**?* (**they're**) Say: *Remember not to confuse these when you write.*

- **Activity B:** After students complete the activity, point out how the specific verbs for **walk** gave a clearer picture of the hike. For example, ask: *What does **trudge** mean?* (walk slowly, heavily) *So, the new verb shows that the hike was difficult.* Then have students identify the verbs they circled that replaced verbs other than **walk.** (e.g., **tore**, which tells exactly how Ben **messed up** his shirt)

DAY 2

Read the rule aloud. Remind students that adverbs can modify verbs, adjectives, and other adverbs. Guide students through the activities.

- **Activity A:** Read the paragraph aloud. Then discuss the adverbs in the box. Point out the three antonym pairs. (**feverishly/halfheartedly; generously/selfishly; completely/somewhat**) Say: *Both antonyms may make sense in the sentence, but they change the meaning completely. Be sure to choose the right adverb.* Then have students complete the activity.

- **Activity B:** Help students think of ways the trial may have ended. (e.g., what it was like in the courtroom when the verdict was announced) You may also want to brainstorm adverbs to use. (e.g., **breathlessly, furiously, triumphantly**)

- **Activity C (Convention):** Review the meanings of **their, there,** and **they're**. Then have students complete the activity.

Name: ______________________ **Week 2 • Day 1**

Word Choice Choose strong, specific verbs to show exactly what is happening. Avoid tired, overused verbs.

A. Read this personal narrative about a hike in the woods. Circle all the forms of the verb *walk*.

Walking Along the Trail

Ben and I chose a tough trail for our hike. At first, we walked along a level path through the trees, smelling the pine-scented air. But soon the path became rocky and steep. We walked up the slope, walking over big rocks as the trail went higher. We started getting tired, but we walked on. We were doing pretty well until Ben fell over a tree root and messed up his shirt. Then, I fell while crossing a stream and got soaked! However, we kept going. Breathing hard as we walked the last few feet to the summit, we saw the view. There were tall trees as far as the eye could see, their leaves a brilliant orange and red against the autumn sky. We were happy until we realized that we'd have to walk back down that same big hill to get home!

B. Read this revision. Circle the verbs that have replaced the forms of *walk*, as well as other verbs that have been improved.

Tripping Along the Trail

Ben and I chose a tough trail for our hike. At first, we strolled along a level path through the trees, inhaling the pine-scented air. But soon the path became rocky and steep. We trudged up the slope, scrambling over big rocks as the trail climbed higher. We started getting tired, but we plodded on. We were doing pretty well until Ben stumbled over a tree root and tore his shirt. Then, I slipped while crossing a stream and got soaked! However, we kept going. Panting as we crept the last few feet to the summit, we marveled at the view. There were tall trees as far as the eye could see, their leaves a brilliant orange and red against the autumn sky. We were happy until we realized we'd have to hike down that same hill to get home!

78 WORD CHOICE Daily 6-Trait Writing • EMC 6026 • © Evan-Moor Corp.

Name: ______________________ **Week 2 • Day 2**

Word Choice Use accurate adverbs to enhance your verbs and make the action more vivid.

A. Read Lucy's narrative. Fill in the blanks with adverbs from the box.

Adverbs				
feverishly	selfishly	somewhat	nervously	clearly
halfheartedly	generously	completely	ruthlessly	cleverly

Sample Answers:

When I awoke this morning, my stomach lurched __nervously__. Our school's mock trial competition was today, and I had been practicing __feverishly__ all month. In our fictional case, Joe Warner, ex-employee of the famous TV producer Arnie Chambers, was charged with vandalism. I was supposed to defend him. Had Warner __ruthlessly__ destroyed Chambers' office when Chambers __selfishly__ stole his script and produced a new show with it? The other team's lawyers thought their case was airtight. "They're in for a surprise," I thought. I was __completely__ convinced of Warner's innocence. But how could I convince the jury? Could I __clearly__ present my case and bring home the trophy?

B. Write an ending to the story above, explaining how the mock trial turned out. Write at least two sentences with adverbs, describing what happened.

Sample Answer: I triumphantly called my last witness and paused dramatically before dropping the bombshell. Warner had been desperately pitching a new show to another network at the time of the attack. Therefore, he was undeniably innocent!

C. Fill in each blank with *there, their,* or *they're*.

1. The prosecutors brought __their__ witnesses forward.
2. __They're__ all students in the seventh grade.
3. __There__ was silence as the judge gave instructions to the jury.

© Evan-Moor Corp. • EMC 6026 • Daily 6-Trait Writing WORD CHOICE 79

Name: ____________________ **Week 2 • Day 3**

Word Choice Look for tired verbs in your writing. Change them to strong, specific verbs, and add adverbs to enhance the action.

Read this personal narrative about a race. Fix the incorrect forms of *their, there,* and *they're.* Then rewrite the narrative, using stronger verbs and adverbs to show the excitement of the race.

Survival of the Fastest

My friend Kumar and I are in an outdoor survival club. Last weekend, the club had a race to see which team could make a lean-to shelter the fastest. ~~They're~~ There were five teams. Everyone hoped ~~there~~ their team would win.

When our club leader said "Go!" Kumar and I ran off, looking for a large rock to put our shelter against. We found the perfect boulder. Next, we ran around getting long, sturdy sticks. We brought the heavy sticks over to the boulder and put them against the rock, a few inches apart. Then, we got a bunch of thinner sticks and put them between the longer ones. After that, we started picking up leaves. ~~Their~~ They're good for warmth, so we put them between the sticks and put large armfuls over the whole structure. Finally, we put branches on top to keep the leaves in place. Then, we used our whistle to signal that we were finished. To our surprise, we had won!

Sample Answer: My friend Kumar and I are in an outdoor survival club. Last weekend, the club held a race to see which of the five teams could build a lean-to shelter the fastest. Kumar and I desperately wanted to win. When our club leader finally shouted "GO!," we quickly sprinted away from the group. We searched high and low for a large rock to prop our shelter against. We finally found the perfect boulder. Next, we dashed around gathering sturdy sticks. We dragged the heavy sticks over to the boulder and quickly leaned them against the rock, a few inches apart. Then, we collected a bunch of thinner sticks and carefully placed them between the longer ones. After that, we began scooping up leaves. They're good for warmth, so we carefully stuffed them between the sticks and tossed armfuls over the whole structure. Finally, we heaved branches on top to secure the leaves in place. Then, we blew hard on our whistle to signal that we had finished. To our surprise, we had won!

80 WORD CHOICE Daily 6-Trait Writing • EMC 6026 • © Evan-Moor Corp.

Name: ____________________ **Week 2 • Day 4**

Word Choice Use strong, specific verbs and accurate adverbs in your writing.

A. Think of a time when you participated in an exciting contest or game. Complete the sequence chart to plan a narrative about that event.

Sample Answers:

My name was called to go down to the basketball court. → I went to the free-throw line. → The referee said I could win $100 if I made the shot. → The crowd got silent. → I threw the ball into the air. → It went in! I won $100!

B. Circle two verbs in your chart that could be stronger or more specific. Write the verbs in the two boxes. Then write stronger verbs and adverbs that could describe the action more clearly. Sample Answers:

Weak Verb: went
Stronger Verbs: stepped up, jogged, sprinted
Adverbs: nervously, excitedly

Weak Verb: got
Stronger Verbs: grew, fell
Adverbs: suddenly, completely

© Evan-Moor Corp. • EMC 6026 • Daily 6-Trait Writing WORD CHOICE 81

DAY 3

Read the rule aloud. Say: *When you revise your writing, check to make sure you've used strong verbs and adverbs.* Then guide students through the activity.

- **Convention:** Review the meanings of **there, their,** and **they're**. Have students read the paragraph and fix the misspelled words.
- Instruct students to reread the paragraph and circle any verbs that seem vague, weak, or overused. (e.g., **said, ran, got, put**) Then model replacing one of the verbs. For example, point out the sentence, "Next, we ran around getting sticks." Ask: *What would be a stronger verb than **getting**?* (e.g., **grabbing, snatching up**) *What adverb could we add to show how the boys were running around?* (e.g., **feverishly, frantically**) Have students complete the activity and read aloud their finished paragraphs.

DAY 4

Read the rule aloud. Then guide students through the activities.

- **Activity A:** Brainstorm with students types of events they could write about. (e.g., sports competition, spelling bee, science fair) Ask volunteers to describe what happened at those events. Then have students complete their sequence charts independently.
- **Activity B:** Model the activity by drawing a set of boxes on the board. Ask a student to name a weak verb from his or her chart. Write it in the top box. If necessary, have the student explain the context of the verb. Then have the class brainstorm better verbs and specific adverbs that the student could use in place of the weak verb.
- **Convention:** Remind students to use **their, there,** and **they're** correctly.

DAY 5 *Writing Prompt*

- *Use your charts from Day 4 to describe an exciting contest or game you have participated in. Use strong, specific verbs and adverbs.*
- *Be sure to use **there, their,** and **they're** correctly.*

Name: ______________________

Word Choice Choose strong, specific verbs to show exactly what is happening. Avoid tired, overused verbs.

A. Read this personal narrative about a hike in the woods. Circle all the forms of the verb *walk*.

Walking Along the Trail

Ben and I chose a tough trail for our hike. At first, we walked along a level path through the trees, smelling the pine-scented air. But soon the path became rocky and steep. We walked up the slope, walking over big rocks as the trail went higher. We started getting tired, but we walked on. We were doing pretty well until Ben fell over a tree root and messed up his shirt. Then, I fell while crossing a stream and got soaked! However, we kept going. Breathing hard as we walked the last few feet to the summit, we saw the view. There were tall trees as far as the eye could see, their leaves a brilliant orange and red against the autumn sky. We were happy until we realized that we'd have to walk back down that same big hill to get home!

B. Read this revision. Circle the verbs that have replaced the forms of *walk,* as well as other verbs that have been improved.

Tripping Along the Trail

Ben and I chose a tough trail for our hike. At first, we strolled along a level path through the trees, inhaling the pine-scented air. But soon the path became rocky and steep. We trudged up the slope, scrambling over big rocks as the trail climbed higher. We started getting tired, but we plodded on. We were doing pretty well until Ben stumbled over a tree root and tore his shirt. Then, I slipped while crossing a stream and got soaked! However, we kept going. Panting as we crept the last few feet to the summit, we marveled at the view. There were tall trees as far as the eye could see, their leaves a brilliant orange and red against the autumn sky. We were happy until we realized we'd have to hike down that same hill to get home!

Name: ________________________

Word Choice Use accurate adverbs to enhance your verbs and make the action more vivid.

A. Read Lucy's narrative. Fill in the blanks with adverbs from the box.

Adverbs				
feverishly	selfishly	somewhat	nervously	clearly
halfheartedly	generously	completely	ruthlessly	cleverly

When I awoke this morning, my stomach lurched ____________. Our school's mock trial competition was today, and I had been practicing ____________ all month. In our fictional case, Joe Warner, ex-employee of the famous TV producer Arnie Chambers, was charged with vandalism. I was supposed to defend him. Had Warner ____________ destroyed Chambers' office when Chambers ____________ stole his script and produced a new show with it? The other team's lawyers thought their case was airtight. "They're in for a surprise," I thought. I was ____________ convinced of Warner's innocence. But how could I convince the jury? Could I ____________ present my case and bring home the trophy?

B. Write an ending to the story above, explaining how the mock trial turned out. Write at least two sentences with adverbs, describing what happened.

____

____

C. Fill in each blank with *there, their,* or *they're.*

1. The prosecutors brought ____________ witnesses forward.
2. ____________ all students in the seventh grade.
3. ____________ was silence as the judge gave instructions to the jury.

Name: ______________________________

Word Choice

Look for tired verbs in your writing. Change them to strong, specific verbs, and add adverbs to enhance the action.

Read this personal narrative about a race. Fix the incorrect forms of *their, there,* and *they're.* Then rewrite the narrative, using stronger verbs and adverbs to show the excitement of the race.

Survival of the Fastest

My friend Kumar and I are in an outdoor survival club. Last weekend, the club had a race to see which team could make a lean-to shelter the fastest. They're were five teams. Everyone hoped there team would win.

When our club leader said "Go!" Kumar and I ran off, looking for a large rock to put our shelter against. We found the perfect boulder. Next, we ran around getting long, sturdy sticks. We brought the heavy sticks over to the boulder and put them against the rock, a few inches apart. Then, we got a bunch of thinner sticks and put them between the longer ones. After that, we started picking up leaves. Their good for warmth, so we put them between the sticks and put large armfuls over the whole structure. Finally, we put branches on top to keep the leaves in place. Then, we used our whistle to signal that we were finished. To our surprise, we had won!

Name: ______________________________

Word Choice Use strong, specific verbs and accurate adverbs in your writing.

A. Think of a time when you participated in an exciting contest or game. Complete the sequence chart to plan a narrative about that event.

	→		→	
	→		→	

B. Circle two verbs in your chart that could be stronger or more specific. Write the verbs in the two boxes. Then write stronger verbs and adverbs that could describe the action more clearly.

Weak Verb:

Stronger Verbs:

Adverbs:

Weak Verb:

Stronger Verbs:

Adverbs:

WEEK 3 WORD CHOICE
Using Figurative Language

DAY 1

Read the rule aloud. Then guide students through the activities.

- **Activity A:** Have students read both versions of the narrative. Ask: *Which one helps you better imagine what it was like to be in the storm? Why?* (the second; uses comparisons that create strong images) Explain: *"As dark as night" uses the word* **as** *to compare the cloudy sky to nighttime, so it's a simile. What does the fourth sentence compare Jeff to?* (a mummy) *It doesn't use* **like** *or* **as**, *so it is a metaphor.* Have students complete the activity.
- **Activity B:** Model writing a metaphor. Say: *In the revised narrative, snowflakes are compared to wet cotton balls. But you could also compare them to fingerprints, since they're all unique. So I'll write, "Snowflakes are Mother Nature's icy fingerprints."*
- **Convention:** Have students find the following phrases in the revised narrative: "wind was," "sidewalks were," "We were," and "storm was." Use them to review the rules of subject-verb agreement. Remind students to use these verb forms correctly in their metaphors and similes.

Name: ______________ **Week 3 • Day 1**

Word Choice Use similes and metaphors to make your writing richer. A simile compares two things using *like* or *as*. A metaphor does not use *like* or *as*.

A. Read the two versions of this personal narrative. In the revised version, underline the similes and metaphors that were added.

Draft

The snow started just as my brother Jeff and I left school. It was growing very dark, and the wind was beginning to blow. Snowflakes fell in heavy clumps and stuck to my face. Jeff wrapped his scarf around his face, and I put on my white wool cap and gloves. The sidewalk was slippery. We skated along carefully, trying not to fall. Ice pellets stung my face. When we were still two blocks from home, the wind began to blow even harder. I knew that we were in for a terrible blizzard.

Revision

The snow started just as my brother Jeff and I left school. It was growing as dark as night, and the wind was beginning to blow. Snowflakes fell in clumps like wet cotton balls that stuck to my face. Jeff had turned into an Egyptian mummy, with his scarf wrapped up to his eyes. I put on my white wool cap and gloves, feeling like a ghost as my hands disappeared against the snow. The sidewalks were as slick as oil. We skated along carefully, trying not to fall. Needles of ice pricked my stinging cheeks along the way. When we were still two blocks from home, the wind began to howl like a hungry wolf. I knew that this storm was about to become a terrible monster.

B. Write a simile or metaphor to describe each subject below. **Sample Answers:**

1. Snowflakes: Snowflakes are Mother Nature's icy fingerprints.
2. Icicles: Icicles hang like daggers above the shivering ground.
3. Snowballs: Snowballs are frozen bombs lobbed by innocent children.
4. Clouds: The clouds look as fluffy as whipped cream sculpted by the wind.

84 WORD CHOICE Daily 6-Trait Writing • EMC 6026 • © Evan-Moor Corp.

DAY 2

Read the rule aloud. Explain that **personification** means to give human form or qualities to a nonliving thing. Then guide students through the activities.

- **Activity A (Convention):** Explain that a traditional haiku has three lines with a 5–7–5 syllable count. Then read "Winter" aloud. Point out the verb **growl**. Ask: *Does the verb agree with the subject* **wind**? (no) *What should it be?* (**growls**)

  Ask: *Does ice actually "bite"?* (no, that's a human action) Say: *Ice is so cold that it can feel as if it's biting. The writer "personified" that feeling.* Have students complete the activity.
- **Activity B:** Model completing "Spring." Say: *This haiku is about spring. I know that the sun often shines in spring, so I could add, "The sun smiles for days."* Point out that you used the correct syllable count (5) and personification. Then have students complete the activity.

Name: ______________ **Week 3 • Day 2**

Word Choice Use personification to bring your ideas to life.

A. Read these haiku. Use proofreading marks to fix the errors in subject-verb agreement. Then underline the examples of personification.

Winter
Ice bites and wind growl s
A bear in her deepest sleep—
Alone until spring

Fall
Flags of red and gold
Leaves on trees wave and salutes
Proclaiming autumn

B. Read these haiku starters. Then finish each poem by writing the line or lines with the number of syllables given. Include personification and be sure to use correct subject-verb agreement.
Sample Answers:

Spring
Tulips peek their heads
Trees put on shiny green coats
The sun smiles for days (5)

Lake
The boats nod and sway
Dancing to the happy songs (7)
The lake softly sings

Sun
The sun breathes deeply
Stretches, then reaches straight down (7)
And touches the fields (5)

Grass
The green army stands (5)
Pushing roots in shallow ground
Protecting the earth (5)

© Evan-Moor Corp. • EMC 6026 • Daily 6-Trait Writing WORD CHOICE 85

Name: ______________________ **Week 3 • Day 3**

Word Choice Use figurative language to make your descriptions come alive for your reader.

Read this story about a girl who has just moved from Alaska to Florida. Then:
- Finish the similes, metaphors, and personification by filling in the blanks.
- Use proofreading marks to correct any errors in subject-verb agreement.

Sample Answers:

Adjusting to a New View

"Welcome to Swampland," Niki sighs as she steps out onto the porch and is immediately struck by a wall of heat and humidity. It is as hot as the inside of a volcano. "I can't believe we moved here from Fairbanks," mutters Niki. "Is my dad trying to kill me?" She turn^s on the outside fan and flops onto a lounge chair. Within minutes, she is covered in sweat and feels like a greased pig.

She gaze^s down the barely paved road, letting her eyes relax until she sees heat waves dancing in the air above the pavement. They rise~~s~~ like smoke from a fire. Across the road, a lethargic alligator slides lazily into a muddy pond, slowly submerging like a submarine. "I guess he ~~don't~~ doesn't like the heat any more than I do," Niki thinks.

Suddenly, the wind picks up and the temperature drop^s. Niki looks out across the marshy fields. Massive storm clouds ~~is~~ are rolling in, as big and dark as night. They seem to be mocking Niki, as if trying to teach her a lesson. The next second, a bolt of lightning flashes on the horizon. A deafening thunderclap shakes the house like an earthquake. More and more lightning bolts begin to tear through the fabric of the sky. Niki grins as she watch^es the performance. "Now THAT," she admits, "is pretty cool."

86 WORD CHOICE — Daily 6-Trait Writing • EMC 6026 • © Evan-Moor Corp.

Name: ______________________ **Week 3 • Day 4**

Word Choice Use similes, metaphors, and personification to develop your ideas.

Choose one of the story prompts below. Then use the chart to plan a setting for your story. What creative comparisons could you make to help your reader picture the setting?

- ❑ One fall day, two kids find an abandoned village while hiking in the woods.
- ❑ A girl goes to her favorite park after a storm and turns her skateboard into a snowboard.
- ❑ Two kids hold a dog wash to raise money during their summer break.
- ❑ A boy watches a baby bird hatch one spring afternoon.

Sample Answers:

Setting: park

Feature of setting	Description	Could be compared to . . .
Example: trees	bare	bony fingers reaching up from the ground
sky	gray	scarf wrapped around the sun
hill	bumpy	riding a roller coaster

© Evan-Moor Corp. • EMC 6026 • Daily 6-Trait Writing — WORD CHOICE 87

DAY 3

Read the rule aloud. Explain that the term **figurative language** refers to personification, similes, and metaphors. Guide students through the activity.

- Read aloud the story. Say: *The writer did a good job of describing the setting. For example, she used the metaphor "wall of heat and humidity" to describe the intensity of the weather outside. There was not an actual wall, but it was so hot and humid that Niki felt like she had walked into a wall.*
- Direct students to the second sentence and work with them to complete the simile. For example, ask: *What are some things that the heat could be compared to?* (e.g., volcano, sauna, furnace) Then have students complete the activity independently or in pairs.
- **Convention:** Review subject-verb agreement. Then have students identify the errors and explain how they corrected the verbs.

DAY 4

Read the rule aloud. Then guide students through the activity.

- Read aloud the story prompts. For each one, help students brainstorm features of the setting that they could describe.
- Re-create the chart on the board and model filling it in. For example, say: *Let's say I choose the first prompt. Since it's set in the fall, I could write about the leaves as a feature. In the "Description" column, I'll describe their colors and how they're falling from the trees. Then I could compare them to colorful butterflies fluttering to the ground.*
- Have students choose one story prompt and complete the activity independently. Circulate to help students think of interesting features and comparisons.

DAY 5 *Writing Prompt*

- *Use your comparisons from Day 4 to write the beginning of a short story. Use similes, metaphors, and personification to describe the setting.*
- *Be sure to use correct subject-verb agreement.*

Name: ______________________

Word Choice

Use similes and metaphors to make your writing richer. A simile compares two things using *like* or *as*. A metaphor does not use *like* or *as*.

A. Read the two versions of this personal narrative. In the revised version, underline the similes and metaphors that were added.

Draft

The snow started just as my brother Jeff and I left school. It was growing very dark, and the wind was beginning to blow. Snowflakes fell in heavy clumps and stuck to my face. Jeff wrapped his scarf around his face, and I put on my white wool cap and gloves. The sidewalk was slippery. We skated along carefully, trying not to fall. Ice pellets stung my face. When we were still two blocks from home, the wind began to blow even harder. I knew that we were in for a terrible blizzard.

Revision

The snow started just as my brother Jeff and I left school. It was growing as dark as night, and the wind was beginning to blow. Snowflakes fell in clumps like wet cotton balls that stuck to my face. Jeff had turned into an Egyptian mummy, with his scarf wrapped up to his eyes. I put on my white wool cap and gloves, feeling like a ghost as my hands disappeared against the snow. The sidewalks were as slick as oil. We skated along carefully, trying not to fall. Needles of ice pricked my stinging cheeks along the way. When we were still two blocks from home, the wind began to howl like a hungry wolf. I knew that this storm was about to become a terrible monster.

B. Write a simile or metaphor to describe each subject below.

1. Snowflakes: ______________________
2. Icicles: ______________________
3. Snowballs: ______________________
4. Clouds: ______________________

Name: ______________________________

Word Choice Use personification to bring your ideas to life.

A. Read these haiku. Use proofreading marks to fix the errors in subject-verb agreement. Then underline the examples of personification.

Winter

Ice bites and wind growl,
A bear in her deepest sleep—
Alone until spring

Fall

Flags of red and gold
Leaves on trees wave and salutes,
Proclaiming autumn

B. Read these haiku starters. Then finish each poem by writing the line or lines with the number of syllables given. Include personification and be sure to use correct subject-verb agreement.

Spring

Tulips peek their heads
Trees put on shiny green coats
______________________ (5)

Lake

The boats nod and sway
______________________ (7)
The lake softly sings

Sun

The sun breathes deeply
______________________ (7)
______________________ (5)

Grass

______________________ (5)
Pushing roots in shallow ground
______________________ (5)

Name: ______________________________

Word Choice Use figurative language to make your descriptions come alive for your reader.

Read this story about a girl who has just moved from Alaska to Florida. Then:

- Finish the similes, metaphors, and personification by filling in the blanks.
- Use proofreading marks to correct any errors in subject-verb agreement.

Adjusting to a New View

"Welcome to Swampland," Niki sighs as she steps out onto the porch and is immediately struck by a wall of heat and humidity. It is as hot as ______________________________. "I can't believe we moved here from Fairbanks," mutters Niki. "Is my dad trying to kill me?" She turn on the outside fan and flops onto a lounge chair. Within minutes, she is covered in sweat and feels like ______________________________.

She gaze down the barely paved road, letting her eyes relax until she sees heat waves ______________________________ above the pavement. They rises like ______________________________. Across the road, a lethargic alligator slides lazily into a muddy pond, slowly submerging ______________________________. "I guess he don't like the heat any more than I do," Niki thinks.

Suddenly, the wind picks up and the temperature drop. Niki looks out across the marshy fields. Massive storm clouds is rolling in, as big and dark as ______________________________. They seem to be ______________________________ Niki, as if ______________________________. The next second, a bolt of lightning flashes on the horizon. A deafening thunderclap shakes the house like ______________________________. More and more lightning bolts begin to ______________________________ the sky. Niki grins as she watch the performance. "Now THAT," she admits, "is pretty cool."

Name: ______________________________

Word Choice Use similes, metaphors, and personification to develop your ideas.

Choose one of the story prompts below. Then use the chart to plan a setting for your story. What creative comparisons could you make to help your reader picture the setting?

- ☐ One fall day, two kids find an abandoned village while hiking in the woods.
- ☐ A girl goes to her favorite park after a storm and turns her skateboard into a snowboard.
- ☐ Two kids hold a dog wash to raise money during their summer break.
- ☐ A boy watches a baby bird hatch one spring afternoon.

Setting: ______________________________

Feature of setting	Description	Could be compared to . . .
Example: trees	bare	bony fingers reaching up from the ground

WORD CHOICE

Choosing the Right Words for Your Audience

DAY 1

Read the rule aloud. Say: *To make the best word choices, you need to think about your audience. That includes deciding how formal or informal your writing needs to be.* Then guide students through the activity.

- Ask: *Who is usually your audience for a report?* (teacher) *What kind of language do you normally use in a report?* (formal) Then have students read both versions and complete the activity.
- Have students identify the words and phrases that they underlined in Version 2. Then discuss the changes that the writer made and how they better suit the audience. (e.g., made it sound more formal, more like something you would write for an adult) Ask: *Whom might Version 1 appeal to?* (young kids, peers)

DAY 2

Read the rule aloud. Say: *Sometimes, writers think that using big or unusual words from a thesaurus will make them sound smarter. Although a thesaurus is a good tool, it can sometimes lead the writer to choose a word that doesn't suit the audience.* Guide students through the activities.

- **Activity A:** Read the essay aloud. Ask: *What is the writer trying to say?* (The airport is too loud. It should have listening stations in the waiting areas.) Say: *Using formal language can be important when communicating a problem and suggesting a solution, but using overly difficult words can sound silly, get in your reader's way, and weaken your message. Don't use big words just to try to sound smarter. It's more important to be clear.*

  Point out the word **tarrying** in the first sentence. Say: *While **tarrying** is correct in this sentence, few people use this word. **Waiting** is a perfectly good word to use. It is clear and accurate.* Have students complete the activity. You may wish students to work in pairs and/or use dictionaries if they don't know the meanings of words.
- **Activity B (Convention):** Remind students that a run-on sentence is made up of two or more sentences that run together without proper punctuation. Say: *You can fix a run-on by breaking it into two sentences or by adding a conjunction to make it a compound sentence.* Have students correct the run-ons. Review the answers as a class.

Name: ____________________ **Week 4 • Day 1**

Word Choice Choose words that will appeal to your audience. Think about whether you need to use formal or informal language.

Read these versions of a research report. Underline the words in Version 2 that replaced the bold words in Version 1. Then answer the question.

Version 1

How Two Guys Got off the Ground

Whenever you hop on a plane, think about Orville and Wilbur Wright. On December 17, 1903, the Wright brothers made history with the first **for real** airplane flights. But how did these two **guys** get their start? Wilbur said that he and Orville first **got thinking about flying** when their **dad** gave them **some toy helicopter thing. But** that was just the beginning. First, they had to **learn stuff.**

Wilbur and Orville **were totally into reading.** Even though they **didn't go to** college, they **got smart** by reading the books in their **dad's** library. Orville then learned to be a printer, and he **talked his brother into working** with him. They also began to sell and **fix bikes**. That may not seem **like a big deal**, but they were learning about machines.

Version 2

The Wright Brothers: The Early Years

The next time you board an airplane, think about Orville and Wilbur Wright. On December 17, 1903, the Wright brothers made history with their first successful airplane flights. But how did these two inventors get their start? Wilbur said that he and his brother first became interested in flight when their father gave them a little helicopter-like toy. Of course, that was just the beginning. First, they had to receive an education.

Wilbur and Orville loved to read. Even though they never attended college, they educated themselves by reading the books in their father's library. Orville then learned to be a printer, and he convinced his brother to work with him. They also began to sell and repair bicycles. That may not seem terribly relevant, but they were learning about machines.

Which version of the report would your teacher probably rather read? Why?

Version 2. It's more formal and uses academic-sounding words.

90 WORD CHOICE Daily 6-Trait Writing • EMC 6026 • © Evan-Moor Corp.

Name: ____________________ **Week 4 • Day 2**

Word Choice Choose words that will appeal to your audience. Don't use difficult language that may get in the way of your ideas.

A. Read this problem-and-solution essay. Cross out the overly formal words or phrases. Replace them with the more direct words in the box, or use your own.

noise	laptops	music	waiting	read a book	travelers
suggest	working	annoying	problem	advertisements	thinking

I was ~~tarrying~~ waiting in the airport when I noticed an ~~irksome~~ annoying problem. Some ~~voyagers~~ travelers were ~~laboring~~ working on their ~~portable electronic computing devices~~ laptops. Like others, I was making an attempt to ~~peruse a text~~ read a book, but I could not concentrate because a television blared above my head. At the same time, I could hear the airport's own radio station. Cell phones rang and flight announcements were made, adding to the ~~cacophony~~ noise.

After ~~ruminating~~ thinking about this ~~conundrum~~ problem, I have come up with a solution to ~~propound~~ suggest. The waiting area could be equipped with multiple personal listening stations. Those who want to listen to the television or the radio could tune in, as well as those who prefer a particular kind of ~~harmonic and melodic entertainment~~ music. The airline announcements would be broadcast through the headsets, as well, to alert the listening travelers.

In this way, the airport would meet the needs and preferences of many people. And while these stations might be expensive to install, the airline could display ~~promotional product placements~~ advertisements to make up the cost.

B. Rewrite each run-on as two sentences or as one compound sentence.

Sample Answers:

1. The chairs are uncomfortable I think the airport should have recliners.

   The chairs are uncomfortable. I think the airport should have recliners.

2. Kids always run around the airport, there should be an indoor play area.

   Kids always run around the airport, so there should be an indoor play area.

© Evan-Moor Corp. • EMC 6026 • Daily 6-Trait Writing WORD CHOICE 91

Name: ____________________ **Week 4 • Day 3**

Word Choice Choose words that will appeal to all members of your audience.

Read this speech that Robbie delivered to students and teachers at a school assembly. Use proofreading marks to fix the run-on sentences. Then complete the activities.

Check this out. You know how we all have to go to the library and peruse a book every week for free reading? It makes you want to barf, right? Most of our books are lame and were written a million years ago by old dudes instead, the library needs more graphic novels.

Your teachers might tell you that graphic novels are just comic books, but that's a lie some graphic novels are about superheroes, but many are about a multitude of academically appropriate topics. Some are way-cool versions of the classic stories we read in class others are about things that happened in history, such as the Vikings, ancient Rome, and the Civil War.

Graphic novels are vastly superior to regular books because the pictures are sick plus, if kids don't comprehend the words in a story, they can look at the pictures and ameliorate their understanding. So, all students should bug their teachers and librarians for more graphic novels in school.

Sample Answers:

1. List three words or phrases that students might not like or understand in the speech.
   peruse, multitude, academically appropriate, vastly superior, ameliorate
2. List three words or phrases that teachers might not like or understand in the speech.
   makes you want to barf, lame, written a million years ago, old dudes, that's a lie, way-cool, pictures are sick, bug
3. Rewrite one sentence from Robbie's speech to include better word choices.

   Old Sentence: Graphic novels are vastly superior to regular books because the pictures are sick.

   New Sentence: Graphic novels are much better than regular books because the illustrations hold your attention.

92 WORD CHOICE Daily 6-Trait Writing • EMC 6026 • © Evan-Moor Corp.

Name: ____________________ **Week 4 • Day 4**

Word Choice Choose words that will appeal to your audience.

A. Think of a problem in your school or community. How would you solve it? Use the problem-and-solution diagram to plan a speech you could give to both students and teachers.

Sample Answers:

Problem: (Explain what is wrong.)
smelly lockers

Solution: (Explain how the problem could be solved.)
hold bimonthly locker cleanouts to throw out trash, take home dirty gym clothes, return library books, and spray lockers with disinfectant

Pros: (Explain why the solution is a good one.)	**Cons:** (Acknowledge other problems the solution might cause.)
kids could get into the habit of keeping their personal areas clean and organized; hallways wouldn't stink	would take away time from classes

B. Exchange papers with a partner. Circle any words or phrases that would not be appropriate for teachers. Then circle any that would not appeal to students.

© Evan-Moor Corp. • EMC 6026 • Daily 6-Trait Writing WORD CHOICE 93

DAY 3

Read the rule aloud. Then say: *Sometimes, your audience will have a mix of people in it. Choose words that will appeal to everyone.* Guide students through the activity.

- **Convention:** Have students read the speech and fix the run-on sentences by breaking them apart or turning them into compound sentences. Review the answers as a class, pointing out that there may be multiple ways to fix each run-on.
- Say: *Robbie tried to write his speech for both teachers and students by including words that each would like. But would all of the words appeal to* both *groups?* (no) Ask: *What kinds of words did Robbie use to appeal to teachers?* (big, formal words) *Would the students know the meanings of all those words?* (no) *What kinds of words did Robbie use to appeal to students?* (slang) *Would teachers appreciate all those words?* (no) Have students answer items 1 and 2.
- For item 3, use the sample answer on the reduced page to model rewriting a sentence with words that would be appropriate for both teachers and students. Have students write their sentences, and ask volunteers to share them.

DAY 4

Read the rule aloud. Then guide students through the activities.

- **Activity A:** Brainstorm with students problems in your school or community. (e.g., bullying, no arts classes, homelessness, litter) Have students choose one problem they feel strongly about and write it in the first box. Model filling in the diagram with the sample answers on the reduced page. Then have students complete the activity.
- **Activity B:** Have partners work together to brainstorm appropriate language for both teachers and students.

DAY 5 *Writing Prompt*

- *Use your diagram from Day 4 to write a speech about a solution to a problem in your school or community. Use the best words for your audience.*
- *Exchange papers to check for run-on sentences. Fix any that are found.*

Name: ______________________________

Week 4 • Day 1

Word Choice

Choose words that will appeal to your audience. Think about whether you need to use formal or informal language.

Read these versions of a research report. Underline the words in Version 2 that replaced the bold words in Version 1. Then answer the question.

Version 1

How Two Guys Got off the Ground

Whenever you hop on a plane, think about Orville and Wilbur Wright. On December 17, 1903, the Wright brothers made history with the first **for real** airplane flights. But how did these two **guys** get their start? Wilbur said that he and Orville first **got thinking about flying** when their **dad** gave them **some toy helicopter thing. But** that was just the beginning. First, they had to **learn stuff.**

Wilbur and Orville **were totally into reading.** Even though they **didn't go to** college, they **got smart** by reading the books in their **dad's** library. Orville then learned to be a printer, and he **talked his brother into working** with him. They also began to sell and **fix bikes**. That may not seem **like a big deal**, but they were learning about machines.

Version 2

The Wright Brothers: The Early Years

The next time you board an airplane, think about Orville and Wilbur Wright. On December 17, 1903, the Wright brothers made history with their first successful airplane flights. But how did these two inventors get their start? Wilbur said that he and his brother first became interested in flight when their father gave them a little helicopter-like toy. Of course, that was just the beginning. First, they had to receive an education.

Wilbur and Orville loved to read. Even though they never attended college, they educated themselves by reading the books in their father's library. Orville then learned to be a printer, and he convinced his brother to work with him. They also began to sell and repair bicycles. That may not seem terribly relevant, but they were learning about machines.

Which version of the report would your teacher probably rather read? Why?

____

Name: ____________________

Word Choice Choose words that will appeal to your audience. Don't use difficult language that may get in the way of your ideas.

A. Read this problem-and-solution essay. Cross out the overly formal words or phrases. Replace them with the more direct words in the box, or use your own.

noise	laptops	music	waiting	read a book	travelers
suggest	working	annoying	problem	advertisements	thinking

I was tarrying in the airport when I noticed an irksome problem. Some voyagers were laboring on their portable electronic computing devices. Like others, I was making an attempt to peruse a text, but I could not concentrate because a television blared above my head. At the same time, I could hear the airport's own radio station. Cell phones rang and flight announcements were made, adding to the cacophony.

After ruminating about this conundrum, I have come up with a solution to propound. The waiting area could be equipped with multiple personal listening stations. Those who want to listen to the television or the radio could tune in, as well as those who prefer a particular kind of harmonic and melodic entertainment. The airline announcements would be broadcast through the headsets, as well, to alert the listening travelers.

In this way, the airport would meet the needs and preferences of many people. And while these stations might be expensive to install, the airline could display promotional product placements to make up the cost.

B. Rewrite each run-on as two sentences or as one compound sentence.

1. The chairs are uncomfortable I think the airport should have recliners.

____

2. Kids always run around the airport, there should be an indoor play area.

____

Word Choice Choose words that will appeal to all members of your audience.

Read this speech that Robbie delivered to students and teachers at a school assembly. Use proofreading marks to fix the run-on sentences. Then complete the activities.

Check this out. You know how we all have to go to the library and peruse a book every week for free reading? It makes you want to barf, right? Most of our books are lame and were written a million years ago by old dudes, instead, the library needs more graphic novels.

Your teachers might tell you that graphic novels are just comic books, but that's a lie some graphic novels are about superheroes, but many are about a multitude of academically appropriate topics. Some are way-cool versions of the classic stories we read in class, others are about things that happened in history, such as the Vikings, ancient Rome, and the Civil War.

Graphic novels are vastly superior to regular books because the pictures are sick plus, if kids don't comprehend the words in a story, they can look at the pictures and ameliorate their understanding. So, all students should bug their teachers and librarians for more graphic novels in school.

1. List three words or phrases that students might not like or understand in the speech.

____

2. List three words or phrases that teachers might not like or understand in the speech.

____

3. Rewrite one sentence from Robbie's speech to include better word choices.

Old Sentence: ______________________________

New Sentence: ______________________________

Name: ______________________________

Word Choice Choose words that will appeal to your audience.

A. Think of a problem in your school or community. How would you solve it? Use the problem-and-solution diagram to plan a speech you could give to both students and teachers.

Problem: (Explain what is wrong.)

Solution: (Explain how the problem could be solved.)

Pros: (Explain why the solution is a good one.)

Cons: (Acknowledge other problems the solution might cause.)

B. Exchange papers with a partner. Circle any words or phrases that would not be appropriate for teachers. Then circle any that would not appeal to students.

WEEK 5 WORD CHOICE
Getting the Reader's Attention

DAY 1

Read the rule aloud. Say: *Use everything you've learned about word choice—vivid verbs, descriptive language, similes, metaphors, and personification—to craft openings, or leads, that make your reader want to keep reading.* Then guide students through the activities.

- **Activity A:** Have students read both openings. Then ask: *Which is more powerful?* (Opening 2) Guide students in comparing the openings. For example, say: *The first boldface phrase in Opening 1 is **fast-moving vehicles.** What is the corresponding phrase in Opening 2? (**careening cars and tilting trucks**) Which is more specific and descriptive?* (the second) Have students continue to compare the openings, underlining the more precise words.

  Convention: Say: *Sometimes, people misspell plural nouns by putting an apostrophe before the **s**. Remember, plural nouns do not have apostrophes.* Point out the words **Moviegoers, robbers,** and **officers** in Opening 1. Ask: *Are these plural nouns or possessive nouns?* (plural) *Are they written correctly?* (yes)

- **Activity B:** Say: *The writer of Opening 2 did more than simply use precise words.* Read through the techniques and explain each one, pointing out examples as necessary. Then have students complete the activity.

DAY 2

Read the rule aloud. Then guide students through the activities.

- **Activity A:** Say: *It's important to grab your reader's attention in the **lead**, or first sentence or two, of an article.* Read the first pair of leads. Then say: *The phrases "Two famous actors," "in town," and "a nice car" don't tell us very much.* Discuss what makes the second lead stronger. (e.g., creates an image, is more specific) Have students mark the stronger leads and explain their choices.

  Convention: Have students find and correct the plural nouns. Review the answers as a class.

- **Activity B:** Use the sample answer on the reduced page to model rewriting the first lead. Then have students complete the activity.

Name: ______________________ **Week 5 • Day 1**

Word Choice To write a strong opening and get your reader's attention, use powerful, precise language.

A. Read each opening for a movie review. Underline the precise words or phrases in Opening 2 that replaced the bold words in Opening 1.

Opening 1

Moviegoers who like scenes full of **fast-moving vehicles** will like this **funny** movie about two oddball bank robbers. These guys **aren't very smart**. They just **drive around** the county in **old** trucks. **Going after** these **robbers** are **a couple of amusing** police officers. The actors who play them are **really good.**

Opening 2

Screech! Blam! If you like to watch careening cars and tilting trucks, then buy your ticket for this wild-and-whacky ride of a movie about two oddball bank robbers. These guys are clueless idiots. They just tumble across the county in broken-down trucks. Cheerfully chasing these luckless criminals are the zaniest police officers you will ever see. The actors who play them are bound to get an Academy Award for their performances.

B. The writer of Opening 2 used certain techniques to get the reader's attention. Write at least two examples of each technique below.

Sample Answers

1. Sound-effect words: Screech, Blam
2. Confident language: buy your ticket, actors are bound to get an Academy Award
3. Alliteration: careening cars, tilting trucks, wild-and-whacky, cheerfully chasing
4. Strong adjectives: careening, tilting, clueless, broken-down, luckless, zaniest

96 WORD CHOICE Daily 6-Trait Writing • EMC 6026 • © Evan-Moor Corp.

Name: ______________________ **Week 5 • Day 2**

Word Choice Grab your reader's attention by choosing strong, specific nouns, verbs, adjectives, and adverbs.

A. Read each pair of leads for an article in an entertainment magazine. Mark the lead that is more specific. Then use proofreading marks to fix the errors in plural nouns.

1. ☐ Two famous actor's arrived in town yesterday, driving a nice car.
   ☒ An A-list Hollywood couple stylishly arrived in Lexington yesterday, behind the wheel of a cherry-red convertible.
2. ☒ After two decades', the old High Street Film Palace will glitter again on Friday.
   ☐ The old movie theater on High Street is open and beautiful again after being closed for a long time.
3. ☒ Henry Horton, the most famous graduate of Kenwood High School, donated one million dollar's to his former school for a new theater.
   ☐ A famous actor donated a large sum of money to a local school.

B. Rewrite these leads. Use your imagination to make them more specific and attention-getting. Sample Answers:

1. In spite of the snowstorm, many people showed up for the movie tryouts.
   In spite of the worst blizzard of the season, hundreds of eager actors trekked through the snow to show off their movie star potential.
2. Many famous people dressed up to go to the opening of the new film.
   Over fifty Hollywood celebrities glittered at the red carpet premier of the latest *Batman* movie.
3. A famous actor spoke on TV to get people to donate to an animal charity.
   This year's Oscar winner for Best Actress tearfully implored TV viewers to give generously to the shelter for abandoned animals.

© Evan-Moor Corp. • EMC 6026 • Daily 6-Trait Writing WORD CHOICE 97

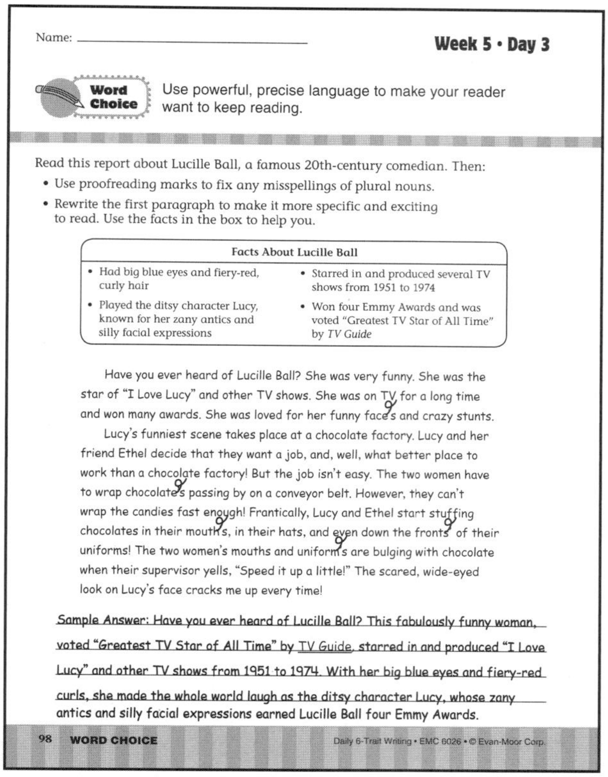

Name: ______________ **Week 5 • Day 3**

Word Choice Use powerful, precise language to make your reader want to keep reading.

Read this report about Lucille Ball, a famous 20th-century comedian. Then:

- Use proofreading marks to fix any misspellings of plural nouns.
- Rewrite the first paragraph to make it more specific and exciting to read. Use the facts in the box to help you.

Facts About Lucille Ball	
• Had big blue eyes and fiery-red, curly hair	• Starred in and produced several TV shows from 1951 to 1974
• Played the ditsy character Lucy, known for her zany antics and silly facial expressions	• Won four Emmy Awards and was voted "Greatest TV Star of All Time" by *TV Guide*

Have you ever heard of Lucille Ball? She was very funny. She was the star of "I Love Lucy" and other TV shows. She was on TV for a long time and won many awards. She was loved for her funny face's and crazy stunts.

Lucy's funniest scene takes place at a chocolate factory. Lucy and her friend Ethel decide that they want a job, and, well, what better place to work than a chocolate factory! But the job isn't easy. The two women have to wrap chocolate's passing by on a conveyor belt. However, they can't wrap the candies fast enough! Frantically, Lucy and Ethel start stuffing chocolates in their mouth's, in their hats, and even down the fronts' of their uniforms! The two women's mouths and uniform's are bulging with chocolate when their supervisor yells, "Speed it up a little!" The scared, wide-eyed look on Lucy's face cracks me up every time!

Sample Answer: Have you ever heard of Lucille Ball? This fabulously funny woman, voted "Greatest TV Star of All Time" by TV Guide, starred in and produced "I Love Lucy" and other TV shows from 1951 to 1974. With her big blue eyes and fiery-red curls, she made the whole world laugh as the ditsy character Lucy, whose zany antics and silly facial expressions earned Lucille Ball four Emmy Awards.

98 **WORD CHOICE** Daily 6-Trait Writing • EMC 6026 • © Evan-Moor Corp.

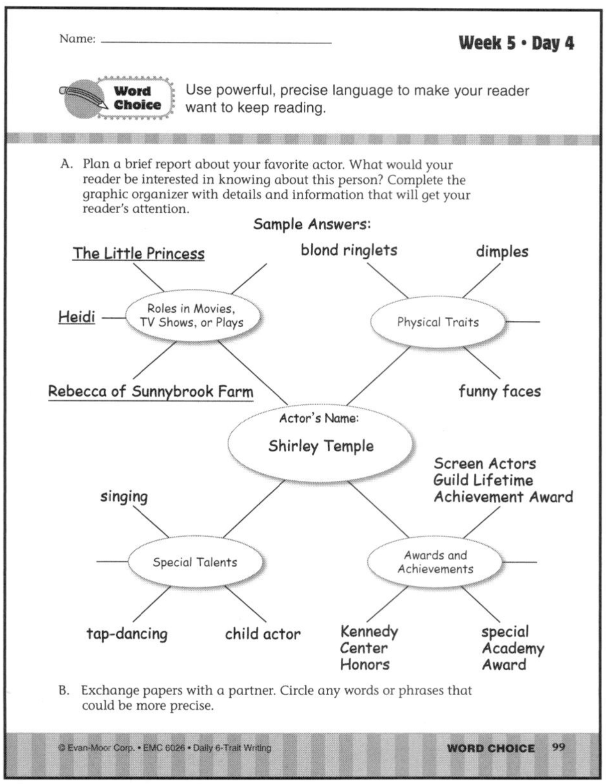

Name: ______________ **Week 5 • Day 4**

Word Choice Use powerful, precise language to make your reader want to keep reading.

A. Plan a brief report about your favorite actor. What would your reader be interested in knowing about this person? Complete the graphic organizer with details and information that will get your reader's attention.

B. Exchange papers with a partner. Circle any words or phrases that could be more precise.

© Evan-Moor Corp. • EMC 6026 • Daily 6-Trait Writing **WORD CHOICE** 99

DAY 3

Read the rule aloud. Then guide students through the activity.

- **Convention:** Have students read the report and fix the plural nouns. Review the answers as a class, noting the two words with apostrophes that should not be changed. (**Lucy's, women's**)
- Ask: *Which part of the report was more interesting to read, the first paragraph or second?* (second) *Why?* (first is vague, lacks attention-getting details; second is more detailed, specific) Have students identify examples of vague phrases in the first paragraph. (e.g., "very funny," "for a long time," "many awards")
- Read aloud the facts in the box and invite students to share anything else they know about Lucille Ball. Then ask: *How might this information be added to the first paragraph to add interest and detail? For example, what could we say instead of "a long time"?* ("from 1951 to 1974") Have students rewrite the paragraph, using powerful, precise language. Remind them also to try to use the writer's techniques learned on Day 1.

DAY 4

Review the rule. Guide students through the activities.

- **Activity A:** Help students brainstorm actors for their reports. For example, ask: *Which actor have you seen in more than one movie or TV show? What did you like about him or her? What makes this actor special?* Have students fill in their graphic organizers.
- **Activity B:** Have students exchange papers and identify words or details that could be improved. Encourage partners to help each other brainstorm better word choices.

DAY 5 *Writing Prompt*

- *Use your ideas from Day 4 to write a brief report about your favorite actor. Use powerful, precise language that will hold your reader's attention.*
- *Be sure to spell plural nouns correctly, without an apostrophe.*

Name: ________________________________

Week 5 • Day 1

Word Choice To write a strong opening and get your reader's attention, use powerful, precise language.

A. Read each opening for a movie review. Underline the precise words or phrases in Opening 2 that replaced the bold words in Opening 1.

Opening 1

Moviegoers who like scenes full of **fast-moving vehicles** will like this **funny** movie about two oddball bank robbers. These guys **aren't very smart**. They just **drive around** the county in **old** trucks. **Going after** these **robbers** are **a couple of amusing** police officers. The actors who play them are **really good.**

Opening 2

Screech! Blam! If you like to watch careening cars and tilting trucks, then buy your ticket for this wild-and-whacky ride of a movie about two oddball bank robbers. These guys are clueless idiots. They just tumble across the county in broken-down trucks. Cheerfully chasing these luckless criminals are the zaniest police officers you will ever see. The actors who play them are bound to get an Academy Award for their performances.

B. The writer of Opening 2 used certain techniques to get the reader's attention. Write at least two examples of each technique below.

1. Sound-effect words: ________________________________

2. Confident language: ________________________________

____

3. Alliteration: ________________________________

____

4. Strong adjectives: ________________________________

____

Name: ______________________

Word Choice Grab your reader's attention by choosing strong, specific nouns, verbs, adjectives, and adverbs.

A. Read each pair of leads for an article in an entertainment magazine. Mark the lead that is more specific. Then use proofreading marks to fix the errors in plural nouns.

1. ☐ Two famous actor's arrived in town yesterday, driving a nice car.
   ☐ An A-list Hollywood couple stylishly arrived in Lexington yesterday, behind the wheel of a cherry-red convertible.
2. ☐ After two decades', the old High Street Film Palace will glitter again on Friday.
   ☐ The old movie theater on High Street is open and beautiful again after being closed for a long time.
3. ☐ Henry Horton, the most famous graduate of Kenwood High School, donated one million dollar's to his former school for a new theater.
   ☐ A famous actor donated a large sum of money to a local school.

B. Rewrite these leads. Use your imagination to make them more specific and attention-getting.

1. In spite of the snowstorm, many people showed up for the movie tryouts.

____

____

2. Many famous people dressed up to go to the opening of the new film.

____

____

3. A famous actor spoke on TV to get people to donate to an animal charity.

____

____

Word Choice Use powerful, precise language to make your reader want to keep reading.

Read this report about Lucille Ball, a famous 20th-century comedian. Then:

- Use proofreading marks to fix any misspellings of plural nouns.
- Rewrite the first paragraph to make it more specific and exciting to read. Use the facts in the box to help you.

Facts About Lucille Ball

- Had big blue eyes and fiery-red, curly hair
- Played the ditsy character Lucy, known for her zany antics and silly facial expressions
- Starred in and produced several TV shows from 1951 to 1974
- Won four Emmy Awards and was voted "Greatest TV Star of All Time" by *TV Guide*

Have you ever heard of Lucille Ball? She was very funny. She was the star of "I Love Lucy" and other TV shows. She was on TV for a long time and won many awards. She was loved for her funny face's and crazy stunts.

Lucy's funniest scene takes place at a chocolate factory. Lucy and her friend Ethel decide that they want a job, and, well, what better place to work than a chocolate factory! But the job isn't easy. The two women have to wrap chocolate's passing by on a conveyor belt. However, they can't wrap the candies fast enough! Frantically, Lucy and Ethel start stuffing chocolates in their mouth's, in their hats, and even down the fronts' of their uniforms! The two women's mouths and uniform's are bulging with chocolate when their supervisor yells, "Speed it up a little!" The scared, wide-eyed look on Lucy's face cracks me up every time!

____

____

____

____

Name: ______________________________ **Week 5 • Day 4**

Word Choice Use powerful, precise language to make your reader want to keep reading.

A. Plan a brief report about your favorite actor. What would your reader be interested in knowing about this person? Complete the graphic organizer with details and information that will get your reader's attention.

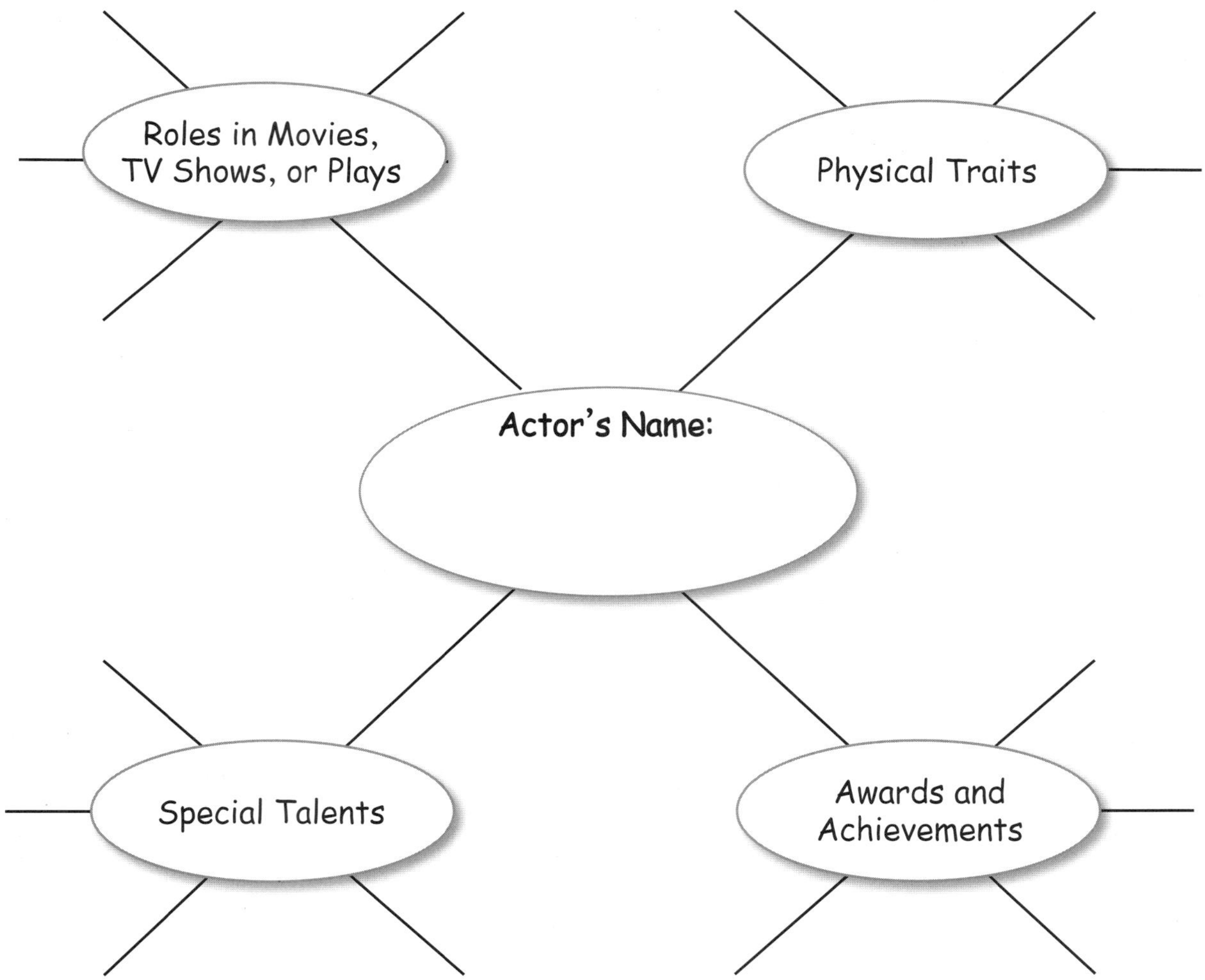

B. Exchange papers with a partner. Circle any words or phrases that could be more precise.

WEEK 1

SENTENCE FLUENCY

Combining Sentences

Refer to pages 6 and 7 to introduce or review the writing trait.

DAY 1

Read the rule aloud and review the definition of a compound sentence. (two complete sentences joined by a comma and the coordinating conjunction **and**, **but**, **or**, or **so**) Say: *Compound sentences can improve your sentence* ***fluency****, or the flow of your writing.* Then guide students through the activities.

- **Activity A:** Read the editorial aloud. Then reread the first three sentences and have students underline the two sentences that sound choppy and disconnected. ("The piping plover... Its future is...") Ask: *Why don't these two sentences flow well?* (too short; relationship between two ideas isn't clear) Have students finish reading the editorial and complete the activity independently.
- **Activity B:** Have students read the revision. Then direct students to the second sentence. Say: *This sentence combines two related ideas into one sentence that flows naturally, using the conjunction* ***but****.* Have students identify the two sentences within the compound sentence.

  Convention: Point out the comma between **bird** and **but**. Say: *When you write a compound sentence, remember to use a comma before the conjunction.* Then have students complete the activity.

DAY 2

Read the rule aloud. Say: *A rambling sentence is several sentences strung together with too many conjunctions. A run-on is two or more sentences that run together without proper punctuation.* Guide students through the activity.

- Have a volunteer read aloud the report. Then model rewriting one of the sentences. For example, point out the second sentence and ask: *Is this a run-on or a rambling sentence?* (rambling) Model breaking the sentence into three separate sentences, emphasizing that one of them can still be a compound sentence. Then have students rewrite the paragraph. Ask volunteers to read aloud their revisions.
- **Convention:** Review the use of commas in compound sentences. Then have students check to make sure they used commas correctly.

Name: ______________________ **Week 1 • Day 1**

Sentence Fluency Make your writing flow by combining short, choppy sentences into compound sentences.

A. Read this draft of an editorial written for the *Seaside Town Gazette*. Underline any pairs of sentences that sound choppy or don't flow naturally together.

Protect the Plover

The citizens of Seaside must support the efforts of the Piping Plover Committee. The piping plover is a beautiful little bird. Its future is threatened. It faces special dangers on our beaches during its nesting season. Someone taking a walk on the wrong part of the beach could destroy a plover's nest and eggs. Pets allowed to roam free on the beach can kill birds. We all want to be able to walk anywhere on the beach. The plover pays the price for our actions. What can we do? Respect the fenced nesting areas of the birds. Always supervise your pets. We can follow these simple rules. We can lose the piping plover forever. The choice is up to you. Make the right one.

B. In this revision, the writer has made her sentences flow better. Underline the compound sentences. Circle the commas and conjunctions.

The citizens of Seaside must support the efforts of the Piping Plover Committee. The piping plover is a beautiful little bird, but its future is threatened. It faces special dangers on our beaches during its nesting season. Someone taking a walk on the wrong part of the beach can destroy a plover's nest and eggs, and pets allowed to roam free on the beach can kill birds. We all might want to be able to walk anywhere on the beach, but the plover pays the price for our actions. What can we do? Respect the fenced nesting areas of the birds, and always supervise your pets. We can follow these simple rules, or we can lose the piping plover forever. The choice is up to you, so make the right one.

102 SENTENCE FLUENCY Daily 6-Trait Writing • EMC 6026 • © Evan-Moor Corp.

Name: ______________________ **Week 1 • Day 2**

Sentence Fluency When you combine sentences to make your writing flow, be careful not to form rambling or run-on sentences.

Read this report. Then:

- Underline the rambling sentences. Draw a wavy line under the run-ons.
- Rewrite the report, changing the rambling and run-on sentences to compound or simple sentences.

The Common Crow

What is that large bird you hear cawing from the top of a tree it is probably a common crow. The common crow weighs about 20 ounces, and its body length is between 15 and 18 inches, and crows look solid black, but their dark feathers shine with deep blues and greens in the sunlight.

Crows travel in flocks, so they often feed together in the winter, hundreds of crows will gather where there is food and crows might raid another bird's nest for eggs, or they might clean up garbage left by careless people. Farmers used to think crows were a nuisance because they eat young corn shoots, now most farmers understand that crows also eat insects that can harm crops.

Sample Answer:

What is that large bird you hear cawing from the top of a tree? It is probably a common crow. The common crow weighs about 20 ounces. Its body length is between 15 and 18 inches. Crows look solid black, but their dark feathers shine with deep blues and greens in the sunlight.

Crows travel in flocks, so they often feed together. In the winter, hundreds of crows will gather where there is food. Crows might raid another bird's nest for eggs, or they might clean up garbage left by careless people. Farmers used to think crows were a nuisance because they eat young corn shoots. Now, however, most farmers understand that crows also eat insects that can harm crops.

© Evan-Moor Corp. • EMC 6026 • Daily 6-Trait Writing SENTENCE FLUENCY 103

Name: ____________________

Week 1 • Day 3

Sentence Fluency When you revise your writing, look for ways to make it flow better by using compound sentences.

A. Read this e-mail. Then rewrite the e-mail by combining the shorter sentences into compound sentences.

> Hey, Ashley!
>
> Thanks for sending me that website link for my report. I learned a lot about crows. I'm still not sure what they like to eat. I've seen them eat garbage. Your website said that crows eat corn. Another website said that they eat bugs. I'll just have to keep researching.
>
> I was able to get started on my report last night. I made an outline I wrote a rough draft. I'd like to finish my paper tomorrow. I don't know if I'll be able to. I'll try! I could work on it in the morning. I could work on it after my piano lesson. It depends on when I get home. Will you go to the pool tomorrow? Will you stay home and finish your report?
>
> Akiko

Sample Answer:

Thanks for sending me that website link for my report. I learned a lot about crows, but I'm still not sure what they eat. I've seen them eat garbage, but your website said crows eat corn. Another website said they eat bugs, so I'll just have to keep researching.

I was able to get started on my report last night. I made an outline, and I wrote a rough draft. I'd like to finish my paper tomorrow, but I don't know if I'll be able to. I'll try! I could work on it in the morning, or I could work on it after my piano lesson. It depends on when I get home. Will you go to the pool tomorrow, or will you stay home and finish your report?

B. Is there another way you could have combined the sentences in the e-mail? Rewrite two of the sentences, combining them in a different way. Sample Answer:

I learned a lot about crows. I'm still not sure what they like to eat, but I've seen them eat garbage. Your website said they eat corn, and another website said they eat bugs. I'll just have to keep researching.

104 SENTENCE FLUENCY Daily 6-Trait Writing • EMC 6026 • © Evan-Moor Corp.

DAY 3

Read the rule aloud. Remind students that a compound sentence can be formed with **and**, **but**, **or**, or **so**. Then guide students through the activities.

- **Activity A:** Read the e-mail aloud, emphasizing its choppiness. Ask: *Does this e-mail flow smoothly from one idea to the next?* (no) Say: *Even in informal e-mails, we need to make sure our reader sees the connection between our ideas.* Draw attention to the second and third sentences. Ask: *What conjunction could we use to connect these two thoughts?* (**but**) Write the sentences on the board and model combining them. Then have students complete the activity.

- **Activity B (Convention):** If students have difficulty thinking of another way to combine sentences, suggest that they try out different conjunctions between each sentence. Then have students exchange papers to check for proper comma usage.

Name: ____________________

Week 1 • Day 4

Sentence Fluency Use compound sentences to make your writing flow more smoothly.

A. Use the form below to plan a short report about a type of bird. It can be a common bird in your area, or an exotic bird that you are interested in studying. Sample Answers:

Name of bird: Emperor penguin

Range: Antarctica

Physical characteristics:	Habitat:
about 4 feet tall	ice and water
webbed feet	
claws	

Interesting facts:	Food:
males hatch eggs	fish and shrimp
slide over ice	

B. Write two compound sentences that you could use in your report.

Sample Answer: Emperor penguins are birds, but they spend much of their life in the icy waters of Antarctica. They have wings, but they can't fly.

© Evan-Moor Corp. • EMC 6026 • Daily 6-Trait Writing SENTENCE FLUENCY 105

DAY 4

Read the rule aloud. Then guide students through the activities.

- **Activity A:** Brainstorm types of birds that students could write about. (e.g., pet birds, birds studied in class, birds that students have seen or read about) If necessary, allow time for brief research using classroom resources or the Internet. You may wish to have students who choose the same bird to work together.

- **Activity B (Convention):** Remind students to choose the conjunction that indicates the correct relationship between the two parts of the sentence and to use a comma before the conjunction.

DAY 5 *Writing Prompt*

- *Use the notes you took on Day 4 to write a short report about a type of bird. Use compound sentences to make your writing flow smoothly.*

- *Be sure to use commas in compound sentences correctly.*

Name: ______________________________

Sentence Fluency Make your writing flow by combining short, choppy sentences into compound sentences.

A. Read this draft of an editorial written for the *Seaside Town Gazette.* Underline any pairs of sentences that sound choppy or don't flow naturally together.

Protect the Plover

The citizens of Seaside must support the efforts of the Piping Plover Committee. The piping plover is a beautiful little bird. Its future is threatened. It faces special dangers on our beaches during its nesting season. Someone taking a walk on the wrong part of the beach could destroy a plover's nest and eggs. Pets allowed to roam free on the beach can kill birds. We all want to be able to walk anywhere on the beach. The plover pays the price for our actions. What can we do? Respect the fenced nesting areas of the birds. Always supervise your pets. We can follow these simple rules. We can lose the piping plover forever. The choice is up to you. Make the right one.

B. In this revision, the writer has made her sentences flow better. Underline the compound sentences. Circle the commas and conjunctions.

The citizens of Seaside must support the efforts of the Piping Plover Committee. The piping plover is a beautiful little bird, but its future is threatened. It faces special dangers on our beaches during its nesting season. Someone taking a walk on the wrong part of the beach can destroy a plover's nest and eggs, and pets allowed to roam free on the beach can kill birds. We all might want to be able to walk anywhere on the beach, but the plover pays the price for our actions. What can we do? Respect the fenced nesting areas of the birds, and always supervise your pets. We can follow these simple rules, or we can lose the piping plover forever. The choice is up to you, so make the right one.

Name: ___________________________

Sentence Fluency

When you combine sentences to make your writing flow, be careful not to form rambling or run-on sentences.

Read this report. Then:

- Underline the rambling sentences. Draw a wavy line under the run-ons.
- Rewrite the report, changing the rambling and run-on sentences to compound or simple sentences.

The Common Crow

What is that large bird you hear cawing from the top of a tree it is probably a common crow. The common crow weighs about 20 ounces, and its body length is between 15 and 18 inches, and crows look solid black, but their dark feathers shine with deep blues and greens in the sunlight.

Crows travel in flocks, so they often feed together in the winter, hundreds of crows will gather where there is food and crows might raid another bird's nest for eggs, or they might clean up garbage left by careless people. Farmers used to think crows were a nuisance because they eat young corn shoots, now most farmers understand that crows also eat insects that can harm crops.

____

____

____

____

____

____

____

____

____

____

Sentence Fluency

When you revise your writing, look for ways to make it flow better by using compound sentences.

A. Read this e-mail. Then rewrite the e-mail by combining the shorter sentences into compound sentences.

> Hey, Ashley!
>
> Thanks for sending me that website link for my report. I learned a lot about crows. I'm still not sure what they like to eat. I've seen them eat garbage. Your website said that crows eat corn. Another website said that they eat bugs. I'll just have to keep researching.
>
> I was able to get started on my report last night. I made an outline I wrote a rough draft. I'd like to finish my paper tomorrow. I don't know if I'll be able to. I'll try! I could work on it in the morning. I could work on it after my piano lesson. It depends on when I get home. Will you go to the pool tomorrow? Will you stay home and finish your report?
>
> Akiko

B. Is there another way you could have combined the sentences in the e-mail? Rewrite two of the sentences, combining them in a different way.

Name: ______________________

Sentence Fluency

Use compound sentences to make your writing flow more smoothly.

A. Use the form below to plan a short report about a type of bird. It can be a common bird in your area, or an exotic bird that you are interested in studying.

Name of bird: ______________________

Range: ______________________

Physical characteristics:

____

____

____

____

Habitat:

____

____

____

____

Interesting facts:

____

____

____

____

Food:

____

____

____

____

B. Write two compound sentences that you could use in your report.

____

____

____

SENTENCE FLUENCY
Writing Complex Sentences

DAY 1

Read the rule aloud. Say: *Just as you can combine short, related sentences into compound sentences, you can use complex sentences to combine your ideas.*

Write the following sentence on the board: *Your family history is important because it shows where you came from.* Underline "Your family history is important" and say: *This is an **independent clause**, or a group of words that can stand alone as a complete sentence.* Then underline "because it shows where you came from" and say: *This is a **dependent clause**, or a group of words that cannot stand alone as a complete sentence. A dependent clause starts with a **subordinating conjunction**, such as **because**.* (Circle **because**.)

Rewrite the sentence: *Because it shows where you came from, your family history is important.* Say: *Sometimes a complex sentence is written with the dependent clause first, beginning with the conjunction and followed by a comma.* Then guide students through the activities.

- **Activity A:** Read aloud the words in the box. Say: *In compound sentences, we use the conjunctions **and, but, or,** and **so**. But in complex sentences, we use conjunctions like the ones in this box.* Have students read the paragraphs and complete the activity.
- **Activity B (Convention):** Say: *To decide whether a complex sentence sounds better with its dependent clause first or last, you can try writing it both ways. If the dependent clause comes first, use a comma after it.* Have students complete the activity.

DAY 2

Read the rule aloud. Then guide students through the activities.

- **Activity A:** Read each clause aloud. Point out the ones that begin with **although** and **if** to introduce these conjunctions. Then model choosing two clauses to form a sentence. First write it starting with the dependent clause; then write it the other way around. Have students discuss which way sounds better or makes more sense. Then have students complete the activity.
- **Activity B (Convention):** Have students exchange papers and check each other's work.

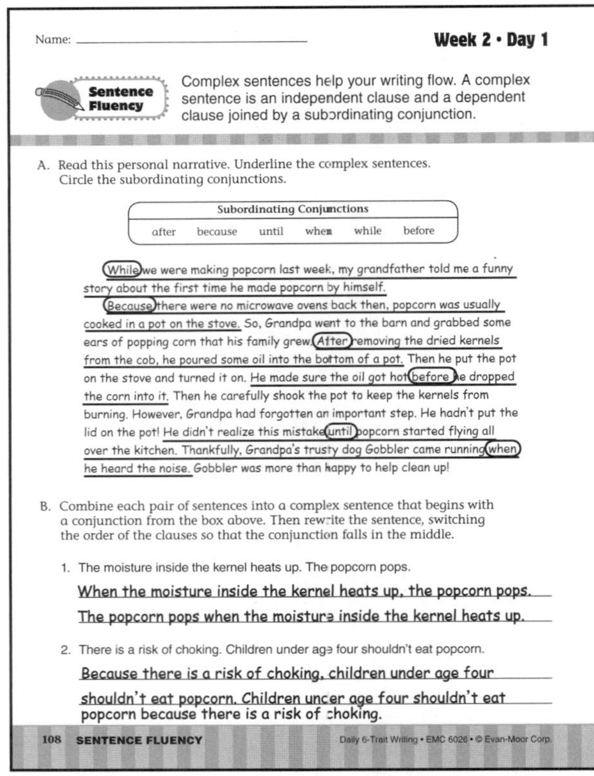

Name: ______________________ **Week 2 • Day 1**

Sentence Fluency

Complex sentences help your writing flow. A complex sentence is an independent clause and a dependent clause joined by a subordinating conjunction.

A. Read this personal narrative. Underline the complex sentences. Circle the subordinating conjunctions.

Subordinating Conjunctions					
after	because	until	when	while	before

While we were making popcorn last week, my grandfather told me a funny story about the first time he made popcorn by himself. Because there were no microwave ovens back then, popcorn was usually cooked in a pot on the stove. So, Grandpa went to the barn and grabbed some ears of popping corn that his family grew. After removing the dried kernels from the cob, he poured some oil into the bottom of a pot. Then he put the pot on the stove and turned it on. He made sure the oil got hot before he dropped the corn into it. Then he carefully shook the pot to keep the kernels from burning. However, Grandpa had forgotten an important step. He hadn't put the lid on the pot! He didn't realize this mistake until popcorn started flying all over the kitchen. Thankfully, Grandpa's trusty dog Gobbler came running when he heard the noise. Gobbler was more than happy to help clean up!

B. Combine each pair of sentences into a complex sentence that begins with a conjunction from the box above. Then rewrite the sentence, switching the order of the clauses so that the conjunction falls in the middle.

1. The moisture inside the kernel heats up. The popcorn pops.
   When the moisture inside the kernel heats up, the popcorn pops.
   The popcorn pops when the moisture inside the kernel heats up.
2. There is a risk of choking. Children under age four shouldn't eat popcorn.
   Because there is a risk of choking, children under age four shouldn't eat popcorn. Children under age four shouldn't eat popcorn because there is a risk of choking.

108 SENTENCE FLUENCY Daily 6-Trait Writing • EMC 6026 • © Evan-Moor Corp.

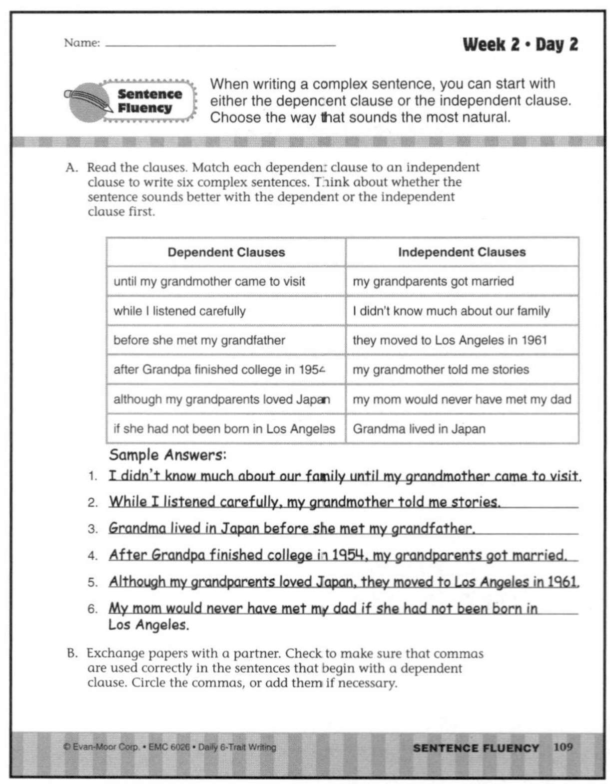

Name: ______________________ **Week 2 • Day 2**

Sentence Fluency

When writing a complex sentence, you can start with either the dependent clause or the independent clause. Choose the way that sounds the most natural.

A. Read the clauses. Match each dependent clause to an independent clause to write six complex sentences. Think about whether the sentence sounds better with the dependent or the independent clause first.

Dependent Clauses	Independent Clauses
until my grandmother came to visit	my grandparents got married
while I listened carefully	I didn't know much about our family
before she met my grandfather	they moved to Los Angeles in 1961
after Grandpa finished college in 1954	my grandmother told me stories
although my grandparents loved Japan	my mom would never have met my dad
if she had not been born in Los Angeles	Grandma lived in Japan

Sample Answers:

1. I didn't know much about our family until my grandmother came to visit.
2. While I listened carefully, my grandmother told me stories.
3. Grandma lived in Japan before she met my grandfather.
4. After Grandpa finished college in 1954, my grandparents got married.
5. Although my grandparents loved Japan, they moved to Los Angeles in 1961.
6. My mom would never have met my dad if she had not been born in Los Angeles.

B. Exchange papers with a partner. Check to make sure that commas are used correctly in the sentences that begin with a dependent clause. Circle the commas, or add them if necessary.

© Evan-Moor Corp. • EMC 6026 • Daily 6-Trait Writing SENTENCE FLUENCY 109

Name: ______________________ **Week 2 • Day 3**

Sentence Fluency Use complex sentences to help your writing flow more smoothly.

A. Rewrite this biography to make it flow more smoothly. Combine some of the sentences into complex sentences using the conjunctions in the box.

An Adventurous Woman

My great-aunt Betty was born in 1922 and grew up in Texas. She was 18. She graduated from high school. She spent two years working in a bakery. She realized she wanted to moved to the big city. Betty enrolled in beauty school and learned to cut hair. She really wanted to travel. She wanted more adventure in her life. She joined the Women's Army Corps in 1943. This was during World War II. Aunt Betty spoke French. She was ordered to serve in Paris. She lived there for two years. The war ended in 1945.

Subordinating Conjunctions					
before	although	because	when	until	since

Sample Answer:

My great-aunt Betty was born in 1922 and grew up in Texas. When she was 18, she graduated from high school. She spent two years working in a bakery before she realized she wanted to move to the big city. Betty enrolled in beauty school and learned to cut hair, although she really wanted to travel. Because she wanted more adventure in her life, she joined the Women's Army Corps in 1943. This was during World War II. Because Aunt Betty spoke French, she was ordered to serve in Paris. She lived there for two years until the war ended in 1945.

B. Exchange papers with a partner. Underline each complex sentence in the rewritten biography, and check to make sure that commas have been used correctly.

110 SENTENCE FLUENCY Daily 6-Trait Writing • EMC 6026 • © Evan-Moor Corp.

DAY 3

Read the rule aloud. Say: *Complex sentences help your writing flow smoothly by creating longer sentences and sentences that begin in different ways.* Guide students through the activities.

- **Activity A:** Have a student read the paragraph aloud. Say: *This paragraph would flow a lot better if we combined some of the sentences.* Say: *The second sentence says that Betty was 18. The third sentence says she graduated from high school. Since most students graduate from high school when they are 17 or 18, a good conjunction to link those sentences is* **when**: *"When she was 18, she graduated from high school."* Have a volunteer write the sentence on the board.

  Have students complete the activity on their own. Invite volunteers to read their revisions aloud.

- **Activity B (Convention):** Have students exchange papers and check each other's sentences for correct comma usage.

Name: ______________________ **Week 2 • Day 4**

Sentence Fluency Use complex sentences to help your writing flow more smoothly.

A. Use the timeline below to plan a biography of someone whom you admire. On the timeline, note significant events or accomplishments in that person's life. You can use either dates or ages in your timeline.

The Life of Shirley Chisholm Sample Answers:

- 1924 — born in Brooklyn
- 1964 — elected to New York State Legislature
- 1968 — first African-American woman elected to U.S. Congress
- 1972 — ran for the Democratic Party's presidential nomination
- 1982 — retired from Congress
- 1993 — inducted into National Women's Hall of Fame

B. Use two of the subordinating conjunctions from the box to write two complex sentences about the subject of your biography.

Sample Answers:

Subordinating Conjunctions				
after	until	when	before	if
unless	although	because	while	once

1. After serving two terms in the New York State Legislature, Chisholm decided to run for the U.S. Congress.
2. Chisholm was a representative for fourteen years before retiring in 1982.

© Evan-Moor Corp. • EMC 6026 • Daily 6-Trait Writing SENTENCE FLUENCY 111

DAY 4

Review the rule. Guide students through the activities.

- **Activity A:** This activity can be completed in several ways: 1) Complete the timeline as a class, choosing one subject and using classroom reference materials; 2) Complete the timeline as a class, using the sample answers on the reduced page shown to the left; 3) Have students complete the timeline independently, choosing their own subjects and using classroom reference materials.

- **Activity B:** Encourage students to think about the relationships between the events they are writing about while choosing conjunctions. Invite volunteers to read their finished sentences aloud.

DAY 5 *Writing Prompt*

- *Use your timeline from Day 4 to write a biography of someone whom you admire. Use complex sentences to help your writing flow smoothly.*
- *Be sure to use commas in complex sentences correctly.*

Name: ___________________________________ **Week 2 • Day 1**

Sentence Fluency

Complex sentences help your writing flow. A complex sentence is an independent clause and a dependent clause joined by a subordinating conjunction.

A. Read this personal narrative. Underline the complex sentences. Circle the subordinating conjunctions.

Subordinating Conjunctions					
after	because	until	when	while	before

While we were making popcorn last week, my grandfather told me a funny story about the first time he made popcorn by himself.

Because there were no microwave ovens back then, popcorn was usually cooked in a pot on the stove. So, Grandpa went to the barn and grabbed some ears of popping corn that his family grew. After removing the dried kernels from the cob, he poured some oil into the bottom of a pot. Then he put the pot on the stove and turned it on. He made sure the oil got hot before he dropped the corn into it. Then he carefully shook the pot to keep the kernels from burning. However, Grandpa had forgotten an important step. He hadn't put the lid on the pot! He didn't realize this mistake until popcorn started flying all over the kitchen. Thankfully, Grandpa's trusty dog Gobbler came running when he heard the noise. Gobbler was more than happy to help clean up!

B. Combine each pair of sentences into a complex sentence that begins with a conjunction from the box above. Then rewrite the sentence, switching the order of the clauses so that the conjunction falls in the middle.

1. The moisture inside the kernel heats up. The popcorn pops.

____

____

2. There is a risk of choking. Children under age four shouldn't eat popcorn.

____

____

Name: ____________________

Sentence Fluency

When writing a complex sentence, you can start with either the dependent clause or the independent clause. Choose the way that sounds the most natural.

A. Read the clauses. Match each dependent clause to an independent clause to write six complex sentences. Think about whether the sentence sounds better with the dependent or the independent clause first.

Dependent Clauses	Independent Clauses
until my grandmother came to visit	my grandparents got married
while I listened carefully	I didn't know much about our family
before she met my grandfather	they moved to Los Angeles in 1961
after Grandpa finished college in 1954	my grandmother told me stories
although my grandparents loved Japan	my mom would never have met my dad
if she had not been born in Los Angeles	Grandma lived in Japan

1. ____________________
2. ____________________
3. ____________________
4. ____________________
5. ____________________
6. ____________________

B. Exchange papers with a partner. Check to make sure that commas are used correctly in the sentences that begin with a dependent clause. Circle the commas, or add them if necessary.

Sentence Fluency

Use complex sentences to help your writing flow more smoothly.

A. Rewrite this biography to make it flow more smoothly. Combine some of the sentences into complex sentences using the conjunctions in the box.

An Adventurous Woman

My great-aunt Betty was born in 1922 and grew up in Texas. She was 18. She graduated from high school. She spent two years working in a bakery. She realized she wanted to moved to the big city. Betty enrolled in beauty school and learned to cut hair. She really wanted to travel. She wanted more adventure in her life. She joined the Women's Army Corps in 1943. This was during World War II. Aunt Betty spoke French. She was ordered to serve in Paris. She lived there for two years. The war ended in 1945.

Subordinating Conjunctions					
before	although	because	when	until	since

____

____

____

____

____

____

____

____

____

____

B. Exchange papers with a partner. Underline each complex sentence in the rewritten biography, and check to make sure that commas have been used correctly.

Name: ______________________

Sentence Fluency Use complex sentences to help your writing flow more smoothly.

A. Use the timeline below to plan a biography of someone whom you admire. On the timeline, note significant events or accomplishments in that person's life. You can use either dates or ages in your timeline.

The Life of ______________________

B. Use two of the subordinating conjunctions from the box to write two complex sentences about the subject of your biography.

Subordinating Conjunctions				
after	until	when	before	if
unless	although	because	while	once

1. ______________________

2. ______________________

SENTENCE FLUENCY

More Ways to Combine Sentences

DAY 1

Read the rule aloud. Review the definition of **subject** and explain that a **compound subject** is two or more subjects joined by a conjunction. Then guide students through the activities.

- **Activity A:** Read the narrative aloud. Have students identify the sentence that already has a compound subject. ("Marcos and Amy thought...) Then return to the second sentence. Ask: *What is the subject?* (**My sister**) *What is the subject of the next sentence?* (**My brother**) Say: *Both sentences are about the same action, so they could be combined. What would the compound subject of the new sentence be?* (**My sister and brother**)

  Point out that there is often more than one way to combine sentences by using words not in the original sentences. Direct students to sentences 9 and 10. Say: *One of these already has a compound subject, but the sentences can still be combined.* Brainstorm ways to do so, such as by changing the subject to **We all.** Then have students complete the activity.

- **Activity B (Convention):** Point out sentences 2 and 3 of the narrative. Say: *If you combined these sentences to form a compound subject, the verb should have become plural to match. What should it be?* (**have been**) Have students complete the activity.

DAY 2

Read the rule aloud. Then guide students through the activity.

- **Convention:** Have students read the review. Then point out the fourth sentence. Say: *"...the manager skates..." may sound OK on its own, but remember, the whole subject is **servers and the manager.** So, what should the verb be?* (**skate**)

- Reread the first three sentences aloud. Ask: *Which sentences have the same subject?* (2 and 3) Say: *We can combine these into one sentence with a **compound predicate**, or two actions joined by a conjunction.* ("drive up to Lulu's and park outside") Use the sample answers on the reduced page to discuss other ways to combine sentences. Then have students complete the activity.

Name: ____________________ **Week 3 • Day 1**

Sentence Fluency Make your writing flow by combining short, choppy sentences into sentences with compound subjects.

A. Read this personal narrative. Then:
- Underline the sentences that could be combined into new sentences with compound subjects.
- Circle the subjects of the sentences you underlined.
- Rewrite the underlined sentences by combining their subjects.

In the Spotlight

Auditioning for our school musical, Grease, was one of the scariest things I have ever done. My sister has been in a play. My brother has been in a play, too. But I am the shy one in the family! Still, I love to sing. So when auditions were announced, I decided to go for it.

My friend Marcos auditioned for a part. My friend Amy also auditioned for a part. I thought the others were better than I was. Marcos and Amy thought the others were better than they were. The next day, the results were posted. As we approached the board, I saw my name. Marcos saw his, too. We both got parts! Amy didn't get a part. I felt bad about that. Marcos did, too. But then we found out that Amy is going to be the assistant director. She'll be telling us what to do!

Sample Answers:

1. My sister and brother have been in plays.
2. My friends Marcos and Amy both auditioned for parts.
3. We all thought the others were better than we were.
4. As we approached the board, Marcos and I saw our names.
5. Marcos and I felt bad about Amy not getting a part.

B. Complete each sentence with the correct form of the verb.

1. **(has / have)** The actors and the director __have__ been rehearsing.
2. **(is / are)** Jorge and Samantha __are__ in charge of props.

114 SENTENCE FLUENCY Daily 6-Trait Writing • EMC 6026 • © Evan-Moor Corp.

Name: ____________________ **Week 3 • Day 2**

Sentence Fluency Make your writing flow by combining sentences with the same subjects.

Read this restaurant review. Then:
- Use proofreading marks to correct the two errors in subject-verb agreement.
- Underline five pairs of sentences with the same subject that could be combined into new sentences.
- Combine the pairs to write five new sentences.

Lulu's Rocks Around the Clock!

If you haven't been to Lulu's, you should check out this old-fashioned 1950s-style diner. Cars drive up to Lulu's. Cars park outside. Then the customers wait in their cars as servers and the manager skates around the lot greeting people. When a customer rolls down the car window, a teenage girl skates up to the car. She hooks a tray to the car door. She takes the order. A few minutes later, the server returns. She brings the food.

Friday nights are especially fun at Lulu's. Every week, the Howard Middle School Drama Club performs to raise money. The students sing songs from the 1950s. The students also dance to the songs. Customers love singing along to "Rock Around the Clock." They also enjoy "Hound Dog." For the final song, a girl and a boy performs with the owner of Lulu's. There isn't a better show in town! Lulu's is definitely the place to be on Friday nights this summer.

1. Cars drive up to Lulu's and park outside.
2. She hooks a tray to the car door and takes the order.
3. A few minutes later, the server returns with the food.
4. The students sing and dance to songs from the 1950s.
5. Customers love singing along to "Rock Around the Clock" and "Hound Dog."

© Evan-Moor Corp. • EMC 6026 • Daily 6-Trait Writing SENTENCE FLUENCY 115

Name: ______________________ **Week 3 • Day 3**

Sentence Fluency Use compound subjects, compound predicates, and other phrases with conjunctions to make your writing flow.

Read this interview about the drama club's fundraiser. Then write a short article about the fundraiser, based on details given in the interview. Include sentences with compound subjects, compound predicates, and other phrases containing conjunctions.

Reporter: What is the Howard Middle School Drama Club doing this summer?

Troy: Every Friday night, we perform a fifties revue at Lulu's Drive-In. We sing songs from the fifties. We dance. It's a lot of fun for us. It's fun for the customers, too.

Reporter: Does everyone participate?

Troy: Of course! All of the boys sing "Earth Angel." We also sing "Rock Around the Clock." Then the girls dance on roller skates to "Hound Dog." They sing while they skate. Two standout performers are Kayli and Thalia. Kayli sings "Mr. Sandman." Thalia sings with her. Our drama coach, Ms. Chandler, walks around the cars to collect donations. Ms. Stewart helps her.

Reporter: About how much money do you raise each night?

Troy: We raise about fifty dollars a night. The money goes toward costumes. It also helps pay production costs for our annual play.

Sample Answer:

Every Friday night, the Howard Middle School Drama Club performs a fifties revue at Lulu's Drive-In. Members of the club sing and dance to songs from the fifties. It provides a lot of fun for students and customers alike. The boys sing "Earth Angel" and "Rock Around the Clock." Then the girls sing "Hound Dog" while dancing on roller skates. Two standout performers, Kayli and Thalia, sing a duet of "Mr. Sandman." Throughout the performance, the drama coach and her assistant collect donations from the audience. This raises about fifty dollars a night. The club then uses the money for costumes and other production costs for the club's annual play.

116 SENTENCE FLUENCY Daily 6-Trait Writing • EMC 6026 • © Evan-Moor Corp.

Name: ______________________ **Week 3 • Day 4**

Sentence Fluency Use compound subjects, compound predicates, and other phrases with conjunctions to make your writing flow.

A. Plan a review of a restaurant. Why do you like going there? Complete the web by filling in details about the food, the atmosphere, the servers, and any entertainment or other special features.

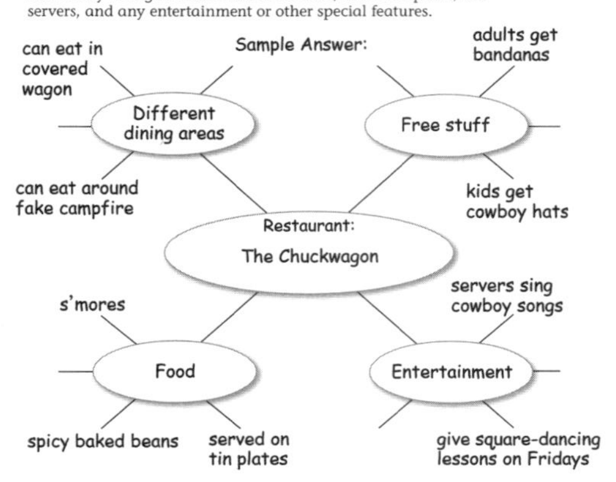

B. Write two sentences about the restaurant. Write one sentence with a compound subject. Write the other sentence with a compound predicate.

Sample Answers:

1. Both kids and adults get special things to wear to make their experience more fun!
2. The servers sing songs and give square-dancing lessons.

© Evan-Moor Corp. • EMC 6026 • Daily 6-Trait Writing SENTENCE FLUENCY 117

DAY 3

Read the rule aloud. Then guide students through the activity.

- To activate prior knowledge, you might want to discuss different types of fundraisers that students have seen or participated in, such as bake sales, car washes, or special performances. Then have two students read the interview aloud.
- Direct students to Troy's first response. Ask: *What verbs could you combine in Troy's answer to form a compound predicate?* (**sing and dance**) *What nouns could you combine to form the object of this sentence: "It's a lot of fun for ___"?* (**students and customers**)
- Have students imagine that they are writing a brief newspaper article to tell people about the fundraiser. Remind students that an article should have a serious, formal-sounding voice. Then have students complete the activity in pairs or individually.
- **Convention:** Have students check each other's articles for correct subject-verb agreement.

DAY 4

Review the rule. Guide students through the activities.

- **Activity A:** Brainstorm unique restaurants in your area or ones that students have been to. For students who do not know any restaurants well enough to write about, have them work with a partner, asking questions to help the partner brainstorm details to write in the web.
- **Activity B:** Invite a volunteer to share the details from his or her web. Have the class brainstorm sentences that the student might write, using compound subjects and predicates. Then have students write their own sentences.

DAY 5 *Writing Prompt*

- *Write a review of a restaurant you like, using compound subjects, predicates, and other combined phrases to make your sentences flow fluently.*
- *Make sure that your subjects and verbs agree.*

Name: ____________________

Week 3 • Day 1

Sentence Fluency

Make your writing flow by combining short, choppy sentences into sentences with compound subjects.

A. Read this personal narrative. Then:

- Underline the sentences that could be combined into new sentences with compound subjects.
- Circle the subjects of the sentences you underlined.
- Rewrite the underlined sentences by combining their subjects.

In the Spotlight

Auditioning for our school musical, Grease, was one of the scariest things I have ever done. My sister has been in a play. My brother has been in a play, too. But I am the shy one in the family! Still, I love to sing. So when auditions were announced, I decided to go for it.

My friend Marcos auditioned for a part. My friend Amy also auditioned for a part. I thought the others were better than I was. Marcos and Amy thought the others were better than they were. The next day, the results were posted. As we approached the board, I saw my name. Marcos saw his, too. We both got parts! Amy didn't get a part. I felt bad about that. Marcos did, too. But then we found out that Amy is going to be the assistant director. She'll be telling us what to do!

1. ____________________
2. ____________________
3. ____________________
4. ____________________
5. ____________________

B. Complete each sentence with the correct form of the verb.

1. **(has / have)** The actors and the director __________ been rehearsing.
2. **(is / are)** Jorge and Samantha __________ in charge of props.

Name: ______________________________

Sentence Fluency Make your writing flow by combining sentences with the same subjects.

Read this restaurant review. Then:

- Use proofreading marks to correct the two errors in subject-verb agreement.
- Underline five pairs of sentences with the same subject that could be combined into new sentences.
- Combine the pairs to write five new sentences.

Lulu's Rocks Around the Clock!

If you haven't been to Lulu's, you should check out this old-fashioned 1950s-style diner. Cars drive up to Lulu's. Cars park outside. Then the customers wait in their cars as servers and the manager skates around the lot greeting people. When a customer rolls down the car window, a teenage girl skates up to the car. She hooks a tray to the car door. She takes the order. A few minutes later, the server returns. She brings the food.

Friday nights are especially fun at Lulu's. Every week, the Howard Middle School Drama Club performs to raise money. The students sing songs from the 1950s. The students also dance to the songs. Customers love singing along to "Rock Around the Clock." They also enjoy "Hound Dog." For the final song, a girl and a boy performs with the owner of Lulu's. There isn't a better show in town! Lulu's is definitely the place to be on Friday nights this summer.

1. ______________________________
2. ______________________________
3. ______________________________
4. ______________________________
5. ______________________________

Sentence Fluency

Use compound subjects, compound predicates, and other phrases with conjunctions to make your writing flow.

Read this interview about the drama club's fundraiser. Then write a short article about the fundraiser, based on details given in the interview. Include sentences with compound subjects, compound predicates, and other phrases containing conjunctions.

Reporter: What is the Howard Middle School Drama Club doing this summer?

Troy: Every Friday night, we perform a fifties revue at Lulu's Drive-In. We sing songs from the fifties. We dance. It's a lot of fun for us. It's fun for the customers, too.

Reporter: Does everyone participate?

Troy: Of course! All of the boys sing "Earth Angel." We also sing "Rock Around the Clock." Then the girls dance on roller skates to "Hound Dog." They sing while they skate. Two standout performers are Kayli and Thalia. Kayli sings "Mr. Sandman." Thalia sings with her. Our drama coach, Ms. Chandler, walks around the cars to collect donations. Ms. Stewart helps her.

Reporter: About how much money do you raise each night?

Troy: We raise about fifty dollars a night. The money goes toward costumes. It also helps pay production costs for our annual play.

Name: ____________________

Week 3 • Day 4

Sentence Fluency

Use compound subjects, compound predicates, and other phrases with conjunctions to make your writing flow.

A. Plan a review of a restaurant. Why do you like going there? Complete the web by filling in details about the food, the atmosphere, the servers, and any entertainment or other special features.

B. Write two sentences about the restaurant. Write one sentence with a compound subject. Write the other sentence with a compound predicate.

1. ____________________

2. ____________________

WEEK 4 Sentence Fluency
Varying Sentence Beginnings

DAY 1

Read the rule aloud. Then guide students through the activities.

- **Activity A:** Have students read the draft. Then write the first two words of each sentence on the board. ("I am," "I learned," "I thought," "They have," "They are," etc.) Ask: *What do all of Keisha's sentences begin with?* (pronoun **I** or **they** followed by verb) Say: *Repeatedly starting sentences in the same way makes your writing sound boring.*

  Have students read the revision and underline the revised sentence beginnings. Then ask: *How did Keisha change the first sentence?* (used an interjection and verb-subject construction) *The second?* (moved **tonight** to the beginning) Repeat for each of the revised sentences. (e.g., 3: rephrased as question; 5: added transition word; 6: changed pronoun to noun; 8: added transition phrase, moved up prepositional phrase; 9: changed pronoun; 10: rephrased as question)

- **Activity B (Convention):** Point out the commas after **Tonight**, **However**, and **In fact** in Version 2 of the letter. Say: *When you begin a sentence with a transition word or phrase, remember to place a comma after it.* Have students complete the activity. Then review the answers as a class.

Name: ______________________ **Week 4 • Day 1**

Sentence Fluency Vary the way your sentences begin so your writing doesn't sound choppy and repetitive.

A. Read each version of Keisha's letter. In the revision, Keisha began her sentences in a variety of ways to make the letter sound more interesting. Underline the sentence parts that she changed.

Draft

Dear Megan,

I am so busy! I am writing a report tonight on the gray squirrel. I learned that gray squirrels are native to the United States. I thought this meant that gray squirrels lived only in the U.S. I was wrong. I learned that they were imported into Europe in the 1800s. They have become huge pests there. They have taken over the habitats of native red squirrels in England. They are causing the red squirrels to die out. I didn't know that squirrels could be such troublemakers!

Your friend,
Keisha

Revision

Dear Megan,

Whew, am I busy! Tonight, I am writing a report on the gray squirrel. Did you know that gray squirrels are native to the United States? I thought this meant that gray squirrels lived only in the U.S. However, I was wrong. Gray squirrels were imported into Europe in the 1800s. They have become huge pests there. In fact, in England, they have taken over the habitats of native red squirrels. This is causing the red squirrels to die out. Who knew that squirrels could be such troublemakers?

Your friend,
Keisha

B. Insert commas where they belong in the sentences below.

1. Often, squirrels try to steal seeds from bird feeders.
2. Surprisingly, squirrels may also eat insects and birds' eggs.
3. However, squirrels generally prefer acorns, nuts, and berries.

120 SENTENCE FLUENCY Daily 6-Trait Writing • EMC 6026 • © Evan-Moor Corp.

DAY 2

Read the rule aloud. If necessary, briefly review prepositional phrases, subordinating conjunctions in complex sentences, and transition words and phrases. Then guide students through the activity.

- Invite a volunteer to read the report aloud. Then ask: *How can the sentence fluency in this report be improved?* (by varying the sentence beginnings) Then read aloud item 1. Ask: *What is the final prepositional phrase in this sentence?* ("in the United States") Then have students rewrite the sentence. Repeat the process for items 2 and 3.

- **Convention:** Review: *When you start a sentence with a long prepositional phrase, a transition word or phrase, or a dependent clause, remember to place a comma after it.* Have students check their revised sentences for correct comma usage.

Name: ______________________ **Week 4 • Day 2**

Sentence Fluency To vary the way your sentences begin, you can start with different subjects, add introductory or transition words, or rearrange sentence parts.

Read this paragraph from a report about gray squirrels. Then follow the directions to rewrite some of the sentence beginnings. Be sure to use commas correctly.

Gray squirrels are common visitors to yards and parks in the United States. Squirrels are rodents. They have slender bodies and strong, flexible limbs. Their forefeet have four digits and a kind of thumb, almost like a human hand. They are good at going up and down tree trunks and hanging onto branches. Their ankles are flexible, and their curved claws are sharp. Their most distinctive feature is their long, bushy tail. Gray squirrels use their tail for protection, balance, and communication.

1. Revise the following sentence by moving the final prepositional phrase to the beginning. **Sample Answers:**

   Gray squirrels are common visitors to yards and parks in the United States.

   In the United States, gray squirrels are common visitors to yards and parks.

2. Revise the following two sentences by combining them into a complex sentence and beginning the new sentence with *Because*.

   They are good at going up and down tree trunks and hanging onto branches. Their ankles are flexible, and their curved claws are sharp.

   Because their ankles are flexible and their curved claws are sharp, they are good at going up and down tree trunks and hanging onto branches.

3. Revise the following sentence by adding a transition word or phrase at the beginning. Be sure that it makes sense with the sentence that comes before it in the report.

   Their most distinctive feature is their long, bushy tail.

   However, their most distinctive feature is their long, bushy tail.

© Evan-Moor Corp. • EMC 6026 • Daily 6-Trait Writing SENTENCE FLUENCY 121

Name: ____________________ **Week 4 • Day 3**

Sentence Fluency When you revise your writing, look for ways to vary your sentence beginnings to improve the flow.

Read this personal narrative. Add the missing commas in the dialogue. Then rewrite the narrative to add more variety in how the sentences begin.

My mom and I walked in the front door. We both screamed loudly.

I asked, "What happened?" The living room was an absolute wreck. The couch was torn to shreds. A potted plant was knocked over. We walked around the room cautiously to survey the damage. The worst was in front of the fireplace. There was soot all over the floor. There were footprints in it.

I said, "I think those are animal tracks!" I looked more closely, and I noticed animal droppings scattered about.

We heard a strange chattering noise coming from the closet. Mom said, "Stand back." She quietly approached the closet. A squirrel rocketed out of it as Mom threw open the closet door. The squirrel looked terrified as it dashed across the living room and out of the house.

Mom said, "I guess we need a new cover for our chimney!" She laughed.

Sample Answer:

When Mom and I walked in the front door, we both screamed loudly!

"What happened?" I cried. Our living room was an absolute wreck. The couch was shredded, and the potted plant was knocked over. Cautiously, we walked around the room to survey the damage. It was the worst in front of the fireplace because there was soot all over the floor. Not only that, but the soot had footprints in it.

I exclaimed, "I think those are animal tracks!" Looking more closely, I noticed animal droppings scattered about.

Suddenly, we heard a strange chattering noise coming from the closet. "Stand back," Mom ordered, quietly approaching the closet. As she threw open the door, a squirrel rocketed out! Terrified, the squirrel dashed across the living room and out of the house.

"I guess we need a new cover for our chimney!" said Mom, laughing.

122 SENTENCE FLUENCY Daily 6-Trait Writing • EMC 6026 • © Evan-Moor Corp.

Name: ____________________ **Week 4 • Day 4**

Sentence Fluency Begin your sentences in different ways to keep your reader interested and engaged.

A. Think of a time that you unexpectedly came face to face with an animal. Answer the following questions to plan a short narrative about the experience. Sample Answers:

1. What kind of animal was it? Was it wild or tame? a wild raccoon
2. What happened during your encounter? My dad asked me to take out the trash one night. As I walked up to the trash can, I noticed something behind it. I peeked around it and saw yellow eyes! I dropped the trash bag on the ground and ran back into the house as fast as I could!
3. What did you, or someone else, say during the encounter? I screamed! Then I yelled, "Go away!"
4. What did you do after the encounter? What did you say? I told my dad what happened. He said it was just a raccoon and told me to go back out there. I said, "No way! I'm not going out there alone!" So he came with me and brought a flashlight.

B. Write a complete sentence describing something that happened during the encounter. Sample Answer:
I saw shining yellow eyes right in front of me!

C. Rewrite the sentence you just wrote, beginning it in a different way. Sample Answer:
Right in front of me was a pair of shining yellow eyes!

© Evan-Moor Corp. • EMC 6026 • Daily 6-Trait Writing SENTENCE FLUENCY 123

DAY 3

Read the rule aloud. Remind students: *You can begin sentences not only with nouns and articles, but with verbs, adverbs, interjections, introductory and transition words and phrases, and subordinating conjunctions.* Then guide students through the activity.

- **Convention:** To review commas in dialogue, write the following sentences on the board and circle the commas: *I said, "This room is a mess." "This room is a mess," I said.* Point out that the comma always goes before the quotation marks.
- Read aloud the narrative, emphasizing the boring, repetitive rhythm of the sentence construction. Then point out that most of the sentences begin with a subject followed by a verb. Call attention to the first two sentences and say: *We could revise these by combining them and making a new sentence that begins differently. For example, we could start with the subordinating conjunction* ***when*** *and form this complex sentence: "When Mom and I walked in the front door, we both screamed loudly."*
- Have students complete the activity. Remind them to use commas correctly in their revisions of the narrative. Then have students share their writing.

DAY 4

Read the rule aloud. Then guide students through the activities.

- **Activity A:** Help students brainstorm animal encounters they may have had, such as coming upon a stray cat or dog, meeting a friend's pet for the first time, finding a rodent in the house, etc. Then have students complete the activity.
- **Activities B and C:** Use the sample answers on the reduced page to model writing and revising a sentence. Then have students write their own sentences.

DAY 5 *Writing Prompt*

- *Write a description of a surprise encounter with an animal. Vary the way you begin your sentences.*
- *Be sure to use commas correctly.*

Sentence Fluency

Vary the way your sentences begin so your writing doesn't sound choppy and repetitive.

A. Read each version of Keisha's letter. In the revision, Keisha began her sentences in a variety of ways to make the letter sound more interesting. Underline the sentence parts that she changed.

Draft

Dear Megan,

I am so busy! I am writing a report tonight on the gray squirrel. I learned that gray squirrels are native to the United States. I thought this meant that gray squirrels lived only in the U.S. I was wrong. I learned that they were imported into Europe in the 1800s. They have become huge pests there. They have taken over the habitats of native red squirrels in England. They are causing the red squirrels to die out. I didn't know that squirrels could be such troublemakers!

Your friend,
Keisha

Revision

Dear Megan,

Whew, am I busy! Tonight, I am writing a report on the gray squirrel. Did you know that gray squirrels are native to the United States? I thought this meant that gray squirrels lived only in the U.S. However, I was wrong. Gray squirrels were imported into Europe in the 1800s. They have become huge pests there. In fact, in England, they have taken over the habitats of native red squirrels. This is causing the red squirrels to die out. Who knew that squirrels could be such troublemakers?

Your friend,
Keisha

B. Insert commas where they belong in the sentences below.

1. Often squirrels try to steal seeds from bird feeders.
2. Surprisingly squirrels may also eat insects and birds' eggs.
3. However squirrels generally prefer acorns, nuts, and berries.

Name: ______________________________

Sentence Fluency

To vary the way your sentences begin, you can start with different subjects, add introductory or transition words, or rearrange sentence parts.

Read this paragraph from a report about gray squirrels. Then follow the directions to rewrite some of the sentence beginnings. Be sure to use commas correctly.

Gray squirrels are common visitors to yards and parks in the United States. Squirrels are rodents. They have slender bodies and strong, flexible limbs. Their forefeet have four digits and a kind of thumb, almost like a human hand. They are good at going up and down tree trunks and hanging onto branches. Their ankles are flexible, and their curved claws are sharp. Their most distinctive feature is their long, bushy tail. Gray squirrels use their tail for protection, balance, and communication.

1. Revise the following sentence by moving the final prepositional phrase to the beginning.

   Gray squirrels are common visitors to yards and parks in the United States.

   ____

2. Revise the following two sentences by combining them into a complex sentence and beginning the new sentence with *Because*.

   They are good at going up and down tree trunks and hanging onto branches. Their ankles are flexible, and their curved claws are sharp.

   ____

   ____

3. Revise the following sentence by adding a transition word or phrase at the beginning. Be sure that it makes sense with the sentence that comes before it in the report.

   Their most distinctive feature is their long, bushy tail.

   ____

WEEK 5 SENTENCE FLUENCY

Writing a Smooth Paragraph

DAY 1

Read the rule aloud. Say: *Paragraphs flow more smoothly when they contain both short and long sentences. Too many short sentences in a row can make a paragraph choppy, and too many long sentences in a row can make a reader tired.* Then guide students through the activities.

- **Activity A:** Review the definitions of compound and complex sentences. Then read aloud the first narrative. Ask: *What kind of sentence is the third sentence?* (compound, with conjunction **so**) *The fourth?* (complex, with conjunction **when**)

  Have students read each narrative and complete the underlining independently. Then ask: *Which narrative sounds better?* (Narrative 1) *Why?* (mix of compound, complex, and simple sentences) Have students work in pairs to combine some of the sentences in Narrative 2. Then invite students to share their revisions.

- **Activity B (Convention):** Review the definition of a run-on sentence. (two or more sentences joined together without proper punctuation) Then have students complete the activity.

Name: ______________________ **Week 5 • Day 1**

Sentence Fluency To write a smooth paragraph, vary the types of sentences you use. Include simple, compound, and complex sentences.

A. Underline the compound sentences in each student's narrative. Draw a wavy line under the complex sentences. Then use proofreading marks to combine at least two pairs of sentences in Narrative 2.

Narrative 1

Last weekend, my mom took me to a climbing gym. I was so excited! My mom climbs a lot, so I wanted to try it. When we got there, I met my instructor, Jim. I had to take a class because it was my first time climbing. Jim fitted me with a harness and took me over to the climbing wall. He clipped my harness to the end of a rope, and he clipped the other end to his own harness. As I climbed up the wall, Jim pulled on the rope. He gave me tips about where to put my hands and feet. It was tough, but I kept going. When I finally reached the top, Jim and my mom cheered. I was hooked!

Narrative 2 **Sample Answers:**

My brother took me to the climbing gym last Saturday. It was awful. I had to wear an uncomfortable harness. I could barely move! Then my brother brought me over to this huge wall. He clipped my harness to the end of a rope. He clipped the other end to himself. He told me to climb. It was too hard! My hands kept slipping. My toes wouldn't stay on the fake rocks. My brother tried to encourage me, but it didn't help. I probably slipped off ten times. I only made it halfway up the wall. Then I quit!

B. Write an *X* next to the run-on sentences.

1. ____ I think I have acrophobia, which is a fear of heights.
2. __X__ Don't look down, it will make you nervous.
3. __X__ My dad is on a climbing team they compete all over the state.
4. ____ Rock climbing takes courage but also requires a lot of strength.

126 SENTENCE FLUENCY Daily 6-Trait Writing • EMC 6026 • © Evan-Moor Corp.

DAY 2

Read the rule aloud. Say: *Transition words and phrases help your paragraphs flow smoothly by connecting your sentences.* Then guide students through the activities.

- **Activity A:** Read the story aloud without the transition words. Say: *This story makes sense, but it would sound better if the ideas were connected by transitions.* Have students fill in the blanks.

  Convention: Use the first sentence in the story to model correcting a run-on. Say: *There are different ways to correct this run-on. We could separate it into two sentences, or we could add the conjunction* **and** *after the comma to make it a compound sentence. We could also change* **It was** *to the prepositional phrase* **On a**. *When you fix a run-on, choose the way that sounds best with the other sentences.* Have students find and fix the other run-on sentences.

- **Activity B:** Have students write their endings independently and then read them aloud.

Name: ______________________ **Week 5 • Day 2**

Sentence Fluency Use transition words and phrases to improve the flow of sentences throughout your paragraphs.

A. Read the story. Then:
- Use the words and phrases in the box to fill in the blanks.
- Use proofreading marks to correct the run-on sentences.

Transition Words and Phrases		
in fact	suddenly	for example
finally	naturally	on the other hand

It was a hot summer Saturday, Cindy and her mom walked into Kinsey's Sports Emporium to buy Cindy a new BMX bike helmet. As they stepped inside the cool, air-conditioned store, the two breathed a sigh of relief.

The bike department was on the fifth floor. __Naturally__, Cindy and her mom headed for the elevator instead of taking the stairs. As soon as they stepped off the elevator, Cindy saw a wide variety of helmets. __In fact__, there were so many that Cindy had trouble deciding on one. __For example__, she could get an open-face helmet similar to her old one. __On the other hand__, she could upgrade to a full-face helmet with a visor and shield. __Finally__, Cindy found the perfect one it was a black, full-face helmet decorated with hot pink flames.

Cindy stepped back into the elevator, excited about her new helmet. The doors closed, the elevator began to move. __Suddenly__, it stopped with a thud. Cindy and her mom were stuck!

B. Write a conclusion to the story above. Use transition words and phrases to help your paragraph flow. **Sample Answer:**

They pressed the emergency call button. However, nothing happened! Cindy and her mom began to panic. In fact, soon they were banging on the doors and shouting, "Help!" Finally, a voice from the speaker said, "Everything's OK. The electricity just went out. However, it will be back on any minute."

© Evan-Moor Corp. • EMC 6026 • Daily 6-Trait Writing SENTENCE FLUENCY 127

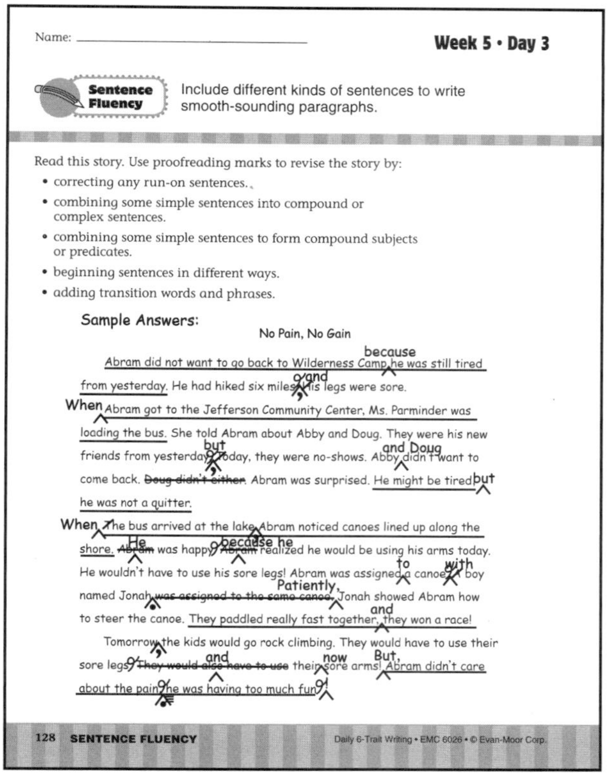

Name: ____________________ **Week 5 • Day 3**

Sentence Fluency Include different kinds of sentences to write smooth-sounding paragraphs.

Read this story. Use proofreading marks to revise the story by:

- correcting any run-on sentences.
- combining some simple sentences into compound or complex sentences.
- combining some simple sentences to form compound subjects or predicates.
- beginning sentences in different ways.
- adding transition words and phrases.

Sample Answers:

No Pain, No Gain

Abram did not want to go back to Wilderness Camp he was still tired from yesterday. He had hiked six miles. His legs were sore. Abram got to the Jefferson Community Center, Ms. Parminder was loading the bus. She told Abram about Abby and Doug. They were his new friends from yesterday. Today, they were no-shows. Abby didn't want to come back. Doug didn't either. Abram was surprised. He might be tired he was not a quitter.

The bus arrived at the lake Abram noticed canoes lined up along the shore. Abram was happy. Abram realized he would be using his arms today. He wouldn't have to use his sore legs! Abram was assigned a canoe. A boy named Jonah was assigned to the same canoe. Jonah showed Abram how to steer the canoe. They paddled really fast together, they won a race!

Tomorrow the kids would go rock climbing. They would have to use their sore legs. They would also have to use their sore arms! Abram didn't care about the pain he was having too much fun.

Corrections: because; and; When; but; and Doug; but; When; He; because he; to; with; Patiently,; and; and; now; But,

128 SENTENCE FLUENCY Daily 6-Trait Writing • EMC 6026 • © Evan-Moor Corp.

DAY 3

Read the rule aloud. Then guide students through the activity.

- Have a volunteer read the story aloud. Then ask: *What's wrong with this story?* (sounds choppy, doesn't flow, has run-ons) Review the list of ways the sentences could be improved.
- Choose one or two sentences to model correcting. For example, say: *The first sentence is a run-on. But if we just divide it into two sentences, it will sound choppy, especially since the next two sentences are short, too.* Brainstorm ways to fix the sentences. For example, model breaking the run-on into two sentences, or use the sample answer on the reduced page to combine the second sentence with the one after it to form a complex sentence.
- **Convention:** Have students underline all the run-on sentences in the narrative. Discuss how each one could be corrected.
- Have students work in pairs or independently to rewrite the narrative. Then invite volunteers to read their revised narratives aloud.

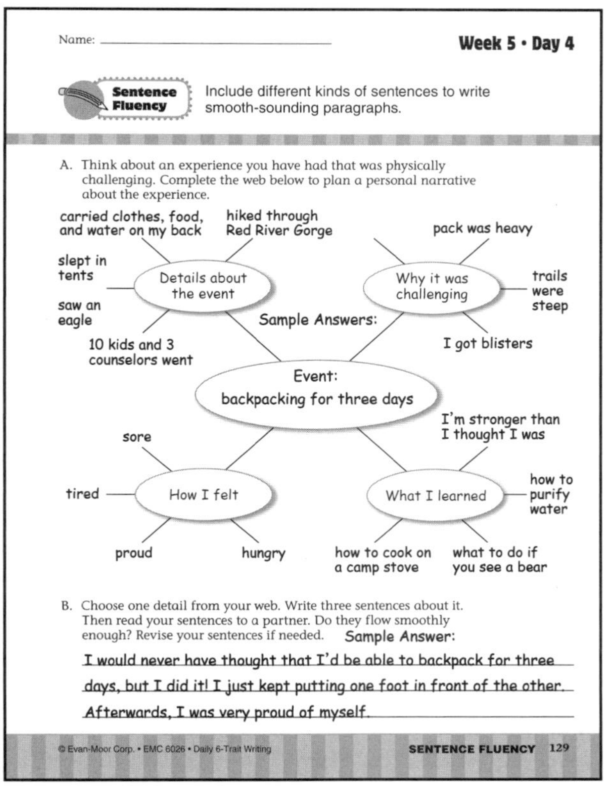

Name: ____________________ **Week 5 • Day 4**

Sentence Fluency Include different kinds of sentences to write smooth-sounding paragraphs.

A. Think about an experience you have had that was physically challenging. Complete the web below to plan a personal narrative about the experience.

B. Choose one detail from your web. Write three sentences about it. Then read your sentences to a partner. Do they flow smoothly enough? Revise your sentences if needed. Sample Answer:

I would never have thought that I'd be able to backpack for three days, but I did it! I just kept putting one foot in front of the other. Afterwards, I was very proud of myself.

© Evan-Moor Corp. • EMC 6026 • Daily 6-Trait Writing SENTENCE FLUENCY 129

DAY 4

Review the rule. Guide students through the activities.

- **Activity A:** Brainstorm with students different physically challenging events they've endured. (e.g., sports competitions or practices, long hikes or bike rides, martial arts classes, etc.) Then have students complete their webs.
- **Activity B:** After students write their sentences, have them exchange papers with a partner. Encourage partners to help each other brainstorm ways to improve the flow of their sentences.

DAY 5 *Writing Prompt*

- *Write a personal narrative about a physically challenging experience you have had. Use different sentence types so your paragraphs flow smoothly.*
- *Exchange papers with a partner to check for run-on sentences. Correct any that are found.*

Name: ________________________________

Sentence Fluency

To write a smooth paragraph, vary the types of sentences you use. Include simple, compound, and complex sentences.

A. Underline the compound sentences in each student's narrative. Draw a wavy line under the complex sentences. Then use proofreading marks to combine at least two pairs of sentences in Narrative 2.

Narrative 1

Last weekend, my mom took me to a climbing gym. I was so excited! My mom climbs a lot, so I wanted to try it. When we got there, I met my instructor, Jim. I had to take a class because it was my first time climbing. Jim fitted me with a harness and took me over to the climbing wall. He clipped my harness to the end of a rope, and he clipped the other end to his own harness. As I climbed up the wall, Jim pulled on the rope. He gave me tips about where to put my hands and feet. It was tough, but I kept going. When I finally reached the top, Jim and my mom cheered. I was hooked!

Narrative 2

My brother took me to the climbing gym last Saturday. It was awful. I had to wear an uncomfortable harness. I could barely move! Then my brother brought me over to this huge wall. He clipped my harness to the end of a rope. He clipped the other end to himself. He told me to climb. It was too hard! My hands kept slipping. My toes wouldn't stay on the fake rocks. My brother tried to encourage me, but it didn't help. I probably slipped off ten times. I only made it halfway up the wall. Then I quit!

B. Write an *X* next to the run-on sentences.

1. ____ I think I have acrophobia, which is a fear of heights.
2. ____ Don't look down, it will make you nervous.
3. ____ My dad is on a climbing team they compete all over the state.
4. ____ Rock climbing takes courage but also requires a lot of strength.

Name: ______________________________

Sentence Fluency

Use transition words and phrases to improve the flow of sentences throughout your paragraphs.

A. Read the story. Then:

- Use the words and phrases in the box to fill in the blanks.
- Use proofreading marks to correct the run-on sentences.

Transition Words and Phrases		
in fact	suddenly	for example
finally	naturally	on the other hand

It was a hot summer Saturday, Cindy and her mom walked into Kinsey's Sports Emporium to buy Cindy a new BMX bike helmet. As they stepped inside the cool, air-conditioned store, the two breathed a sigh of relief.

The bike department was on the fifth floor. ____________________, Cindy and her mom headed for the elevator instead of taking the stairs. As soon as they stepped off the elevator, Cindy saw a wide variety of helmets. ____________________, there were so many that Cindy had trouble deciding on one. ____________________, she could get an open-face helmet similar to her old one. ____________________, she could upgrade to a full-face helmet with a visor and shield. ____________________, Cindy found the perfect one it was a black, full-face helmet decorated with hot pink flames.

Cindy stepped back into the elevator, excited about her new helmet. The doors closed, the elevator began to move. ____________________, it stopped with a thud. Cindy and her mom were stuck!

B. Write a conclusion to the story above. Use transition words and phrases to help your paragraph flow.

____

____

____

Sentence Fluency

Include different kinds of sentences to write smooth-sounding paragraphs.

Read this story. Use proofreading marks to revise the story by:

- correcting any run-on sentences.
- combining some simple sentences into compound or complex sentences.
- combining some simple sentences to form compound subjects or predicates.
- beginning sentences in different ways.
- adding transition words and phrases.

No Pain, No Gain

Abram did not want to go back to Wilderness Camp he was still tired from yesterday. He had hiked six miles. His legs were sore.

Abram got to the Jefferson Community Center, Ms. Parminder was loading the bus. She told Abram about Abby and Doug. They were his new friends from yesterday. Today, they were no-shows. Abby didn't want to come back. Doug didn't either. Abram was surprised. He might be tired, he was not a quitter.

The bus arrived at the lake Abram noticed canoes lined up along the shore. Abram was happy. Abram realized he would be using his arms today. He wouldn't have to use his sore legs! Abram was assigned a canoe. A boy named Jonah was assigned to the same canoe. Jonah showed Abram how to steer the canoe. They paddled really fast together, they won a race!

Tomorrow the kids would go rock climbing. They would have to use their sore legs. They would also have to use their sore arms! Abram didn't care about the pain, he was having too much fun.

Name: ______________________

Week 5 • Day 4

Sentence Fluency

Include different kinds of sentences to write smooth-sounding paragraphs.

A. Think about an experience you have had that was physically challenging. Complete the web below to plan a personal narrative about the experience.

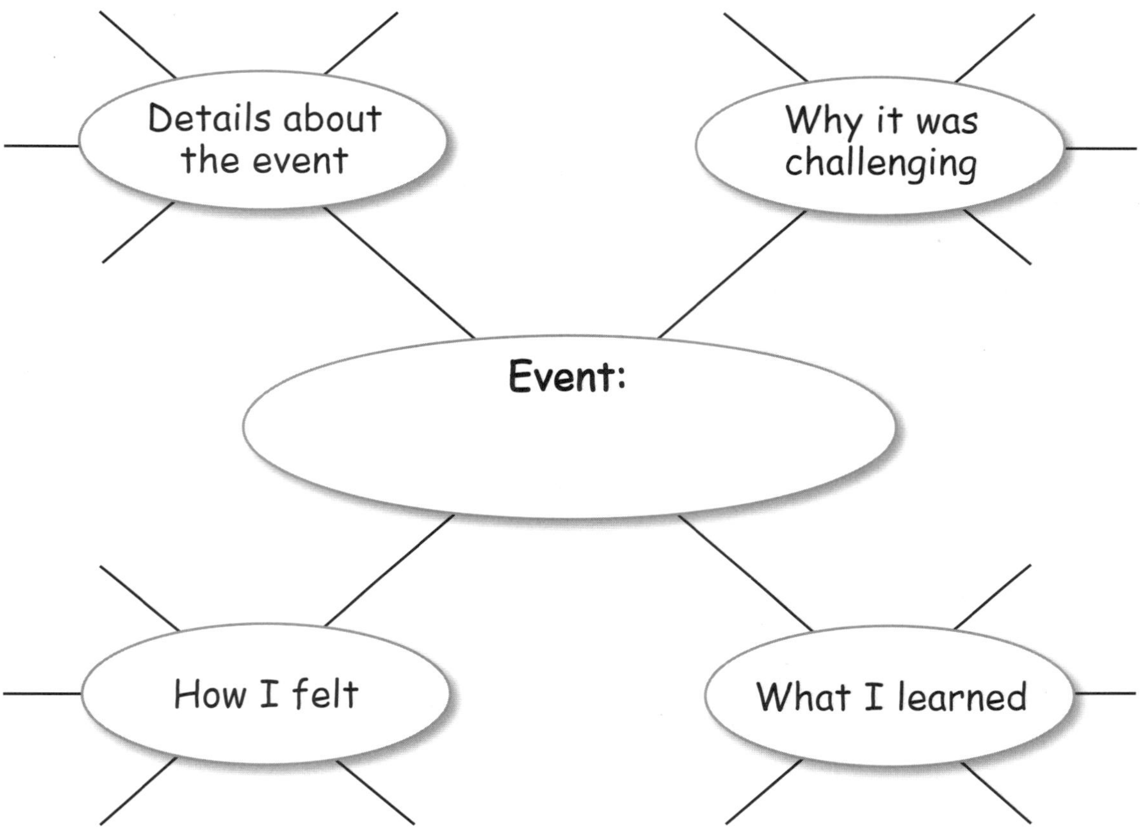

B. Choose one detail from your web. Write three sentences about it. Then read your sentences to a partner. Do they flow smoothly enough? Revise your sentences if needed.

____

____

____

WEEK 1

VOICE

Identifying Different Writing Voices

Refer to pages 6 and 7 to introduce or review the writing trait.

DAY 1

Say: ***Voice** is the way a writer's personality, or style, comes through in writing. Voice is shaped by the writer's purpose and audience.* Read the rule aloud. Then say: *You might write an informal e-mail to a friend about a trip you took. But you'd write a report on that same trip in a more serious, formal voice.* Then guide students through the activity.

- **Convention:** Have students read the paragraphs. Then write the words **no**, **not**, **never**, and **nothing** on the board. Remind students: *These are **negative words.** Using two negatives in a sentence is called a **double negative** and is incorrect.* Point out **isn't nothing** in the e-mail. Say: *Remember, the word **not** is in the contraction **isn't**, so it creates a double negative.* Have students suggest ways to fix the double negative. (**is nothing; isn't anything**)
- Discuss with students how the voice in the two paragraphs differs. Say: *This writer did several things to create an informal and a formal voice. For example, he used slang words such as **cool** in the e-mail, but in the report, he used more scholarly, academic words such as **approximately**.* Discuss the other types of language listed below each paragraph, and have students complete the activity.

DAY 2

Read the rule aloud. Then guide students through the activities.

- **Activity A:** Read the essay aloud. Then say: *The writer used several techniques to make her writing fun. For example, she used **irony**. Irony is when you describe something as the opposite of what you mean in order to surprise and amuse the reader. For example, it is ironic to call a kitty "sweet" when it is in fact mischievous.* Explain that irony is similar to **sarcasm**. Review the other terms as necessary.

  Convention: Write **hardly**, **scarcely**, and **barely** on the board. Explain that these are also negative words and therefore should not be used with other negative words. Have students complete the activity and share their responses.
- **Activity B:** Use the sample answer on the reduced page to model writing a sentence. Then have students write their own sentences.

Name: ______________________ **Week 1 • Day 1**

Voice Your voice can come through your writing in a variety of ways. Sometimes you need to write with a formal voice. Other times, it's OK to use an informal voice.

Read the paragraphs and fix the double negative in each one. Then write examples of the writing techniques used to create the voice of each paragraph.

Informal E-mail

Dublin, Ireland, is such a cool city! My favorite part is Trinity College. It's right in the city and is very old—more than 400 years old! Queen Elizabeth I founded it. In the library, which ~~isn't~~ is (OR isn't anything) nothing like our school library, I saw a book called The Book of Kells. It's even older than the college. Monks started working on it around the year 800. Do the math! That's about 1,200 years old! Anyway, you've got to see it. It's all decorated with colored pictures and designs and stuff. The monks made it all by hand because there weren't any printing presses back then. Can you imagine?

1. Slang: cool, stuff
2. First person: My favorite part, I saw a book
3. Addressing the reader: Do the math!, you've got to see it, Can you imagine?
4. Contractions: it's, isn't, that's, you've, weren't

Formal Report

Dublin is a fascinating city. One of its most interesting features is Trinity College, which Queen Elizabeth I founded in 1592. An ancient manuscript called The Book of Kells is housed at its library. Monks created this manuscript approximately 1,200 years ago, at which time there were ~~not~~ no printing presses. Therefore, the monks hand-lettered the pages on vellum, or animal skin, and added colorful, elaborate illustrations and designs. Experts call this type of text an illuminated manuscript.

1. Academic-sounding words: fascinating, is housed, approximately, at which time, therefore, elaborate illustrations, text
2. Defined terms: vellum; illuminated manuscript

132 VOICE Daily 6-Trait Writing • EMC 6026 • © Evan-Moor Corp.

Name: ______________________ **Week 1 • Day 2**

Voice Some writers use a humorous voice to make their writing fun to read.

A. How did the writer of this essay make it humorous and playful? Write examples of each writing technique that she used. Then use proofreading marks to fix the double negatives.

After months of begging, pleading, and driving your parents crazy, you've finally convinced them to let you have a pet. Now you just have to decide between a dog or a cat. Let's compare these two animals.

Take your average dog. We'll call him Fido. It's Saturday morning, and he licks your nose. Aw, how cute! You open one eye. The sun ~~isn't~~ is barely up, but Fido wants to go out. In fact, he MUST go out. He gives a little whine. Then the barking starts. Uh oh, better get dressed for that early morning stroll!

Now consider Fluffy, your average cat. It's Saturday morning, but instead of insisting on a walk, she is curled up peacefully at your feet. She ~~doesn't~~ hardly makes ~~no~~ a sound. She's such a sweet kitty . . . Or is she? You turn over and stretch, wiggling your toes just a bit. Oh no! You've woken the wild jungle beast! To Fluffy, your toes are tasty mice that she must catch for her breakfast. Sorry, no sleeping late for you!

1. Irony: "Early morning stroll" (walking eager dog won't be a "stroll") "She's such a sweet kitty. . . . Or is she?"
2. Funny phrases and sarcasm: "begging, pleading, and driving your parents crazy"; "that early morning stroll"; "wiggling your toes just a bit"; "Sorry, no sleeping late for you!"
3. Interjections and contractions: You've, Let's, Aw, Uh oh, Oh no
4. Funny metaphors: house cat compared to wild jungle beast; toes compared to tasty mice

B. If the essay above were written with a serious voice, what might it sound like? Write three sentences in a serious voice about taking care of pets.

Sample Answer: Dogs are regarded as cute and lovable. However, you should carefully consider the responsibility before adopting one. For example, dogs must be walked several times a day, including the early morning.

© Evan-Moor Corp. • EMC 6026 • Daily 6-Trait Writing VOICE 133

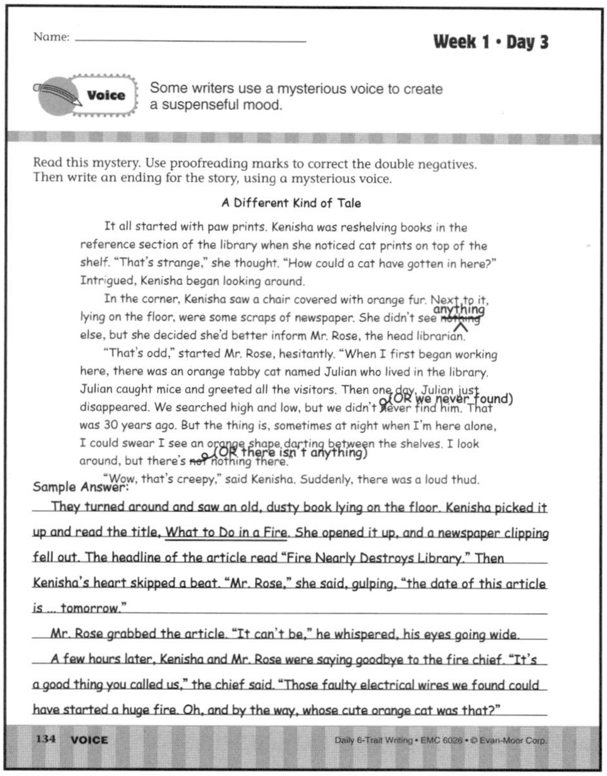

Name: ______________ **Week 1 • Day 3**

Voice Some writers use a mysterious voice to create a suspenseful mood.

Read this mystery. Use proofreading marks to correct the double negatives. Then write an ending for the story, using a mysterious voice.

A Different Kind of Tale

It all started with paw prints. Kenisha was reshelving books in the reference section of the library when she noticed cat prints on top of the shelf. "That's strange," she thought. "How could a cat have gotten in here?" Intrigued, Kenisha began looking around.

In the corner, Kenisha saw a chair covered with orange fur. Next to it, lying on the floor, were some scraps of newspaper. She didn't see ~~nothing~~ anything else, but she decided she'd better inform Mr. Rose, the head librarian.

"That's odd," started Mr. Rose, hesitantly. "When I first began working here, there was an orange tabby cat named Julian who lived in the library. Julian caught mice and greeted all the visitors. Then one day, Julian just disappeared. We searched high and low, but we didn't ~~n~~ever find him. (OR we never found) That was 30 years ago. But the thing is, sometimes at night when I'm here alone, I could swear I see an orange shape darting between the shelves. I look around, but there's ~~not~~ nothing there. (OR there isn't anything)"

"Wow, that's creepy," said Kenisha. Suddenly, there was a loud thud.

Sample Answer:

They turned around and saw an old, dusty book lying on the floor. Kenisha picked it up and read the title, What to Do in a Fire. She opened it up, and a newspaper clipping fell out. The headline of the article read "Fire Nearly Destroys Library." Then Kenisha's heart skipped a beat. "Mr. Rose," she said, gulping, "the date of this article is ... tomorrow."

Mr. Rose grabbed the article. "It can't be," he whispered, his eyes going wide.

A few hours later, Kenisha and Mr. Rose were saying goodbye to the fire chief. "It's a good thing you called us," the chief said. "Those faulty electrical wires we found could have started a huge fire. Oh, and by the way, whose cute orange cat was that?"

134 VOICE Daily 6-Trait Writing • EMC 6026 • © Evan-Moor Corp.

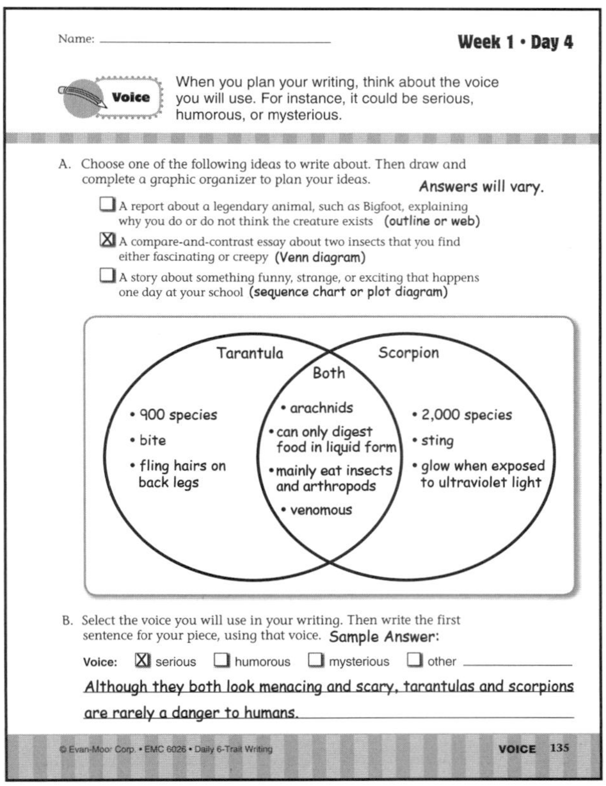

Name: ______________ **Week 1 • Day 4**

Voice When you plan your writing, think about the voice you will use. For instance, it could be serious, humorous, or mysterious.

A. Choose one of the following ideas to write about. Then draw and complete a graphic organizer to plan your ideas. Answers will vary.

- ☐ A report about a legendary animal, such as Bigfoot, explaining why you do or do not think the creature exists (outline or web)
- ☒ A compare-and-contrast essay about two insects that you find either fascinating or creepy (Venn diagram)
- ☐ A story about something funny, strange, or exciting that happens one day at your school (sequence chart or plot diagram)

Tarantula
• 900 species
• bite
• fling hairs on back legs

Both
• arachnids
• can only digest food in liquid form
• mainly eat insects and arthropods
• venomous

Scorpion
• 2,000 species
• sting
• glow when exposed to ultraviolet light

B. Select the voice you will use in your writing. Then write the first sentence for your piece, using that voice. Sample Answer:

Voice: ☒ serious ☐ humorous ☐ mysterious ☐ other ______

Although they both look menacing and scary, tarantulas and scorpions are rarely a danger to humans.

© Evan-Moor Corp. • EMC 6026 • Daily 6-Trait Writing VOICE 135

DAY 3

Read the rule aloud. Say: *Another type of voice is the one you use to sound mysterious.* Write these sentences on the board: *1) I lost my favorite necklace. 2) My favorite necklace had disappeared, never to be seen again.* Ask: *Which sounds more mysterious?* (sentence 2) *Why?* (the phrases "had disappeared" and "never to be seen again") Then guide students through the activity.

- **Convention:** Have students read the story and correct the double negatives. Review the answers as a class, pointing out the various ways each double negative can be fixed.
- Have a volunteer reread the story aloud. Then ask: *Which words and ideas give this writing a mysterious voice?* (e.g., **It all started with paw prints, intrigued, odd, creepy**)
- Brainstorm with students how the story might end. To prompt ideas, ask: *What might have made the noise?* (e.g., book falling off shelf, cat jumping onto floor) Then have students work independently or in pairs to write their endings. Invite volunteers to share what they wrote.

DAY 4

Read the rule aloud. Review the types of voices and when they might be used. Then guide students through the activities.

- **Activity A:** Brainstorm with students specific ideas for each prompt and which graphic organizers to use for each type of writing. Then have students complete their organizers. Circulate to provide assistance as needed.
- **Activity B:** After students write their sentences, have each student read his or her sentence aloud. Have the class identify the type of voice used and discuss ways to make the voice even stronger.

DAY 5 *Writing Prompt*

- *Use your graphic organizer from Day 4 to write a response to the prompt you chose. Write in a clear voice that reflects your ideas and personality.*
- *Remember to avoid double negatives.*

Name: ______________________________

Week 1 • Day 1

Voice

Your voice can come through your writing in a variety of ways. Sometimes you need to write with a formal voice. Other times, it's OK to use an informal voice.

Read the paragraphs and fix the double negative in each one. Then write examples of the writing techniques used to create the voice of each paragraph.

Informal E-mail

Dublin, Ireland, is such a cool city! My favorite part is Trinity College. It's right in the city and is very old—more than 400 years old! Queen Elizabeth I founded it. In the library, which isn't nothing like our school library, I saw a book called The Book of Kells. It's even older than the college. Monks started working on it around the year 800. Do the math! That's about 1,200 years old! Anyway, you've got to see it. It's all decorated with colored pictures and designs and stuff. The monks made it all by hand because there weren't any printing presses back then. Can you imagine?

1. Slang: ______________________________
2. First person: ______________________________
3. Addressing the reader: ______________________________
4. Contractions: ______________________________

Formal Report

Dublin is a fascinating city. One of its most interesting features is Trinity College, which Queen Elizabeth I founded in 1592. An ancient manuscript called The Book of Kells is housed at its library. Monks created this manuscript approximately 1,200 years ago, at which time there were not no printing presses. Therefore, the monks hand-lettered the pages on vellum, or animal skin, and added colorful, elaborate illustrations and designs. Experts call this type of text an illuminated manuscript.

1. Academic-sounding words: ______________________________
2. Defined terms: ______________________________

Name: ______________________

Week 1 • Day 2

Voice

Some writers use a humorous voice to make their writing fun to read.

A. How did the writer of this essay make it humorous and playful? Write examples of each writing technique that she used. Then use proofreading marks to fix the double negatives.

After months of begging, pleading, and driving your parents crazy, you've finally convinced them to let you have a pet. Now you just have to decide between a dog or a cat. Let's compare these two animals.

Take your average dog. We'll call him Fido. It's Saturday morning, and he licks your nose. Aw, how cute! You open one eye. The sun isn't barely up, but Fido wants to go out. In fact, he MUST go out. He gives a little whine. Then the barking starts. Uh oh, better get dressed for that early morning stroll!

Now consider Fluffy, your average cat. It's Saturday morning, but instead of insisting on a walk, she is curled up peacefully at your feet. She doesn't hardly make no sound. She's such a sweet kitty . . . Or is she? You turn over and stretch, wiggling your toes just a bit. Oh no! You've woken the wild jungle beast! To Fluffy, your toes are tasty mice that she must catch for her breakfast. Sorry, no sleeping late for you!

1. Irony: ______________________

____

2. Funny phrases and sarcasm: ______________________

____

3. Interjections and contractions: ______________________

4. Funny metaphors: ______________________

____

B. If the essay above were written with a serious voice, what might it sound like? Write three sentences in a serious voice about taking care of pets.

____

____

Voice

Some writers use a mysterious voice to create a suspenseful mood.

Read this mystery. Use proofreading marks to correct the double negatives. Then write an ending for the story, using a mysterious voice.

A Different Kind of Tale

It all started with paw prints. Kenisha was reshelving books in the reference section of the library when she noticed cat prints on top of the shelf. "That's strange," she thought. "How could a cat have gotten in here?" Intrigued, Kenisha began looking around.

In the corner, Kenisha saw a chair covered with orange fur. Next to it, lying on the floor, were some scraps of newspaper. She didn't see nothing else, but she decided she'd better inform Mr. Rose, the head librarian.

"That's odd," started Mr. Rose, hesitantly. "When I first began working here, there was an orange tabby cat named Julian who lived in the library. Julian caught mice and greeted all the visitors. Then one day, Julian just disappeared. We searched high and low, but we didn't never find him. That was 30 years ago. But the thing is, sometimes at night when I'm here alone, I could swear I see an orange shape darting between the shelves. I look around, but there's not nothing there."

"Wow, that's creepy," said Kenisha. Suddenly, there was a loud thud.

Voice

When you plan your writing, think about the voice you will use. For instance, it could be serious, humorous, or mysterious.

A. Choose one of the following ideas to write about. Then draw and complete a graphic organizer to plan your ideas.

- ☐ A report about a legendary animal, such as Bigfoot, explaining why you do or do not think the creature exists
- ☐ A compare-and-contrast essay about two insects that you find either fascinating or creepy
- ☐ A story about something funny, strange, or exciting that happens one day at your school

B. Select the voice you will use in your writing. Then write the first sentence for your piece, using that voice.

Voice: ☐ serious ☐ humorous ☐ mysterious ☐ other ______________

____

____

VOICE

Using Different Voices for Different Purposes

DAY 1

Read the rule aloud. Then say: *You should always write in your own voice; however, you must adjust your voice to suit your purpose and audience. For example, a good writer will use a different voice to inform readers objectively about a challenging problem than the voice he or she might use to persuade people about how to solve that problem.* Then guide students through the activity.

- Have students read the descriptions. Then say: *While these two writers wrote about the same topic for the same purpose and audience, their voices are different because they are different people. The way they used language is different.* Review the definitions of **alliteration** (two or more words beginning with the same sound) and **irony** (describing something as the opposite of what it is). Then have students complete the activity.
- **Convention:** Point out the sentence beginning "They design..." in the first description. Say: *"design special machines, measure weather conditions, and calculate air resistance" is a series of actions. A* ***series*** *is a list of three or more words or phrases in a sentence, each separated by a comma.* Have students underline the sentence and circle the commas in the series. Repeat for the sentence containing a series in the second description.

DAY 2

Read the rule aloud. Then guide students through the activities.

- **Activity A (Convention):** Remind students that a series can be several short words, or it can be several long phrases with parallel structure. Then have students complete the activity.
- **Activity B:** Reread the essay aloud. Then ask: *Is this essay persuasive?* (yes) *How could you describe the voice of the writer?* (persuasive, but not overly forceful; polite, confident) Guide students in answering the questions. For example, for the first question, say: *Whenever the writer states her opinion, she begins with a phrase that contains* ***I*** *or* ***me*** *to indicate that she is speaking only for herself.* Have students underline these phrases. Then guide them through the remaining questions.

Name: ______________________ **Week 2 • Day 1**

Voice The voice you use depends on your purpose for writing. For example, when your purpose is to entertain, you can use an exciting or humorous voice.

Read these descriptions. Think about how each writer's voice sounds different, even though they are both entertaining. Then answer the questions.

Writer 1

Have you ever tried to launch a ten-pound pumpkin across a football field? Next week's Pumpkin Toss, sponsored by the Science Club, is the biggest competition of the year for serious science students who want an exciting challenge. Teams compete to see who can catapult a pumpkin the farthest. They design special machines, measure weather conditions, and calculate air resistance. Last year's contest was a real nail-biter. In the last round, our team smashed the record with a 255-foot pumpkin rocket!

Writer 2

Have you ever heard of the Westwind Middle School Science Club Pumpkin Toss? Believe it or not, this crazy contest is all about seeing who can fling a ten-pound pumpkin the farthest. But it's not about muscles. It's about brains, which gives wimps like me a fighting chance! My team built a catapult to launch our pumpkin. Unfortunately, it didn't go so well. What happened, you ask? Our launch limped, our fling flopped, and our pumpkin plopped! We achieved a remarkable distance of five whole feet.

Sample Answers:

1. Which words or phrases make Writer 1 sound more serious or scientific?
   sponsored, serious science students, calculate air resistance
2. List three examples of alliteration that Writer 2 used.
   crazy contest, launch limped, fling flopped, pumpkin plopped
3. List three words or phrases that Writer 1 used to convey excitement or drama.
   biggest competition of the year; exciting challenge; nail-biter
4. Which sentence in Writer 2's description shows irony?
   "We achieved a remarkable distance of five whole feet."

138 VOICE Daily 6-Trait Writing • EMC 6026 • © Evan-Moor Corp.

Name: ______________________ **Week 2 • Day 2**

Voice The voice you use depends on your purpose for writing. For example, you can use your voice to be persuasive.

A. Read this essay by a Westwind Middle School student. Insert or delete commas to fix the sentences that contain a series.

Let me say that I believe science and technology are very important. I think it is wonderful that our Science Club challenges us to use technology to solve problems think creatively, and, learn. However, I want the club to think twice about next year's Pumpkin Toss Competition.

Why? It may seem like a small thing, but 40 pumpkins are wasted each year. To me, this sends a message that wasting food is OK. I have a suggestion. I've done a little research talked to some people and made a discovery. Nearly 20,000 people in our county rely on the Food Bank to survive. Therefore, why not invite the spectators and participants of the Pumpkin Toss to donate to the Food Bank in return for the wasted pumpkins? Ask each team to donate a bag of food, have spectators bring canned goods for admission and pass around jars, for collecting money. After all, wouldn't it be nice to use the pumpkins for a good cause instead of simply smashing them?

B. The writer of the essay above is persuasive because she connects with her reader. Answer the questions to give examples of how she does this.

1. What phrases does the writer use to be polite and to acknowledge that she is expressing her personal feelings?
   "I believe," "I think," "To me," "I have a suggestion."
2. Give an example of a question that the writer poses to her readers.
   "Why not invite the spectators and participants....?"
   "After all, wouldn't it be nice...?"
3. What does the writer say to make you think you can trust or believe her?
   "I've done a little research, talked to some people..."
4. Give two examples of what the writer says to acknowledge other people's views or opinions.
   "I think it is wonderful that our Science Club challenges us..."
   "It may seem like a small thing, but..."

© Evan-Moor Corp. • EMC 6026 • Daily 6-Trait Writing VOICE 139

Name: ____________ **Week 2 • Day 3**

Voice Choose the proper voice to suit your purpose, and maintain that voice throughout your writing.

A. Underline the sentences in this letter where the writer changes his voice. Then rewrite those sentences to match the writer's purpose.

Dear Dr. Morgenstern:

I am a sixth-grade student at Westwind Middle School. I am writing a research report on the ways that computer technology can help people who are blind, hearing-impaired, paralyzed, or physically challenged in some other way.

The work that your company does interests me very much. Most impressive and inspiring is the computer program you developed that makes communicating easier for people who cannot speak or write. I would like to know more about how your company became interested in using technology to help people. I think computers and stuff are amazing! Plus, I seriously want to help people, too! I'm sure that you are totally busy, but if you could just squeeze me into your schedule so we could chat for a minute, that would be awesome.

Sincerely,
Larry Simpson

Sample Answer: Computers can do amazing things! I am interested in a career using or developing computers to help people in some way. I know how busy you are, but I would be grateful if you could take a moment to answer a few questions.

B. Insert commas where they belong in the following sentences.

1. New technology enables kids with disabilities to communicate with others, to use a computer for academic purposes, and to enjoy many types of entertainment.
2. Kids who previously had difficulty learning now benefit from new computer programs, special software, and larger keyboards and monitors.
3. I hope that someday I can have a career that uses my strong computer skills, my interest in helping people, and my ability to think creatively.

140 VOICE Daily 6-Trait Writing • EMC 6026 • © Evan-Moor Corp.

Name: ____________ **Week 2 • Day 4**

Voice When you plan your writing, think about your purpose and how you can use your voice to suit that purpose.

Have you ever experienced or witnessed some sort of technical difficulty, such as a microphone not working, a computer crashing, or a DVD not playing? Plan an entertaining paragraph about the experience. Fill in the chart with details and descriptive language that will create an entertaining voice.
Sample Answers:

EVENT: the time our science team's robot fell over and "died"	
Humorous or exciting details about what happened	Just as we were demonstrating how it could pick up any object, the claw fell off and the robot toppled over.
Fun or dramatic words	clang, rattle, shudder, pop, expire
Phrases that use alliteration	Weird Wired Wally; tripped, tipped, and toppled
Similes that could be used to describe what happened or to show irony	Our robot looked like a one-armed toaster oven. We turned as red as tomatoes.

© Evan-Moor Corp. • EMC 6026 • Daily 6-Trait Writing VOICE 141

DAY 3

Read the rule aloud. Say: *No matter what your purpose for writing is, be sure your voice doesn't stray from that purpose.* Then guide students through the activities.

- **Activity A:** Have a student read the letter aloud. Then ask: *What is this student's purpose for writing? What does he want Dr. Morgenstern to think of him?* (wants to show that he's intelligent and interested in technology so Dr. Morgenstern will take him seriously) Then ask: *Where does Larry stray from that purpose and voice?* ("Computers and stuff...")

  Have students complete the activity. Then ask volunteers to share their revisions. Have the class determine whether the revised sentences match the intended voice and purpose.

- **Activity B (Convention):** Say: *Using commas to separate items in a series is important, because otherwise all the information runs together and the reader can get confused.* Have students complete the activity independently and then exchange papers to check each other's work.

DAY 4

Read the rule aloud. Then guide students through the activity.

- Brainstorm with students bad experiences they have had with technology that resulted in either minor or serious consequences. (e.g., TV dying in the middle of a favorite show; computer crashing and wiping out an entire paper)
- Have students complete their charts. Circulate to assist students as needed, reminding them to keep in mind their purpose for writing (to entertain) as they try to think of ways to describe what happened.

DAY 5 *Writing Prompt*

- *Use your ideas from Day 4 to write about a time when a piece of electronic equipment failed to function properly. Remember to use an entertaining voice.*
- *Include at least one sentence with a series. Be sure to use commas correctly.*

Name: ________________________________

Voice

The voice you use depends on your purpose for writing. For example, when your purpose is to entertain, you can use an exciting or humorous voice.

Read these descriptions. Think about how each writer's voice sounds different, even though they are both entertaining. Then answer the questions.

Writer 1

Have you ever tried to launch a ten-pound pumpkin across a football field? Next week's Pumpkin Toss, sponsored by the Science Club, is the biggest competition of the year for serious science students who want an exciting challenge. Teams compete to see who can catapult a pumpkin the farthest. They design special machines, measure weather conditions, and calculate air resistance. Last year's contest was a real nail-biter. In the last round, our team smashed the record with a 255-foot pumpkin rocket!

Writer 2

Have you ever heard of the Westwind Middle School Science Club Pumpkin Toss? Believe it or not, this crazy contest is all about seeing who can fling a ten-pound pumpkin the farthest. But it's not about muscles. It's about brains, which gives wimps like me a fighting chance! My team built a catapult to launch our pumpkin. Unfortunately, it didn't go so well. What happened, you ask? Our launch limped, our fling flopped, and our pumpkin plopped! We achieved a remarkable distance of five whole feet.

1. Which words or phrases make Writer 1 sound more serious or scientific?

____

2. List three examples of alliteration that Writer 2 used. ____________________

____

3. List three words or phrases that Writer 1 used to convey excitement or drama.

____

4. Which sentence in Writer 2's description shows irony? ____________________

____

Name: ____________________

Week 2 • Day 2

Voice The voice you use depends on your purpose for writing. For example, you can use your voice to be persuasive.

A. Read this essay by a Westwind Middle School student. Insert or delete commas to fix the sentences that contain a series.

Let me say that I believe science and technology are very important. I think it is wonderful that our Science Club challenges us to use technology to solve problems think creatively, and, learn. However, I want the club to think twice about next year's Pumpkin Toss Competition.

Why? It may seem like a small thing, but 40 pumpkins are wasted each year. To me, this sends a message that wasting food is OK. I have a suggestion. I've done a little research talked to some people and made a discovery. Nearly 20,000 people in our county rely on the Food Bank to survive. Therefore, why not invite the spectators and participants of the Pumpkin Toss to donate to the Food Bank in return for the wasted pumpkins? Ask each team to donate a bag of food, have spectators bring canned goods for admission and pass around jars, for collecting money. After all, wouldn't it be nice to use the pumpkins for a good cause instead of simply smashing them?

B. The writer of the essay above is persuasive because she connects with her reader. Answer the questions to give examples of how she does this.

1. What phrases does the writer use to be polite and to acknowledge that she is expressing her personal feelings?

   ____

2. Give an example of a question that the writer poses to her readers.

   ____

3. What does the writer say to make you think you can trust or believe her?

   ____

4. Give two examples of what the writer says to acknowledge other people's views or opinions.

   ____

   ____

Name: ______________________________

Week 2 • Day 3

Voice Choose the proper voice to suit your purpose, and maintain that voice throughout your writing.

A. Underline the sentences in this letter where the writer changes his voice. Then rewrite those sentences to match the writer's purpose.

> Dear Dr. Morgenstern:
>
> I am a sixth-grade student at Westwind Middle School. I am writing a research report on the ways that computer technology can help people who are blind, hearing-impaired, paralyzed, or physically challenged in some other way.
>
> The work that your company does interests me very much. Most impressive and inspiring is the computer program you developed that makes communicating easier for people who cannot speak or write. I would like to know more about how your company became interested in using technology to help people. I think computers and stuff are amazing! Plus, I seriously want to help people, too! I'm sure that you are totally busy, but if you could just squeeze me into your schedule so we could chat for a minute, that would be awesome.
>
> Sincerely,
> Larry Simpson

____

____

____

____

B. Insert commas where they belong in the following sentences.

1. New technology enables kids with disabilities to communicate with others to use a computer for academic purposes and to enjoy many types of entertainment.

2. Kids who previously had difficulty learning now benefit from new computer programs special software and larger keyboards and monitors.

3. I hope that someday I can have a career that uses my strong computer skills my interest in helping people and my ability to think creatively.

Name: ______________________________

Voice When you plan your writing, think about your purpose and how you can use your voice to suit that purpose.

Have you ever experienced or witnessed some sort of technical difficulty, such as a microphone not working, a computer crashing, or a DVD not playing? Plan an entertaining paragraph about the experience. Fill in the chart with details and descriptive language that will create an entertaining voice.

EVENT:	
Humorous or exciting details about what happened	
Fun or dramatic words	
Phrases that use alliteration	
Similes that could be used to describe what happened or to show irony	

VOICE
Using Voice in Poetry

DAY 1

Read the rule aloud. Then guide students through the activity.

- Read the first poem aloud. Ask: *What is this poem about?* (washing clothes) Say: *Most of us would consider this a chore. But the poet makes it sound fun. How does she do that?* (e.g., with light, happy language; by calling herself "queen of my tub")
- Say: *The poet uses three techniques to give the poem its voice.* Review the techniques listed. Explain that **imagery** refers to images, or pictures, that a writer creates with words, while **rhyme** gives emphasis to certain words at the ends of sentences. For example, **sing, swing, high,** and **sky** together emphasize a positive, uplifting image. Then read the second poems aloud and have students complete the activity independently or in pairs.
- **Convention:** Write the word pairs **wring/ring** and **clothes/close** on the board. Review: ***Homophones*** *are words that sound alike but have different spellings and meanings.* Have students circle the word from each pair that appears in the first poem (**wring, clothes**). Say: *When you write, be sure to use the correct word for your intended meaning.* Help students identify other words in the poems that have homophones. (e.g., **air/heir; to/too/two; poor/pour; passed/past**)

DAY 2

Read the rule aloud. Then guide students through the activities.

- **Activity A:** Read the incomplete poem aloud. Help students brainstorm words to describe the voice. (e.g., **chilling, scary**) Then explain: *This poem has an AABB rhyming pattern. In each stanza, the first and second lines rhyme, and the third and fourth lines rhyme.* Model completing the first stanza, using the sample answers on the reduced page. Then have students complete the activity.
- **Activity B (Convention):** Have students find **missed** and **sight** in the poem, as well as other words that have homophones. (e.g., **right/write; where/wear; veins/vanes; night/knight**) Then have students complete the activity.

Name: ______________________ **Week 3 • Day 1**

Voice A poet's choice of words, images, and rhymes gives a poem its particular voice.

Read these two poem excerpts. Identify the voice in each one, and list examples of the writing techniques that give the poem its voice.

from "A Song from the Suds"
by Louisa May Alcott

Queen of my tub, I merrily sing,
While the white foam raises high,
And sturdily wash, and rinse, and (wring)
And fasten the (clothes) to dry;
Then out in the free fresh air they swing,
Under the sunny sky.

Sample Answers:
Voice: humorous, happy
Word Choice: merrily, sing, high, free, fresh, swing, sunny sky
Imagery: queen of a tub, foam rising high, swinging under a sunny sky
Rhyme: sing/wring/swing; high/dry/sky; voice goes up

from "The House with Nobody in It"
by Joyce Kilmer

Whenever I walk to Suffern along the Erie track
I go by a poor old farmhouse with its shingles broken and black.
I suppose I've passed it a hundred times, but I always stop for a minute
And look at the house, the tragic house, the house with nobody in it.

Sample Answers:
Voice: sad, serious, depressing
Word Choice: poor, old, broken, black, tragic, nobody
Imagery: walking alone beside a train track; old, broken-down, abandoned farmhouse
Rhyme: track/black; minute/in it; voice goes down

144 VOICE Daily 6-Trait Writing • EMC 6026 • © Evan-Moor Corp.

Name: ______________________ **Week 3 • Day 2**

Voice Choose words, images, and rhymes carefully to bring out the voice of your poem.

A. Read the incomplete poem. What kind of voice does it have? Write your answer. Then complete the poem in the same voice.

Voice: chilling, frightening, dark **Sample Answers:**

Pirate Jack Robin

Oh, Pirate Jack Robin filled sailors with fear.
Their knees went a-shaking when Robin came near.
Knives and ropes hung across his broad chest.
Birds used his filthy, dark beard for a nest.

His lips, they turned downward, in a constant frown.
And his hairy fists could knock you right down.
Scars slashed his cheeks where swords hadn't missed.
And Jack never talked; he just growled and hissed.

His breath, it reeked; his teeth, they were green.
The veins in his forehead bulged angry and mean.
Oh, Pirate Jack Robin was a fearsome sight.
He terrorized everyone, both day and night.

B. Circle the correct homophone for each meaning.

1. a light rain or fog — missed — (mist)
2. a location — sight — (site)
3. didn't make it — (missed) — mist
4. the ability to see — (sight) — site

© Evan-Moor Corp. • EMC 6026 • Daily 6-Trait Writing VOICE 145

Name: ______________________ **Week 3 • Day 3**

Voice Use word choice, imagery, and rhyme to maintain the same voice throughout your poem.

Read each poem. Then:

- Use proofreading marks to fix the incorrect homophones.
- Write a second stanza for each poem, maintaining the voice and rhyming pattern.

In the Deep

Swimming deep in inky coldness,
~~Wear~~ Where the light is faint and dim.
Eerie creatures move with boldness.
Life down ~~hear~~ here is harsh and grim.

Sample Answer: Octopuses slowly creep
Along the murky ocean floor.
This dreary place to hunt and sleep
Is miles from any sunny shore.

I'm the One

I'm totally smart, as anyone can ~~sea~~ see.
Crosswords and quiz shows are easy for me.
I know all the states and ~~there~~ their capitals, too.
I can speak Farsi and French. Can you?

Sample Answer:
I'm totally smart, the smartest of all.
If you need answers, just give me a call.
I can name every ocean, river, and lake.
There isn't a test that I couldn't take.

146 VOICE Daily 6-Trait Writing • EMC 6026 • © Evan-Moor Corp.

DAY 3

Read the rule aloud. Say: *Be careful not to change voices in the middle of your poem without a good reason. Carefully consider each word as you write.* Then guide students through the activity.

- **Convention:** Have students read the poems and correct the homophones. Then review the answers as a class.
- Have a volunteer reread the first poem aloud. Ask: *How would you describe this poem's voice?* (e.g., cold, serious, spooky) Then have students identify the rhyming pattern. (ABAB) Help students brainstorm things they could write about in the next stanza. (e.g., specific deep-sea dwellers, why life is "harsh and grim") Repeat the process for the second poem. (voice: silly, bragging; rhyme scheme: AABB)
- Have students write their second stanzas. Then invite volunteers to read aloud what they wrote. Challenge the rest of the class to listen for any homophones and confirm the correct spellings.

Name: ______________________ **Week 3 • Day 4**

Voice When you write a poem, think ahead of time about the voice you want your poem to have.

A. Choose one of the topics below, or think of your own, to write a poem about. Choose the voice that you want your poem to have. Then complete the web with ideas for your poem.

Topic:	Voice:
☒ an unusual animal	☐ humorous, lighthearted
☐ a winter snowstorm	☐ frightening, mysterious
☐ my best friend	☐ quiet, gentle
☐ my favorite food	☐ exciting, powerful
☐ other: ________	☒ other: sad

Sample Answers:

Title: Ode to a Dodo Bird
- small wings, flightless
- became extinct around 17th century
- gray feathers, hooked bill
- often called clumsy, dumb, fearless

B. Plan rhymes for your poem by jotting down any words you can think of that rhyme with some of the words in your web.

flightless	extinct	gray	bill
mightless	distinct	say	still
frightless	blinked	dismay	skill

© Evan-Moor Corp. • EMC 6026 • Daily 6-Trait Writing VOICE 147

DAY 4

Read the rule aloud. Then guide students through the activities.

- **Activity A:** Read through the list of topics with students, and help them brainstorm more specific ones. Then discuss what kind of voice might work best for each topic. Use the sample answers on the reduced page to model completing the web. Then have students complete their own webs.
- **Activity B:** Use the sample answers on the reduced page to model brainstorming words that rhyme with words in the web. Remind students to keep in mind the voice they chose to help them consider the best rhyming words for their poem.

DAY 5 *Writing Prompt*

- *Use your ideas from Day 4 to write an original poem with words, images, and rhymes that give it a strong voice.*
- *Be sure to spell homophones correctly.*

Name: ______________________________

Voice

A poet's choice of words, images, and rhymes gives a poem its particular voice.

Read these two poem excerpts. Identify the voice in each one, and list examples of the writing techniques that give the poem its voice.

from "A Song from the Suds"

by Louisa May Alcott

Queen of my tub, I merrily sing,
While the white foam raises high,
And sturdily wash, and rinse, and wring,
And fasten the clothes to dry;
Then out in the free fresh air they swing,
Under the sunny sky.

Voice: ______________________________

Word Choice: ______________________________

Imagery: ______________________________

Rhyme: ______________________________

from "The House with Nobody in It"

by Joyce Kilmer

Whenever I walk to Suffern along the Erie track
I go by a poor old farmhouse with its shingles broken and black.
I suppose I've passed it a hundred times, but I always stop for a minute
And look at the house, the tragic house, the house with nobody in it.

Voice: ______________________________

Word Choice: ______________________________

Imagery: ______________________________

Rhyme: ______________________________

Name: ______________________________

Voice Choose words, images, and rhymes carefully to bring out the voice of your poem.

A. Read the incomplete poem. What kind of voice does it have? Write your answer. Then complete the poem in the same voice.

Voice: ____________________

Pirate Jack Robin

Oh, Pirate Jack Robin filled sailors with fear.
Their knees went a-shaking when ______________________.
______________________ hung across his broad chest.
Birds used his filthy, dark beard for a nest.

His lips, they turned downward, in a constant frown.
______________________ could knock you right down.
Scars slashed his cheeks where swords hadn't missed.
And Jack never talked; ______________________.

His breath, it reeked; ______________________.
The veins in his forehead bulged angry and mean.
Oh, Pirate Jack Robin was a fearsome sight.
______________________, both day and night.

B. Circle the correct homophone for each meaning.

1. a light rain or fog **missed** **mist**
2. a location **sight** **site**
3. didn't make it **missed** **mist**
4. the ability to see **sight** **site**

Name: ______________________________

Voice

Use word choice, imagery, and rhyme to maintain the same voice throughout your poem.

Read each poem. Then:

- Use proofreading marks to fix the incorrect homophones.
- Write a second stanza for each poem, maintaining the voice and rhyming pattern.

In the Deep

Swimming deep in inky coldness,
Wear the light is faint and dim.
Eerie creatures move with boldness.
Life down hear is harsh and grim.

____

____

____

____

I'm the One

I'm totally smart, as anyone can sea.
Crosswords and quiz shows are easy for me.
I know all the states and there capitals, too.
I can speak Farsi and French. Can you?

____

____

____

____

Name: ______________________

Week 3 • Day 4

Voice

When you write a poem, think ahead of time about the voice you want your poem to have.

A. Choose one of the topics below, or think of your own, to write a poem about. Choose the voice that you want your poem to have. Then complete the web with ideas for your poem.

Topic:

- ☐ an unusual animal
- ☐ a winter snowstorm
- ☐ my best friend
- ☐ my favorite food
- ☐ other: ______________

Voice:

- ☐ humorous, lighthearted
- ☐ frightening, mysterious
- ☐ quiet, gentle
- ☐ exciting, powerful
- ☐ other: ______________

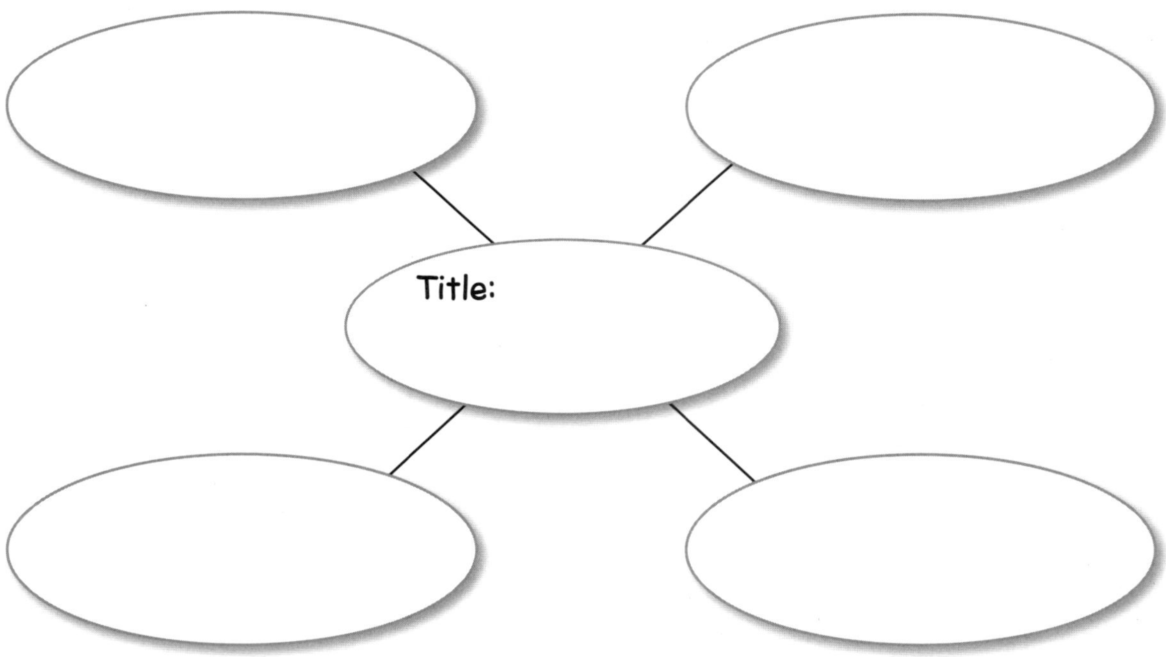

B. Plan rhymes for your poem by jotting down any words you can think of that rhyme with some of the words in your web.

____________ ____________ ____________ ____________

____________ ____________ ____________ ____________

____________ ____________ ____________ ____________

WEEK 4

VOICE
Writing from Different Points of View

DAY 1

Read the rule aloud. Say: ***Point of view** is how someone sees things and the voice he or she uses to describe those things. **First person** is when you write from your own point of view, using pronouns such as **I, me,** and **we. Second person** is when you write as if speaking directly to the reader, using the pronoun **you. Third person** is when you write from someone else's point of view, using pronouns such as **he, she, his, her,** and **they.*** Then guide students through the activities.

- **Activity A:** Have students read the narratives. Point out that both are written in first person. Ask: *What can you tell about Terra's personality from her voice and how she describes her situation?* (sarcastic, not a nature lover) *What can you tell about Mary?* (easygoing, enjoys nature) Read the questions aloud and have students write their responses. Remind students to use first-person point of view and to try to match each girl's voice.

- **Activity B (Convention):** Review first-, second-, and third-person pronouns. Then have students complete the activity.

Name: ____________________ **Week 4 • Day 1**

Voice Everyone has a unique point of view and a unique voice.

A. Read these personal narratives about camp. Then answer the questions.

Terra's Narrative

It was about 135 degrees at Camp Clear Creek the day my parents dropped me off. Going to nature camp was not my first choice, but it had to be better than babysitting my little brother all summer. Then I saw the cabin where I'd be staying. It had been described as "rustic" in the brochure, but "primitive" was more like it. Not only was there no air conditioning, but there wasn't even electricity! How was I going to dry my hair or recharge my cell phone? I couldn't live for two weeks like this!

Mary's Narrative

For months, I had been looking forward to going to Camp Clear Creek so I could experience the outdoors and learn all about ecology. Finally, the day had come! When I arrived at my assigned cabin, I rolled my sleeping bag out on a bed and stowed my backpack. I would have preferred a tent in the woods to a cabin with screened windows, but that was OK. At least I was happier than my bunkmate, Terra. I think she expected a fancy hotel!

Sample Answers:

1. How would Terra feel about not having any running water in the cabin? Write what she might say about having to use an outdoor shower.

   "Are you kidding me? There is no way I'm taking a shower outside!"

2. How might Mary feel if she saw a huge spider? Write what she might say about it.

   "Wow, I just saw the coolest spider! I wonder what kind it was."

B. Circle the pronouns in each sentence. Then write whether each sentence is written in first, second, or third person.

1. If you go camping at Otter Lake, take your bug spray! — second person
2. Gary wondered whether he should tell his friends about the difficult trail they were about to hike. — third person
3. I wish we could stay in a cabin instead of my dad's stinky tent. — first person

150 VOICE — Daily 6-Trait Writing • EMC 6026 • © Evan-Moor Corp.

DAY 2

Read the rule aloud. Say: *Usually when we write to inform, we use third person. But our writing still needs to have a clear voice.* Guide students through the activities.

- **Activity A:** Have students read Andre's draft. Say: *This report is fine. It gives us plenty of information. But anyone could have written it. Just because you're writing a report doesn't mean your writing has to be overly serious or boring. You can still use your voice to show who you are.*

  Have students read the revision. Ask: *What can we now tell about Andre?* (greatly admires founders, loves nature, cares about camp) *How do you know?* (e.g., words such as **amazing, brave, nature's gifts**) Then have students complete the activity.

- **Activity B (Convention):** Write the following sentence on the board: *Fall is my favorite season to go camping.* Say: *To rewrite this in third person, what would I have to change?* (**my**) *To what?* (**his, her,** or **their**). Model rewriting the sentence. Then have students complete the activity.

Name: ____________________ **Week 4 • Day 2**

Voice Use your voice to show who you are, even when you present information from a third-person point of view.

A. Read both versions of Andre's report. Underline the words and phrases in his revision that help his voice come through more clearly.

Draft

On January 8, 1986, the members of the Clear Creek Ecology Club voted to establish a nature camp for children. The camp opened on June 1, 1987. At that time, there were only six small cabins. Volunteers from the club acted as counselors. They taught 24 campers how to blaze trails and identify trees, flowers, and animal tracks. By the following summer, the camp had several hiking trails, a dining hall, and ten more cabins. Today, campers come from all over to learn about nature and experience the outdoors.

Revision

On January 8, 1986, the members of the Clear Creek Ecology Club voted to establish a nature camp for children. This small but amazing group built the camp because they were dedicated to helping children learn about the environment. The camp opened on June 1, 1987, with only six small cabins. Brave volunteers from the club acted as the counselors. They taught those first lucky campers how to blaze trails and identify trees, flowers, and animal tracks. By the following summer, the camp had beautiful hiking trails, a dining hall, and ten more cabins. Today, campers come from all over to study nature's gifts and experience the great outdoors.

B. Rewrite each sentence, changing the first-person point of view to third person.

Sample Answers:

1. When I am older, I would like to be an ecologist like my uncle.

   When she is older, she would like to be an ecologist like her uncle.

2. My brother and I went backpacking with our uncle in 2007.

   Her brother and she went backpacking with their uncle in 2007.

3. My uncle taught us how to identify edible plants.

   Her uncle taught them how to identify edible plants.

© Evan-Moor Corp. • EMC 6026 • Daily 6-Trait Writing — VOICE 151

Name: ______________________

Week 4 • Day 3

Voice When you write to give instructions, use the second-person point of view to connect with your reader.

A. Read Liam's how-to essay. Then answer the questions.

How to Go on a Creek Walk

Going on a creek walk at Camp Clear Creek is a great way to learn about stream ecology and have a lot of fun. Just follow these simple guidelines to protect yourself and the habitat. First of all, wear old shoes and clothes, because you're going to get wet and dirty! Then, be very careful as you step into and move slowly through the creek. You don't want to slip on any loose rocks or algae. You also don't want to stir up the water too much. Remember, you're a visitor. You're there to observe creek life, not disturb it.

Look for tadpoles and minnows in the water, as well as insects skimming along the top. Keep your eye out for frogs and crawfish, too. Bring a jar so that you can collect a small water sample to examine under a microscope back at camp. You'll be amazed to discover how much life there is in just one drop of Clear Creek!

Sample Answers:

1. What can you tell about Liam's personality from his writing? He's curious, likes the outdoors, respects nature, and doesn't mind getting wet and dirty.
2. List at least three phrases or sentences that show how Liam addresses the reader personally.
   "...you're going to get wet and dirty!"; "Remember, you're a visitor."; "You'll be amazed to discover..."

B. How might someone who doesn't like the outdoors describe a creek walk? Think about what his or her voice would sound like. Then use that voice to write at least four sentences, advising someone *not* to go on a creek walk.
Sample Answer:
Going on a creek walk is a horrible idea. You will get all wet and dirty and ruin your clothes. Plus, you could slip on a rock and hurt yourself, not to mention get disgusting green slime all over you. Also, there's gross stuff in the creek! Crawfish and minnows are just waiting to bite your toes. EW!

152 VOICE Daily 6-Trait Writing • EMC 6026 • © Evan-Moor Corp.

Name: ______________________

Week 4 • Day 4

Voice When you plan your writing, think about how you will use your voice and point of view to connect with your reader.

A. Use the graphic organizer to plan a how-to paragraph about something you love to do that others might be hesitant to try.
Sample Answers:

What You Need		Rules or Guidelines
net	display board	Wear protective clothing when collecting bugs.
jar with lid	labels	Try not to harm habitat.
cotton balls	dead bugs	Keep the insect jar away from small children.
rubbing alcohol	book to identify insects	
tweezers		
straight pins		

Steps or Actions

Soak cotton ball in alcohol and place in jar.
↓
Look for insects. Use net to capture.
↓
Use tweezers to put insect in jar. Close lid tightly.
↓
After insect dies, pin onto display board.

B. Write the first sentence of your how-to, using your voice to connect with your readers and to help them see your point of view. Remember, you need to persuade them that this is a fun activity. Sample Answer:
Collecting insects may sound disgusting, but it is a fascinating way to learn more about them so we can protect their habitats.

© Evan-Moor Corp. • EMC 6026 • Daily 6-Trait Writing VOICE 153

DAY 3

Read the rule aloud. Say: *Even when you give instructions, your writing doesn't have to be boring. Because you are addressing the reader directly, you can connect with him or her more personally. Let your enthusiasm for your subject shine through!* Guide students through the activities.

- **Activity A:** Have students read the how-to essay and answer the questions on their own. Then have students share their responses and discuss whether they connected with Liam or not.
- **Activity B:** To prompt ideas, say: *Think about someone like Terra from Day 1. How might she feel about going on a creek walk?* Invite volunteers to pretend to be Terra walking through the creek. Ask: *What might she say?* (e.g., "This is gross! I think something just bit me!")

  Convention: Remind students to write in second person, using the pronoun **you** to address the reader. Have students complete the activity and then share what they wrote.

DAY 4

Read the rule aloud. Then guide students through the activities.

- **Activity A:** Brainstorm with students things that they love to do but that others may not enjoy. (e.g., sports or hobbies that are strenuous, scary, tedious, messy, or time-consuming) If necessary, use the sample answers on the reduced page to model completing the graphic organizer. Then have students complete their own graphic organizers. Circulate to assist as needed.
- **Activity B:** Say: *Remember, your reader has his or her own point of view. Putting yourself in your reader's shoes will help you think of ways to connect with him or her.* Have students write their sentences.

DAY 5 *Writing Prompt*

- *Use your graphic organizer from Day 4 to write a how-to paragraph about something you love to do. Let your voice shine through your writing.*
- *Be sure to use second-person pronouns correctly.*

Name: ______________________________

Week 4 • Day 1

Voice Everyone has a unique point of view and a unique voice.

A. Read these personal narratives about camp. Then answer the questions.

Terra's Narrative

It was about 135 degrees at Camp Clear Creek the day my parents dropped me off. Going to nature camp was not my first choice, but it had to be better than babysitting my little brother all summer. Then I saw the cabin where I'd be staying. It had been described as "rustic" in the brochure, but "primitive" was more like it. Not only was there no air conditioning, but there wasn't even electricity! How was I going to dry my hair or recharge my cell phone? I couldn't live for two weeks like this!

Mary's Narrative

For months, I had been looking forward to going to Camp Clear Creek so I could experience the outdoors and learn all about ecology. Finally, the day had come! When I arrived at my assigned cabin, I rolled my sleeping bag out on a bed and stowed my backpack. I would have preferred a tent in the woods to a cabin with screened windows, but that was OK. At least I was happier than my bunkmate, Terra. I think she expected a fancy hotel!

1. How would Terra feel about not having any running water in the cabin? Write what she might say about having to use an outdoor shower.

____

2. How might Mary feel if she saw a huge spider? Write what she might say about it.

____

B. Circle the pronouns in each sentence. Then write whether each sentence is written in first, second, or third person.

1. If you go camping at Otter Lake, take your bug spray! ______________

2. Gary wondered whether he should tell his friends about the difficult trail they were about to hike. ______________

3. I wish we could stay in a cabin instead of my dad's stinky tent. ______________

Name: ______________________________

Voice Use your voice to show who you are, even when you present information from a third-person point of view.

A. Read both versions of Andre's report. Underline the words and phrases in his revision that help his voice come through more clearly.

Draft

On January 8, 1986, the members of the Clear Creek Ecology Club voted to establish a nature camp for children. The camp opened on June 1, 1987. At that time, there were only six small cabins. Volunteers from the club acted as counselors. They taught 24 campers how to blaze trails and identify trees, flowers, and animal tracks. By the following summer, the camp had several hiking trails, a dining hall, and ten more cabins. Today, campers come from all over to learn about nature and experience the outdoors.

Revision

On January 8, 1986, the members of the Clear Creek Ecology Club voted to establish a nature camp for children. This small but amazing group built the camp because they were dedicated to helping children learn about the environment. The camp opened on June 1, 1987, with only six small cabins. Brave volunteers from the club acted as the counselors. They taught those first lucky campers how to blaze trails and identify trees, flowers, and animal tracks. By the following summer, the camp had beautiful hiking trails, a dining hall, and ten more cabins. Today, campers come from all over to study nature's gifts and experience the great outdoors.

B. Rewrite each sentence, changing the first-person point of view to third person.

1. When I am older, I would like to be an ecologist like my uncle.

____

2. My brother and I went backpacking with our uncle in 2007.

____

3. My uncle taught us how to identify edible plants.

____

Name: ______________________________

Week 4 • Day 3

Voice When you write to give instructions, use the second-person point of view to connect with your reader.

A. Read Liam's how-to essay. Then answer the questions.

How to Go on a Creek Walk

Going on a creek walk at Camp Clear Creek is a great way to learn about stream ecology and have a lot of fun. Just follow these simple guidelines to protect yourself and the habitat. First of all, wear old shoes and clothes, because you're going to get wet and dirty! Then, be very careful as you step into and move slowly through the creek. You don't want to slip on any loose rocks or algae. You also don't want to stir up the water too much. Remember, you're a visitor. You're there to observe creek life, not disturb it.

Look for tadpoles and minnows in the water, as well as insects skimming along the top. Keep your eye out for frogs and crawfish, too. Bring a jar so that you can collect a small water sample to examine under a microscope back at camp. You'll be amazed to discover how much life there is in just one drop of Clear Creek!

1. What can you tell about Liam's personality from his writing? ______________________________

____

2. List at least three phrases or sentences that show how Liam addresses the reader personally.

____

____

B. How might someone who doesn't like the outdoors describe a creek walk? Think about what his or her voice would sound like. Then use that voice to write at least four sentences, advising someone *not* to go on a creek walk.

____

____

____

____

Name: ______________________________

Voice

When you plan your writing, think about how you will use your voice and point of view to connect with your reader.

A. Use the graphic organizer to plan a how-to paragraph about something you love to do that others might be hesitant to try.

What You Need	Rules or Guidelines

Steps or Actions

↓
↓
↓

B. Write the first sentence of your how-to, using your voice to connect with your readers and to help them see your point of view. Remember, you need to persuade them that this is a fun activity.

____

____

WEEK 5

VOICE

Using Voice in Persuasive Writing

DAY 1

Read the rule aloud. Then guide students through the activity.

- Read aloud both editorials. Then ask: *Which one is more persuasive?* (Editorial 2) *Why?* (The voice is more passionate.) Call students' attention to the last three words of Editorial 1. ("to prevent accidents.") Ask: *What words did the writer of Editorial 2 use to say the same thing?* ("before an awful tragedy occurs.") Discuss the differences. Then have students complete the activity.
- **Convention:** Point out the phrase **should have** toward the end of Editorial 2. On the board, write **should have, should've, should of,** and **shoulda.** Circle **should have** and **should've** and say: *Only these two are correct. One is a contraction of the other. In speech, we often shorten* ***should have, would have,*** *and* ***could have*** *to* ***shoulda, woulda,*** *and* ***coulda,*** *but in writing they're incorrect. It is also incorrect to write* ***should of, would of,*** *or* ***could of.*** *Use* ***should've, would've,*** *and* ***could've*** *instead.*

Name: ______________________ **Week 5 • Day 1**

Voice When you write persuasively, think about the emotions you want your reader to feel.

Which editorial below appeals more to the reader's emotions? Underline the words and phrases that show how strongly the writer of that editorial feels about the issue. Then answer the questions.

Editorial 1

The railroad crossing on North Street is not safe now that there is a new ball field next to it. There are no barriers to keep people from crossing the tracks in their cars or on foot when a train is coming. Many people are going to use the crossing. While everyone is supposed to stop and look both ways to check for a train, people are sometimes careless. Someday there might be an accident at this spot. The railroad company should install barriers with flashing lights on them to prevent accidents.

Editorial 2

The North Street railroad crossing has been a problem for years, but now that there is a new ball field next to it, the situation is even more urgent. This crossing has no barriers that come down to prevent a driver or pedestrian from being the victim of a terrible accident. With more children in the area because of the ball field, citizens should be alarmed. Children often cross the tracks without looking, and even cautious drivers can be careless sometimes. The railroad company, which should have done something about this years ago, must take responsibility now and install the proper barriers and lights before an awful tragedy occurs.

Sample Answers:

1. Which editorial is more persuasive? Why? It uses more emotional language. It is more specific about what could happen at the crossing, which makes the reader feel alarmed, upset, and angry at the railroad company.
2. Why do you think the writer of the second editorial included the fact that the railroad crossing has already been a problem for some time?
   It makes the problem seem that much more urgent and puts the railroad company in an even poorer light by showing how it has been irresponsible for years.

156 VOICE Daily 6-Trait Writing • EMC 6026 • © Evan-Moor Corp.

DAY 2

Read the rule aloud. Say: *When you write with a confident voice, your writing is more convincing to readers.* Then guide students through the activities.

- **Activity A:** Ask: *Which opinion statement is stronger? 1) I think school buses should probably have seat belts. 2) All school buses should have seat belts for our protection.* (Statement 2; it takes a specific, confident stand.) Then point out the topic of item 1. (carpooling) Discuss possible opinions about carpooling. (e.g., should be done to save gas; shouldn't be required because too inconvenient) Then have students complete the activity.
- **Activity B:** Read each advertisement aloud. Ask: *Which seems less confident and persuasive?* (the first) *Which words and phrases make the voice sound weak?* (e.g., **might consider, usually, pretty good**) Have students rewrite the ad.
- **Activity C (Convention):** Review the common mistakes people make with **could have, would have,** and **should have.** Then have students complete the activity.

Name: ______________________ **Week 5 • Day 2**

Voice Use a strong, confident voice when you write persuasively.

A. Read each topic for a persuasive paragraph. What would your topic sentence be? Write it as a strong, confident opinion statement.

1. **Topic:** carpooling Sample Answers:
   Opinion Statement: To save gas, it's important to carpool to school with other kids.
2. **Topic:** providing more school buses
   Opinion Statement: Taylor County School District should add more school buses so students' rides to and from school are not so long.

B. Write an *X* next to the advertisement that does not have a confident voice. Then rewrite the ad to sound more confident.

X **Ad 1** The next time you take a trip, you might consider booking your flight with A-Plus Airlines. Our flights are usually on time, and we try not to lose anyone's luggage. Also, our snacks are pretty good. If you fly with us, we hope you'll give us a passing grade!

Ad 2 If your last flight was horrible, you should have flown Aero Air. Then your luggage would have arrived at the same time as you—and on time! Even better, you could have enjoyed plenty of legroom and a free movie. So book your next flight on Aero Air, where all passengers fly first class.

Sample Answer:
The next time you take a trip, be sure to book your flight with A-Plus Airlines. You can trust that you and your luggage will arrive safely and on time. Also, we offer delicious snacks on every flight. At A-Plus Airlines, we guarantee a perfect grade on every trip!

C. Use proofreading marks to fix the incorrect forms of *could have, should have,* and *would have.*

1. You should ~~of~~ have taken Aero Air.
2. You ~~woulda~~ would have gotten to your destination sooner.
3. You ~~coulduv~~ could have watched a free movie on the flight.

© Evan-Moor Corp. • EMC 6026 • Daily 6-Trait Writing VOICE 157

Name: ______________________ **Week 5 • Day 3**

Voice When writing persuasively, use a strong, confident voice to appeal to your reader's emotions.

Read this persuasive paragraph. Then:

- Use proofreading marks to fix the incorrect forms of *could have, would have,* and *should have.*
- Rewrite the paragraph so it has a stronger persuasive voice. Be sure to appeal to your reader's emotions and sound confident.

If someone you know drove to work today, you might tell that person that he or she could ~~of~~ have taken public transportation instead. For one thing, it ~~woulda~~ would have cost less, because the fare for buses, trains, and subways is cheaper than gas. Also, taking public transportation reduces pollution. If more people ride the bus, train, or subway, there will be fewer cars releasing carbon dioxide into the atmosphere. While it may take more time and be less convenient, riding public transportation is also easier in some ways. For example, you don't have to worry about traffic or parking. It might take some adjustment, but eventually you'll realize you ~~shoulda~~ should have made the switch to public transportation sooner.

Sample Answer:

Did someone you know drive to work today? If so, let that person know that he or she should have taken public transportation. Why? For one thing, that person would have saved a ton of money, because a single gallon of gas these days costs more than most bus, train, or subway fares! Also, more people taking public transportation means fewer cars on the road. This significantly reduces the amount of toxic emissions, which means less carbon dioxide released into the atmosphere. Now, who wouldn't want cleaner air and less global warming? Plus, while it might require some time and planning, it's also much less stressful. No more getting stuck in traffic jams or searching for parking spaces! Instead, someone else does all the work. So tell the drivers you know to make the switch today. They'll wish they'd done it sooner!

158 VOICE Daily 6-Trait Writing • EMC 6026 • © Evan-Moor Corp.

Name: ______________________ **Week 5 • Day 4**

Voice When you plan your persuasive writing, think about the reasons and voice you will use to convince your reader.

Complete the opinion diagram to plan a paragraph persuading others to take an action you feel strongly about. Use one of the ideas below, or think of your own.

- Join a cycling club.
- Conserve gasoline.
- Help raise money to pay for a class field trip.
- Add a new train, bus, or subway line in your area.

Sample Answers:

Opinion Statement: The students who live in the River Hills neighborhood should join together to form a cycling club.

Reason: We need to get to know each other better.

Supporting Evidence: Several new families have moved into the neighborhood. It's a great way to make new friends.

Reason: We would get more exercise.

Supporting Evidence: We would be riding regularly, and it would be safer to go on longer and harder rides. We would help motivate each other.

Reason: We could compete in races.

Supporting Evidence: We could race against other cycling clubs. We could help each other train for races.

Possible Objection: Not everyone has a bike.

Response to Objection: Some of us have old bikes that kids could borrow. We could also ask local bike shops to donate old bikes.

© Evan-Moor Corp. • EMC 6026 • Daily 6-Trait Writing VOICE 159

DAY 3

Read the rule aloud. Say: *When you want to write persuasively, put your small doubts and hesitations aside. It's important to anticipate your reader's objections, but then address them confidently to make your argument stronger.* Then guide students through the activity.

- Read the paragraph aloud. Say: *The writer gives reasons for taking public transportation, but the voice isn't very passionate and doesn't appeal to the reader's emotions.* Guide students through the paragraph, discussing words or statements that sound weak or could be changed to have more impact. (e.g., **you might tell, less convenient, in some ways, might take some adjustment**)
- Have students rewrite the paragraph on their own. Then invite students to read their revisions aloud. Discuss the changes that each student made to make the voice sound more confident.

DAY 4

Read the rule aloud. Then guide students through the activity.

- Read through the ideas in the list, and then work with students to write opinion statements for these and any other topics generated by students.
- Use the sample answer on the reduced page to model completing the diagram. Remind students that a good argument also includes possible **objections**, or reasons your audience might disagree with you, and then provides a response that addresses those concerns. Then have students complete the diagram independently.

DAY 5 *Writing Prompt*

- *Use your diagram from Day 4 to write a paragraph persuading your reader to take a certain action. Remember to write with a confident voice that appeals to your reader's emotions.*
- *Be sure to use* ***should have, could have,*** *and* ***would have*** *correctly.*

Voice

When you write persuasively, think about the emotions you want your reader to feel.

Which editorial below appeals more to the reader's emotions? Underline the words and phrases that show how strongly the writer of that editorial feels about the issue. Then answer the questions.

Editorial 1

The railroad crossing on North Street is not safe now that there is a new ball field next to it. There are no barriers to keep people from crossing the tracks in their cars or on foot when a train is coming. Many people are going to use the crossing. While everyone is supposed to stop and look both ways to check for a train, people are sometimes careless. Someday there might be an accident at this spot. The railroad company should install barriers with flashing lights on them to prevent accidents.

Editorial 2

The North Street railroad crossing has been a problem for years, but now that there is a new ball field next to it, the situation is even more urgent. This crossing has no barriers that come down to prevent a driver or pedestrian from being the victim of a terrible accident. With more children in the area because of the ball field, citizens should be alarmed. Children often cross the tracks without looking, and even cautious drivers can be careless sometimes. The railroad company, which should have done something about this years ago, must take responsibility now and install the proper barriers and lights before an awful tragedy occurs.

1. Which editorial is more persuasive? Why? ______________________________

____

2. Why do you think the writer of the second editorial included the fact that the railroad crossing has already been a problem for some time?

____

____

Name: ______________________________

Voice Use a strong, confident voice when you write persuasively.

A. Read each topic for a persuasive paragraph. What would your topic sentence be? Write it as a strong, confident opinion statement.

1. **Topic:** carpooling

   Opinion Statement: ______________________________

   ____

2. **Topic:** providing more school buses

   Opinion Statement: ______________________________

   ____

B. Write an *X* next to the advertisement that does not have a confident voice. Then rewrite the ad to sound more confident.

Ad 1 The next time you take a trip, you might consider booking your flight with A-Plus Airlines. Our flights are usually on time, and we try not to lose anyone's luggage. Also, our snacks are pretty good. If you fly with us, we hope you'll give us a passing grade!

Ad 2 If your last flight was horrible, you should have flown Aero Air. Then your luggage would have arrived at the same time as you—and on time! Even better, you could have enjoyed plenty of legroom and a free movie. So book your next flight on Aero Air, where all passengers fly first class.

____

____

____

C. Use proofreading marks to fix the incorrect forms of *could have, should have,* and *would have.*

1. You should of taken Aero Air.
2. You woulda gotten to your destination sooner.
3. You coulduv watched a free movie on the flight.

Voice

When writing persuasively, use a strong, confident voice to appeal to your reader's emotions.

Read this persuasive paragraph. Then:

- Use proofreading marks to fix the incorrect forms of *could have, would have,* and *should have.*
- Rewrite the paragraph so it has a stronger persuasive voice. Be sure to appeal to your reader's emotions and sound confident.

If someone you know drove to work today, you might tell that person that he or she could of taken public transportation instead. For one thing, it woulda cost less, because the fare for buses, trains, and subways is cheaper than gas. Also, taking public transportation reduces pollution. If more people ride the bus, train, or subway, there will be fewer cars releasing carbon dioxide into the atmosphere. While it may take more time and be less convenient, riding public transportation is also easier in some ways. For example, you don't have to worry about traffic or parking. It might take some adjustment, but eventually you'll realize you shoulduv made the switch to public transportation sooner.

Name: ______________________

Voice

When you plan your persuasive writing, think about the reasons and voice you will use to convince your reader.

Complete the opinion diagram to plan a paragraph persuading others to take an action you feel strongly about. Use one of the ideas below, or think of your own.

- Join a cycling club.
- Conserve gasoline.
- Help raise money to pay for a class field trip.
- Add a new train, bus, or subway line in your area.

Opinion Statement:

Reason:

Supporting Evidence:

Reason:

Supporting Evidence:

Reason:

Supporting Evidence:

Possible Objection:

Response to Objection:

PROOFREADING MARKS

Mark	Meaning	Example
(delete mark)	Take this out (delete).	I love ~~to~~ to read.
⊙	Add a period.	It was late⊙
≡	Make this a capital letter.	First prize went to maria. (≡ under m)
/	Make this a lowercase letter.	We saw a Black Cat. (/ through B and C)
———	Fix the spelling.	This is our ~~hause~~ house.
^ with comma	Add a comma.	Goodnight^, Mom.
v with apostrophe	Add an apostrophe.	That's Lil's bike.
! ? over ^ ^	Add an exclamation point or a question mark.	Help^! Can you help me^?
^	Add a word or a letter.	The ^red pen is mine.
# over ^	Add a space between words.	I like^#pizza.
———	Underline the words.	We read <u>Old Yeller</u>.
“ ” over v v	Add quotation marks.	“Come in,” he said.